Testimonials

"Gracie, with undaunted courage, lives everyday where only our deepest fears take us—and that is, a world of unrelenting pain. To spend time with her, though, is to feel a lot of that courage infuse into your own heart. That's why I love this story—you can't help but sense the divine strength which is her daily comfort and consolation. Thank you, Peter and Gracie, for lifting our own burdens as you bear your hearts in this remarkable book."

—Joni Eareckson-Tada

"Gracie is true to her name—a gracious, loving woman that has overcome adversity through dignity and strength. Her book is a must-read for continued inspiration in all of our lives."

—Dana Perino
Fox News Commentator, former White House Press Secretary
for President George W. Bush

"Powerful! You'll likely laugh, cry, and find yourself deeply affected as you read this book; and you're likely not to see things quite the same way afterward. As a former Commanding General of Walter Reed, I saw God use Gracie in the rehabilitation of many other amputees. But this book isn't just for or about amputees. After reading their book, it becomes clear how God is using Gracie and Peter—and how He can use us all—for so much more than we could have envisioned. A must read for anyone going through almost any trial and tribulation—and that covers most everyone."

—Kenneth L. Farmer, Jr., M.D.
Major General, U.S. Army (Retired)

"Gracie knows tragedy and pain; she understands what it takes to survive life's most traumatic circumstances. Rising from the ashes of despair, she's brought courage, faith, hope and strength to America's Wounded Warriors. I'm overwhelmed by her personal struggle and determination to let Christ flood her soul. Her story is gripping, emotional, encouraging; super-charged with God's healing Grace."

—Chaplain (Colonel) Craig N. Wiley
United States Army

"I have met many brave, inspirational people through the years but Gracie Rosenberger has to be the most extraordinarily courageous individual I have ever known. The way she approaches the challenges in her life is a testament to her faith and commitment to live the most abundant life possible. The next time you're tempted to have a 'pity party' pick up Gracie's book instead."

—Kathie Lee Gifford

"An extraordinary, magical memoir of bravery, perseverance, faith, and love. Peter and Gracie continue to inspire us through their glorious music, hearts, and bold commitment to change the lives of amputees who would otherwise have no hope. We feel blessed to have been a small part of their courageous journey together, and admire them for bringing their powerful story to others so honestly. We can all learn much from their magnanimous example as they are proof positive that life's unexpected challenges can be overcome."

—Senator Bill and Karyn Frist
Former Majority Leader, U.S. Senate

"An inspiring, heart-rending story of pain, hope and victory that demonstrates that 'Love DOES conquer all.' Gracie's story of a broken body and broken lives triumphing over the ordinary and extraordinary challenges of life ...will leave one in tears, sorrow, but ultimately rejoicing. As the senior United States' service member to the wounded in Afghanistan, I've witnessed Peter's and Gracie's inspiring presence and powerful witness at Walter Reed Army Medical Center. Their family and life story will encourage everyone, even someone who is 'just another broken soldier.'"

—Thomas P. Maney
Brigadier General (Retired), Army of the United States

GRACIE ROSENBERGER
as told to Peter W. Rosenberger

Gracie
Standing with Hope
by Gracie Parker Rosenberger
as told to Peter W. Rosenberger

ISBN-13: 978-0-9819357-9-9

Standing with Hope
peterandgracie@standingwithhope.com
PO Box 159115 Nashville, TN 37215
www.standingwithhope.com
www.gracieandpeter.com

Cover & Interior Design:
Megan Johnson
Johnson2Design
Johnson2Design.com

Cover Photo:
Tamara Reynolds Photography
www.TamaraReynoldsPhotography.com

LIBERTY
UNIVERSITY™
Press
Lynchburg, VA

For Parker and Grayson.

So you would know

Contents

PART III

Permitted

109

Contents

Acknowledgments
From the Author

WOW! This is the most difficult page to write. It's my belief that everyone makes an impression on your life, relatively speaking. For me, everyone I've EVER met …the "good, the bad, the ugly" deserve some type of literary recognition …because each experience played a part in shaping the story. (Isn't it fantastic our Savior works through not only the good experiences in our lives …but the horrible and ugly ones, as well?)

All that notwithstanding, a few wonderful individuals deserve special recognition for their part in helping this book come into being:

A God-send of a roommate in college, Nancy Comish, who, nearly three-decades later relived those awful times and worked tirelessly on this book for months… all with only our enormous, eternal gratitude. My family in Florida, my Rosenberger family, scattered around the world, my Texas family, and my church family (especially the *New Life* class and the fabulous cooks in

that group)–you all help carry, push, pull, or counsel me to the Cross…
and I am SO very grateful! ('Darlings,' you know who you are!)

But through all the heartache, loss, laughter, and adventure, three
men stand out …my three men. They not only had the greatest contribu-
tion to this book …but also in helping me _survive_ to even _tell_ a story.

Parker and Grayson …you will always be my "babies" no matter
how old you get. I may have lost both legs bringing you into this world,
but I gained a whole new ability to live life to the fullest. God mercifully
gave me you two …and you both helped me to get "back on my feet
again." You continually give me the courage to realize the "God-size"
dreams He puts on my mind and heart …and you even take them on as
your own, as God starts showing you how BIG your own individual part
is in all of this.

Peter …you help keep my head above water, when I feel like I'm
going under …but I know sometimes you struggle to breathe yourself.
Only God, you, and I know what this has cost you. Gratefully, we see
the strength you have gained through this often lonely … but NEVER
alone …road. I love you all dearly, and am grateful beyond words for the
beauty you and our sons helped pull out of the ashes.

And Peter, you've written down my words and given up a lot of "guy
time" to help me say something very important to every reader; the same
things you say to me …which you also need to hear:

You matter to God.

You matter to your family, especially me.

_And this world we live in would not make nearly enough sense with-
out you._

Acknowledgments

Thank you for helping make sense of my life, and loving me …even when I'm being the "bad and ugly" one. You do what Scripture says for you to do …you love me like Christ loves the church. Bless you for being there!

Gracie

Gracie Rosenberger, July 2010

From the Writer

I've been telling this story for a quarter of a century, and sometimes I've used words. When the time came to put those words on paper, a lot of wonderful people stepped up to help.

My parents, Dr. Beryl and Mary Rosenberger, pushed, challenged, and expressed such confidence in me to write this book; I appreciate and love you both …more than I can say.

My brothers John, Richard, Jim, Tom, and my beautiful sister, Liz. You, along with your families, provide such a sense of community and great love to me.

My Florida family, Jim and Carol Parker, Anne Parker, Bobby and Andrea Killingsworth, Greg and Lisa Killingsworth … You had to relive some of these events with me. Thank you for weeping once more.

Our church family, Covenant Presbyterian, who continues to hold us through many painful moments.

Sam and Marianne Clarke for decades of love.

Nancy Strode Comish. Thank you for the long hours that you shared your skills as a teacher, and for loving my wife and this story.

Bill and Nancy James, and everyone at Liberty University Press. In our first conversation, you stated, "This story will touch hurting hearts and share the Gospel." May it be so.

Mike, Priscilla, and Jadyn Stevens. Thank you for the times weeping, praying, and laughing while editing ...and ultimately embracing the Cross a little tighter as *family* in the Lord.

Joni Eareckson-Tada. I am neither sufficiently eloquent ...nor skillful enough as a writer to properly express my admiration and gratefulness to you. May God continue to richly bless you!

Jeff and Gregg Foxworthy. Rarely does one meet such loving people. Your friendship helped make all this possible. Although my family evidently served as an inspiration for your act, you saw past that and trusted us with your hearts ...you are both dearly loved. Quoting you (without giving a spoiler!), "I read the end ...*I know Who wins!*"

Parker and Grayson. So many times while I carried your mother ...I discovered you were both carrying me. Your father loves ...and is extremely proud of both you men!

Gracie. No matter how many people are inspired and touched through your pain, suffering, courage, and heart ... none will be more grateful to know you than this redeemed piano player from South Carolina who gets to hear you sing everyday!

Peter W. Rosenberger, July 2010

Foreword

I have many things taped to my bathroom mirror. Among them are love notes from my wife and daughters, lists of people to pray for and "don't forget" messages to myself. (The chances of me forgetting seem to grow stronger by the day.) Upon finishing this book I added something else. A simple yellow post-it note with the verse from Proverbs 3:5, "Trust in the Lord with all your heart and lean not on your own understanding."

I seem to struggle with that one. It is a lesson I need to re-learn every day.

I once heard someone say, "If you could figure God out …he really wouldn't be worthy of your worship would he?" I have chewed on that a great deal.

The day Gracie Parker Rosenberger was born, the doctor should have handed her mother a certificate of authenticity. If it's honesty you're craving, then she's your gal. Much like my wife, you rarely have to ask whether she is in a good mood or a bad mood …or how she feels about a subject. You just know. I personally love those kinds of people.

In a world of hype, honesty framed in love is refreshing. Others are drawn to it like bugs to a porch light. Gracie's light just happens to shine a little brighter than most.

You see, what you are about to read is not a story that you will hear told where the "Prosperity Gospel" is preached; at least not the type of prosperity that the world most often chases. The funny thing about people, all people, is we don't seem to do well in that type of prosperity. We tend to assume we deserve it or have earned it. We believe we are self-sustaining and eventually we are all proven wrong.

If you study the scriptures you will find that Jesus actually told the ones nearest to him that they would suffer for his name. Turns out, not only was he The Messiah, The Savior of the world, but he was also proven to be a man of his word. The disciples did suffer indeed after Christ departed. Most of them experienced horrible deaths. But during their time with Jesus they had seen, heard and experienced "something" that made that pain and suffering pale in comparison to what was to come. It was something worth living and dying for. They bet their lives on it.

The riches that God desires for us are so different than what the world is selling.

I believe above all else, the heart of God yearns for deep intimacy with us, and he will allow almost anything to achieve it. Most often it seems we have to reach the end of ourselves before we are willing to reach out and grab the hand of the Creator.

I have been to Africa many times and worked in some of the worst slums on the planet. I have seen, firsthand, poverty at such a level that it makes your heart hurt and sears itself into your brain forever. I have also led a small group Bible study for homeless gentlemen in downtown Atlanta for quite a while. Men left with nothing in the world but the dirty clothes on their backs.

Yet these two groups have something in common. They totally "get" the story of Jesus. They not only get it, they embrace it. You should hear them pray. It is powerful and desperate. My oldest daughter says it is because they don't have a "Plan B." They can't depend on a new car or home to temporarily fill the void in their soul. They desperately need a Savior. Maybe just realizing that makes them blessed.

I think Gracie and Peter would agree.

The truth is we all suffer. Some of us physically, some of us mentally, some of us emotionally, but we all suffer. It is the plight of man. Any gospel that tells you otherwise is false. God doesn't promise to rid us of our suffering. He promises that his grace is sufficient to sustain us through it.

I love Gracie and Peter. I am honored to call them friends. I am so thankful they finally took the time to put the story of their lives on to paper. Because what they have done here is not easy. It takes a tremendous amount of courage to show your scars, to admit to the world your shortcomings. Because the fact is, we all want to be accepted. I believe the turning point in life comes when you decide whose acceptance it is that you seek. I love Galatians 1:10; "Am I now trying to win the approval of men or of God? Or am I trying to please men? If I were still trying to please men, I would not be a servant of Christ."

This is a story that chronicles the journey of a remarkable woman, husband and family. This is a story of faith tested by fire. This is a story of pain and restoration. This is the story of Amazing Grace.

You're going to share this story. I promise.

Jeff Foxworthy, June 2010

The Lord says, I'll give you brokenness,
I'll give you emptiness, I'll give you weakness...
then you'll be useful to Me.

—S. James Bachmann, Jr.
Senior Pastor,
Covenant Presbyterian Church, PCA
Nashville, Tennessee

Prologue

Ninety Seconds

Yea, though I walk through the valley of the shadow of death,
I will fear no evil for Thou art with me;

—Psalm 23:4 (KJV)

November 18, 1983, 12:30 PM, Ninety miles west of Nashville, TN

Fatigue washed over me. Nine weeks into my freshman year in college, months of maintaining a frenzied pace finally registered …and hit like a ton of bricks. In addition to an already full schedule of classes, my decision to declare a double major in vocal performance and piano required lengthy and exhaustive hours of practice. My heavy academic load, along with a strict jogging regimen and a budding college social life, pushed any kind of rest to the bottom of my detailed priority list. Now, driving alone with just my thoughts to keep me company, the weariness crept in relentlessly.

"You know Gracie, you *really* need to roll the window down," I told myself.

Glancing at the window, a voice in my brain kept telling me to lower it and allow the cold autumn air to rouse me from the increasing comfort of the warm car. Not heeding the mental warning bells, my hands gripped the steering wheel …as I continued driving while looking glassy-eyed at the road ahead. The highway, bordered by trees with bare branches rising from autumn-browned fields, stretched ahead and merged with the dull gray sky. I tried to stir myself to alertness by returning to composing lyrics to a tune given to me by a friend.

Father here I am seeking you once more,

Giving up to you these burdens, I've given up before.

Why must there be a constant struggle in me; a giving of myself?

The song seemed about as cheerful as the landscape.

Oh well, at least I looked colorful and cheery! Glancing down, I smiled at the new Aigner shoes my mother bought for my college wardrobe. Earlier that morning I decided to arrange my whole outfit based upon my new shoes; wonderful new burgundy tights, a fabulous deep turquoise corduroy skirt, an Aigner-colored sweater with a stylish large cowl turtleneck, and several pieces of my favorite jewelry …one of which was a gold add-a-bead necklace I had been adding to since sixth grade. To this day, my attire for the trip remains one of my all-time favorite outfits (although it was four sizes smaller.)

As the miles crept by, I noticed the gas gauge was low. With all the running around, I forgot to fill the tank. Scolding myself for failing to stop at the exit rapidly shrinking in my rearview mirror, I made a mental note to fill up at the next one. Being my first time to drive west on this highway, I was unaware that the nearest gas station lay nearly ten miles away.

The gentle humming engine noise of my Honda Accord combined with the dreary landscape to increase the drowsiness that seemed to envelope my body. Feeling my head bob slightly, I quickly shook it off and shifted to the right of a ten truck convoy, thinking how odd for those tractor trailers to be in the left lane. Speeding to seventy MPH (the speed limit was 55) I passed them in the right lane. Racing around them and then cutting back to the left in front of another car, I glanced again at my fuel level and knew I had to find an exit quickly.

If I just didn't feel so sleepy!

With no exit in sight, I settled in after speeding past the tractor trailers, nervously looking at the gas gauge. Staring ahead, the highway seemed to stretch on endlessly, without even a curve to break up the monotony. Relaxing in the warm car and feeling the comfort of sleep moving stealthily over my body, my mind chose to stop fighting it. With blurring eyes, I gave myself permission to rest for "just a moment," and I lay my head on the steering wheel.

Adorned in a beautiful new shoe, my foot pressed heavily on the accelerator, and slowly urged the car back to more than seventy miles per hour. As I drifted from the left lane, the car behind me slipped by, apparently oblivious to my condition …unlike the men driving the eighteen wheelers I had just passed, who could only watch helplessly as I rested my head on the wheel. Frantically blowing their horns trying to startle me awake, the truckers radioed each other and coordinated to form a rolling barrier behind me with their trucks; preventing anyone else from being hit by my aimless car. With their constant horn blasts failing to wake me, the truckers watched my car slowly weaving for about a minute and then steadily drifting to the right. Making its way through the right lane, my Honda Accord raced into the roadside gravel. The crunch of tire against rock caused me to stir a little and, half-way opening my heavy—

lidded eyes, I vaguely noticed a large green sign with white letters. In a drowsy haze, I failed to react in time to keep the car from charging ahead. With no guard rail to prevent disaster, my car left the road and mowed over a mile marker. Bent by the front of the car, the small sign whipped back into the Accord…slicing through the Honda's undercarriage and carving out a large section of my right thigh; nearly cutting me in two.

Ramming head-on into the end of the concrete abutment framing a culvert, the front of the little Honda wrapped itself around the eight-inch barrier; slamming my body against the rapidly crumpling car. Milliseconds later, internal organs also bowed to the law of physics and pounded into my body as it quickly decreased speed …allowing me to fully experience the smashing impact of high velocity meeting a dense, fixed obstacle.

With no buffer to burn off speed, the frontal impact lifted the back end of the car, and, like an Olympic gymnast, the car twisted and flipped through the air so that the back end of the car crushed into the opposite side of the culvert's cement wall. Already bearing the impression of the abutment in the front of the car, the nearly ninety degree impact shoved the trunk of the car almost into the back seat.

With the car hurtling through the air, as if in slow motion, the momentum from pounding backwards into the culvert flipped the crushed automobile again …and then sent it careening along a fifteen-foot embankment. Rolling into a small ravine that served as a run off during rainy weather, the Honda finally tumbled to a stop, amazingly right side up. The gully was deep enough that had the wreck been at night, no one driving by would have noticed or rescued me in time.

Disoriented and in shock, I awoke with my body leaning towards the passenger seat, but both of my legs were grotesquely pinned over my right shoulder. Something seemed dreadfully wrong with each of them; particularly my right foot …which was dangling limply at a bizarre angle. Feeling a wet, sticky substance trickling down my face and into my eyes, I blinked through the blood now oozing from a gash on the top of my head. With curious detachment, I noticed the right, front tire crammed into the passenger seat. A strange flashing in front of me caught my attention and painfully shifting my eyes forward, a wave of fear rushed over me—*MY CAR WAS ON FIRE!*

Although my brain clanged all sorts of alarms, nothing in my body moved. Panic enveloped me, and hopelessness flooded over me. Staring straight into the flames shooting from the engine, I saw a shape of a person. Although the face shone too bright to be distinguishable, I somehow knew the silhouette I saw was Christ. With one last surge of energy, willing myself to speak through a mouth that felt strange and unresponsive …I cried out, "Jesus, only you can save me now!"

Mercifully, everything went black.

It took ninety seconds for my life to be violently and irreparably changed.

Part I

History

Oh yes, you shaped me first inside, then out;
you formed me in my mother's womb.
I thank you, High God—you're breathtaking!
Body and soul, I am marvelously made!
I worship in adoration—what a creation!
You know me inside and out,
you know every bone in my body;
You know exactly how I was made, bit by bit,
how I was sculpted from nothing into something.
Like an open book, you watched me grow from conception to birth;
all the stages of my life were spread out before you,
The days of my life all prepared
before I'd even lived one day.

—Psalm 139:13-16
The Message

Chapter 1

Working Mom

The mother's heart is the child's school-room.

—Henry Ward Beecher

January 18, 1966, Johnson City, TN

"There's something wrong with her eyes."

The normal commotion of a delivery room abruptly halted as the obstetrician and nurses noticed my eyes; severely crossed so that only the whites showed. The news crushed my parents, Jim and Carol Parker, and they struggled to comprehend the heartbreaking report about their new baby girl. In my very first moments on this planet, conversations about me declared an imperfection; a disability, a flaw. By simply entering into the world, I thrust open a door to heartache and sorrow. Arriving with absolutely no control or choice, my presence alone served as a reminder of a broken world …and as a catalyst for people around me to question the goodness and will of God.

Trying to push past the disappointment of my eyes, my parents, grandparents, and big sister did their best to be excited about my arrival, and, borrowing a name from each grandmother, my family welcomed Mary Grace Parker into their little home in Elizabethton, Tennessee. (My maternal grandmother's first name was Othella, and I'm still grateful they chose to bless me with her middle name: "Grace.") My mother wanted to nickname me "Marcie," but it didn't stick. Being Southerners, my full name was frequently used, but eventually everyone settled on "Gracie."

My name, however, was often quickly glossed over as attention naturally focused on my defectiveness when presenting me to others; almost like a caveat with every introduction: "Here's little Mary Grace, isn't it sad about her eyes?"

Barely having time to explore my crib at our home in Elizabethton, my world was quickly framed by doctors and hospitals ...and would be so for the rest of my life. Unprepared for this daunting challenge, my young parents experienced an even greater anxiety over the uncertainty of what was actually wrong with my eyes. *What was her condition? Was she mentally challenged? Would little Mary Grace ever see properly?* These and many other questions plagued them as they frantically visited doctor after doctor; uneasily searching for answers. With the bills mounting, Daddy's parents helped ease some of the financial load for us as my mother and father grew increasingly overwhelmed; floundering in a medical world they did not understand.

Beginning at only three months old, we trekked through the South seeking answers to the dilemma of Mary Grace and her horribly crossed eyes. To the relief of all, my father's cousin, a neurosurgeon, connected us with a specialist in Miami who correctly diagnosed the problem. Once everyone understood my condition, he referred us to Dr. McKee at the McKee-Wilson Eye Hospital in East Tennessee where he successfully operated on my eyes. (This renowned clinic is now known as the Johnson City Specialty Hospital.)

My first operation occurred at the young age of fourteen months. During my initial assessment, doctors discovered many peripheral muscles were undeveloped. Pulling and tying different muscles to compensate, Dr. McKee successfully treated my right eye first. Before starting first grade, I endured four eye operations …as well as the seemingly endless recoveries that followed. In order to strengthen my left eye, the doctor forced me to wear a patch over the right one, along with peculiar looking, horn-rimmed glasses; clearly not the fashion accessory parents hope to provide for their little girl.

Shortly before my third birthday, Daddy chose to leave the job security of his parents' car dealership, and launch out on his own. Packing up our small family and relocating to the panhandle of Northwest Florida, we settled in the obscure little town of Navarre …which is nestled near Fort Walton Beach and Eglin Air Force Base. Highway 98 wove through Navarre, but wasn't even paved through the sparsely populated area at the time we arrived there. Traveling west on 98 led to Pensacola …and Fort Walton Beach lay to the east.

More than a decade earlier, my grandparents had purchased a parcel of land surrounding this sparsely settled area; land which Daddy determined to develop. In many respects, Daddy was born a century too late; he has the heart of a pioneer. Uprooting his wife and two daughters, leaving a steady job and a settled town, we plopped into a fledgling community with only fifty families and lived for nearly a year in a tiny (only fourteen feet long) Shasta travel trailer …while Daddy set out to build a career as a real estate developer.

Building a mobile home park on the property by themselves, my parents moved us into the back of the park's new laundry and recreation hall (we still cooked meals in the travel trailer), and then eventually into a sixty foot mobile home …which seemed like a palace after the Shasta camper.

Moving to Florida did not lessen the challenges of my life. The eye condition, not quite resolved, required frequent trips back to Johnson City to see Dr. McKee who operated on me three more times before entering grade school. Despite progressive treatments, most of my baby pictures were posed in profile, and a self-image of defectiveness slowly took shape. My older sister, Andrea, grew more beautiful with long flowing brown hair always nicely held by pretty bows and clips. In contrast, due to multiple surgeries, patches, and for whatever other reasons, my hair was chopped off into a bob. In so many of my earlier pictures, I looked like a boy. Naturally, my personality seemed to adapt to this tomboy persona, and I fell in love with the outdoors, adventure, and especially getting sweaty and dirty.

> Discouragement and challenges either cripple a person or help build fortitude.

Although outwardly reveling in tomboyish fun, I recall crying often and feeling different and ostracized. Rarely playing with other children due to being frequently ridiculed and called names, I spent a great deal of time alone. Every night, I prayed for God to miraculously heal my eyes while I slept; yet awoke each morning to the hateful condition of a defect …living the reality over and over.

"Mommy, am I cross-eyed?" Tears brimmed when I asked my mother after hearing other kids tease me.

Broken-hearted, her eyes also filled with tears as pain and sadness darkened her face …and if you ask her today, the hurt is still apparent.

Chapter 1

Understandably, that teasing, as well as increased learning challenges, contributed to a "defensive" attitude early on, and helped form what would become an incredibly forceful personality. Discouragement and challenges either cripple a person or help build fortitude. The problem with fortitude building, however, is that it's rarely a smooth road. Potholes of defiance often wreak havoc along the journey and lead to some absurd decisions. Once, not even five years old, I became angry with my parents over something trivial, so I packed up my miniature, flowery and polka-dotted suitcase ...and ran away from home to marry (then) teenage superstar Donny Osmond.

In my suitcase, along with toys and dolls, I had a magazine with Donny's picture on the cover. (I didn't pack food or clothes ...I just assumed Donny would take care of all those things!) Of course, I didn't know Donny's address, but the magazine article mentioned he lived in Utah, and I knew it was somewhere past Pensacola!

Only getting about one hundred yards down the road on Highway 98, the local sheriff discovered an extremely determined little girl heading west. Knowing my family (my father served as a deputy sheriff for the rural community), the officer loaded me into his squad car and drove me home; all the while trying to stifle laughter at the incredibly defiant preschooler with the Donny Osmond crush. Thankfully, northwest Florida in the early seventies was much safer than today's world, and I'm so grateful my childhood rebellion only resulted in embarrassment and, after recovering from the hurt feelings of my attempt to run away, my family had a good laugh.

I never did meet Donny Osmond, though! (I have met Presidents of the United States, but just can't seem to meet Donny Osmond!)

"And they call it ...Pup-py Lo-ve!" If you don't know that song, well... you're just not a faithful Donny Osmond fan!

The physical challenges of underdeveloped eyes complicated my education and led to a learning disability; I struggled in reading. In the early seventies, special needs programs were still in the infant stages, many children with learning disabilities sadly landed in a catch all "special-ed" class. Assuming my difficulties in learning indicated a slow learner, my teacher followed suit and simply transferred me to a special-education class. Gratefully, before my entire life could be shaped by such a decision, a remarkable teacher with her own challenging path, Freida Lloyd, intervened and properly assessed the situation.

Feeling relief that someone else understood this journey, Mom hung on every word from Mrs. Lloyd as the two of them met to discuss what to do with little Mary Grace. Listening with rapt attention as she recounted her personal trials of refusing to accept the current education system's path for her son, who also had a learning disability, my mother felt a glimmer of hope; someone to help sort through the unfamiliar issues that now confronted my family. Admirably at her own expense, Mrs. Lloyd traveled to Miami to glean strategies in cutting-edge educational programs designed for children with special needs and learning disabilities. She incorporated her new-found skills into her son's life …and providentially into the lives of other children in our small community.

> At critical moments, what seemed to present a burden for one family, served as a springboard to help other families.

Recalling this years later, I remain amazed at how God uses one person's heartache as not only a catalyst in their own lives, but in the lives of so many others. At critical moments, what seemed to present a burden for one family served as a springboard to help other families. Over my "forty-something" years, I've observed that pattern repeating uncounted times in the lives of others I meet, as in my own. By intervening in my life, Freida Lloyd, a dedicated mother and teacher, would touch a great many lives, and I believe the highest honor you can give teachers is to acknowledge the impact they made in the time they devoted to you.

As in the case of accurately diagnosing my eyes, teachers properly assessing my learning issues helped Mom and Dad feel a huge relief from the burden of uncertainty. They also took a great deal of comfort discovering others were successfully navigating this path. Grasping a great truth, my parents discovered that when life presents challenges, often painful ones, connecting with others who understand and walk the same journey can bring an extraordinary sense of camaraderie and companionship.

"There's nothing wrong with Mary Grace or her ability to learn," Mrs. Lloyd calmly told my wide-eyed and anxious mother. "She will just have to work a little harder to train herself on how to read effectively."

A *little* harder?! I worked my tail off!

With nothing more than a passion to keep her daughter from failing, Mom threw herself into the task of educating me by participating in a brand new volunteer tutoring program. Under Mrs. Lloyd's supervision, Mom and other eager parents learned tutoring skills to help children with learning disabilities. With Mrs. Lloyd spearheading from the classroom, Mom then shared the load by tutoring assigned students. Parents didn't tutor their own child in the classroom, but rather worked with other children.

Mrs. Lloyd helped transfer me to a different school; one implementing a new program of learning called an "open-classroom" concept. Progressing at the speed of individual students, this new way of teaching worked with me, and I took my first tentative steps in a challenging, but successful academic path.

Choosing not to split us up, Mom made the decision for Andrea to change schools also. Transferring schools was hard for Andrea, and I regret she sacrificed so much on my behalf ...both then and much later. The school bus stopped at the county line, which was nearly a mile from our home, and Mom wouldn't settle for her two daughters to walk that distance alone ...even if I had a picture of Donny Osmond with me. So, since she had to pick us up anyway, she made the choice to drive us the ten miles to school every day, and be there every afternoon to pick us up. This arrangement also avoided a long bus ride full of teasing for the little girl with the eye patch and odd glasses.

Gaining courage and understanding from her network of other parents and Mrs. Lloyd, Mom rolled up her sleeves and not only learned to tutor others in my school, but then worked with me one-on-one after school and into the evenings for nearly my entire schooling. Mom utilized her newfound skills as a special needs educator to spend countless hours with me as I learned to read, write, take notes, and memorize. She incorporated creative tasks, purchased boxes of supplies, and helped me not only keep up with other students, but surpass them.

Through this journey, Mom modeled a foundation of diligence, hard work, and perseverance for me that helped define who I am today. Without any formal training in education, special needs children, or even a college degree, Mom, with just the sheer determination to love and nurture me, found herself becoming an expert in tutoring. Mrs. Lloyd and my mother helped organize the whole initiative that convinced the local school board to integrate special needs students into the system ...and they had to fight that battle every year for several years.

We realized early on that bright and multiple colors helped stimulate parts of my brain that could compensate for my vision issues. Certain nerves simply were not connected or "wired properly," so we learned to make new paths for my mind to learn. Rather than simply reading black and white text, we added audio, colors, and every other sensory input available. I took notes using a tape recorder and read with a marker in hand. The greatest tools that helped me overcome my learning disability were "magic-markers." By using bright and bold colors, my brain processed the text better and, slowly but steadily, I progressed academically.

To this day, I keep a ready supply of "Sharpies" in my purse. I love Sharpies …and I love their commercials telling consumers to use Sharpies when they want to "write out-loud!" That is so funny to me. Imagine opening a grocery list that SHOUTS at you not to forget the toilet paper and milk …that's my kind of list!!

During grade school, we pushed ahead with my training and I continued showing progress. Bringing home consistent "B's" and "C's" on tests and report cards, we all felt a level of comfort with "at least Gracie's not failing." Knowing that I would not be put at the back of the class seemed to help put the family's minds at ease, and Mom's attitude slowly reflected a compensation for my eyes and learning issues; she let compassion for my difficulties dictate expectations and goals. It was almost as if I received a free pass for mediocrity because I had "special challenges."

Growing increasingly frustrated with the amount of work required just to learn words for a spelling test, I allowed the "just get by" mentality to justify cheating on a spelling test. Of course, the only time I'd ever cheated on a test I was immediately caught by my teacher who read me the riot act …and then did the worst possible thing: she told my parents.

"Gracie is more than capable, but must be pushed," she told my very upset mother. With tears forming in Carol Parker's eyes, she listened to this teacher state in no uncertain terms that my eyes or learning disability were not to be used as a crutch; I must set high goals, and be pushed to achieve them.

"You must not feel sorry for Gracie; I don't …and she doesn't feel sorry for herself. She can do anything she wants to!" This teacher affirmed what Mrs. Lloyd said a few years earlier. With those simple words, a life philosophy was imparted. Taking this second teacher's admonition to heart, Mom re-doubled her efforts and refused to allow my eyes or reading difficulties to dictate accomplishment. Although it hurt Mom to push me so hard, her diligent prodding resulted in regained academic traction and, little by little, the successes mounted. Within a short time, the "B's" and "C's" gave way to an increasing number of "A's," as well as a stronger, more focused work ethic.

> I believe teachers should know the impact they make on their students.

While even to this day struggling with certain kinds of tests, like standardized exams, I excelled at academics, and even at advanced-placement classes (AP). More than my eyes, my argumentative personality caused a collision with multiple choice and "pick your best answer" type of questions. The best answer to me was subjective, and I wanted to make a case for the answer I selected. Sometimes I wrote my reasons in the tiny margin spaces. I learned the hard way, however, that the computers grading standardized tests don't like it when students argue with the format and write in the margin.

Repeatedly rising to the occasion, Carol Parker placed herself in the gap and saved me from a life of mediocrity and failure. I believe teachers should know the impact they make on their students. Even though two key teachers intercepted me at a young age to help keep me on the path to excellence, Mom deserves to know the effect of the many times she hid her tears while pushing her daughter to achieve; the uncounted nights around the kitchen table when her heart broke as she watched me struggle with even the simplest task …yet refused to let me quit. To this day, Mom still humbly minimizes her accomplishment, and points to her younger sister, Dottie, as the one with the teaching "gift." Dottie, who sadly passed away in 2007, taught school for years …but I think she was exceptionally proud of her older sister, Carol, and all she accomplished.

With literally the force of her will, she reached down, grasped an unknown courage …and led her daughter, and others, out of what could have resulted in tragic outcomes. In doing so, she modeled persistence, diligence, bravery, and a belief that "quitting was not an option—regardless of the challenges."

Those things would be needed again …in a much more brutal circumstance.

Chapter 2

Sing, Gracie... Sing

You must look into other people ...as well as at them.

—Lord Chesterfield

Maria: I can't seem to stop singing wherever I am. And what's worse,
I can't seem to stop saying things—anything and everything I think and feel.
Mother Abbess: *Some people would call that honesty.*
Maria: *Oh, but it's terrible, Reverend Mother.*

—Julie Andrews as Maria, *The Sound of Music*

rior to and during my early emotional and scho-
lastic upheavals, I learned as a young girl I could
sing and play the piano. I eventually chose to focus exclusively on voice, but during those difficult childhood
and teenage years when staring and teasing were abundant, I
often spent long, lonely hours at the piano; accompanying myself as I sang songs that felt as if they emanated from the basement of my heart. Although finding those solo performances
enjoyable and meaningful, it took a special intervention from
one person to kick-start my singing from something I did in the

living room, to what would eventually take me to some of the world's biggest stages.

Within a short time of our arrival in Florida, my father's parents chose to sell the car dealership they owned in East Tennessee, and they built a home near us in Navarre. Andrea and I being their only grand-children probably had a lot to do with their decision. Granddaddy Parker became a fixture of encouragement to me during those difficult early years. My dad's father, Orion Creet Parker, Jr. often sat me on a stool and had me sing to him ...and he never asked me to stop. I obliged by singing at the only volume I knew: wide-open and *loud*. That seemed to delight him even more, and we spent many incredibly happy hours together. He loved listening to me sing, and seemed always patient, enthusiastic, and supportive.

We even took our show on the road to Carl's Café, one of the two businesses in Navarre (the only other establishment in the tiny town was a gas station). Nearly every weekday, Granddaddy ate lunch at Carl's, which was nothing more than a seaside "greasy spoon" held together with what looked like driftwood paneling and fish nets. Serving as the social center for all of Navarre, Florida, Carl's regulars included local fishermen and retirees who arrived daily for a cup of coffee and a sand-wich, along with a combination of fishing news, weather reports ...and more than a little gossip.

Andrea, four years older, set off every morning to elementary school, but I bounced around with excitement knowing that Granddaddy would come by and take me to lunch at Carl's. Often my father arrived for lunch at the diner to see me in my petite sundress perched on the gold-and-silver-speckled Formica countertop joyously belting out songs, laugh-ing while swinging my legs under the counter, and generally having the time of my life! Shaking his head in disbelief, Daddy watched me holding court and performing for a group of applauding old men, while my grandfather beamed with pride at his young granddaughter with the outrageous personality. Adorned with my eye patch and singing for a group of salty fishermen, I probably looked like *Shirley Temple* meets *Pirates of the Caribbean!*

Grandmother Parker used to chide Granddaddy to make sure none of the men swore around me, and she fretted over things I might overhear and inadvertently learn while hanging around a bunch of "redneck old coots." Granddaddy Parker, however, took great care of me and ensured all the men minded their language …and if one of them made any comments about my eye patch, he received a stern look from my grandfather. Believe me, it never took more than a look.

Granddaddy even went a step further and let me drink coffee. Oh … it tasted so good! My father *(knowing he would never convince Granddaddy otherwise)* quit trying to keep me out of Carl's, but he openly protested to his father when he saw me perched on the counter clutching a mug of coffee with both hands.

"Daddy," he pleaded respectfully, "three year olds shouldn't drink coffee!"

"Hush Jimmy, it's mostly cream and sugar, so settle down …and go on back to work!" Granddaddy said while laughing at my father.

*So Granddaddy was getting his preschooler loaded up on caffeine **and** sugar!*

To this day, I LOVE coffee …and I will always stop and sing for any group of old men who ask.

With as close to a perfect love as I can imagine on this earth, my grandfather remains the dearest man I have ever known. He never seemed to notice any problem with my eyes, or how loud I sang, or anything else that may have appeared abnormal. Of all the people in my life, it was my grandfather who saw past my defectiveness. Rather than compensate for it, try to address it … or even hide it, he encouraged me, "Sing as loud as you can, Gracie. Sing with all your heart!"

Not knowing it at the time, my grandfather elicited a great deal of respect not only in our small town, but across the entire state of Florida, where he had served as the state's attorney before retiring to start his car dealership near my grandmother's family in Elizabethton, Tennessee.

Although not one to solicit favors lightly, his high-profile reputation and statewide admiration usually paved the way for his requests to be granted. So, upon mentioning to our pastor that he would appreciate the opportunity for little Mary Grace to sing at First Baptist Church in Fort Walton Beach, Florida, the pastor graciously offered, "We'd love for her to sing."

My singing career officially started at age five as I stood up in church and performed my first solo. Not one to step onto a stage, my mother was nervous for me. (Carol Parker could never be labeled as a typical "stage-mom.") Closing my eyes, I sang the old Gospel hymn "Heaven Came Down and Glory Filled My Soul" the only way I knew how; full voice …as loud as my young lungs could produce. With an Ethel Merman quality, I belted it out like an Irish drinking song (not normally heard in Baptist churches!).

The audience seemed to love it, and my path as a singer was charted. The girl with the patch over her eye discovered that something in her wanted *and needed* to eclipse her defective appearance. Later, as I took voice lessons, my voice teacher often affirmed my style, "Gracie, sing as if there's a deaf old woman on the back row!" Hardly needing encouragement in that area; I knew something in me wanted out, and singing became the door.

Chapter 2 Sing, Gracie... Sing

Throughout the many years of performances, Granddaddy Parker remains my best audience …ever. I couldn't hit a sour note for him, I never sang too loud, but most importantly, it mattered not in the *slightest* how I looked. At the end of every performance, I received bear hugs, pinched cheeks, smiles, laughter, and love; affirmation beyond anything I could describe. Everything needed for a little girl with a patch over her eye … to see beyond any limitations.

Granddaddy Parker's presence alone provided such joy for Andrea and me, as well as my parents. Losing him all too soon when he suffered a massive heart attack in 1975 …crushed my family. Nothing was ever the same after his death, yet memories still remain vivid and powerful for me. Though brief, the time I had with him inspired the courage to approach challenges differently. Ignoring the patch, the eyes, or anything else, and recalling the love and affection of my grandfather, I decided to step on to even larger stages than that of First Baptist Church of Fort Walton Beach.

By age thirteen, after my fifth eye surgery (performed this time by a doctor in Pensacola), I stowed the eye patch; no longer the pirate girl who looked different. This surgery would last me more than twenty years. Using the confidence gained from academic success and performance affirmation, I immersed myself in music lessons …which provided plenty of experience as a singer, but not necessarily as a refined performer who skillfully commanded the stage. My stage presence evolved from my "do it on my terms" approach to life …as well as the performance experiences that shaped me: perched on a countertop at Carl's! "Polished" is not a word that comes to mind when most people critique my early appearances (and probably more than a few current ones!). I just kind of stepped out on stage and was "Gracie." Regardless of how well I performed, I remained authentic, and did what I wanted to do. My grandfather instilled that in me.

Harmonizing my singing ability with a strong personality and a "full-throttle" performance style, I auditioned for and was selected to join a touring music group called *The Continentals.* In my first tour with them, we traveled all over the United States, and I not only sang with the group, but also served as a featured soloist ... which helped smooth some of those rough edges of my performance style.

Traveling from town to town, we stayed in hotels, churches, and in people's homes. Each member, regardless of how many solos, was required to pitch in for every day's performance and set up equipment, sell products, and make sure to hit every cue and choreographed note. The long days and nights, constant meeting of new people, and rigid performance schedule felt challenging ...and sometimes down-right grueling. I loved every moment!

The confidence gained from my experience with *The Continentals* gave me the courage to compete in the Miss Fort Walton Beach High School Pageant the school year following my tour. I approached the pageant the same way I did everything else ...on my terms. Instead of picking a classical piece and trying to win over an audience with skill and poise, Mom suggested I go a different direction. Featuring personality over poise (a particularly good alternative for me), we selected the song "Honey Bun" from *South Pacific.*

Staying with a sense of practicality, I chose not to buy a new formal and instead opted for the gown from my ninth grade prom; I felt it ridiculous to spend hard-earned money on an event I clearly had no chance of winning. Andrea was much more suited for this type of thing, so much so that she was voted homecoming queen during her senior year. Throughout a lot of my school career, I lived in Andrea's shadow; a model student, she was (and still is) beautiful, poised, soft-spoken ... seemingly perfect.

Chapter 2 Sing, Gracie... Sing

Sounds a lot like Jan Brady from the 1970's "The Brady Bunch" sit-com complaining about her sister, "Marsha, Marsha, Marsha!"

Andrea, like Mom, avoided getting up on stage to perform, but me, well, I grew up holding court on a cheap countertop in a dilapidated diner …singing for a rapt audience of old men while wearing a patch over one eye. Although doubtful about my chances of winning, I still maintained ample confidence in my ability to have a good time and entertain an audience, so I obtained the proper faculty sponsors to ensure my eligibility to compete …and threw my name into the hat for the pageant. With sponsors, a formal gown, and excellent grades, the only thing remaining was the talent portion. In the show/movie *South Pacific,* the character I would emulate, *Nellie,* dressed as a sailor while performing a comedy spoof about a sailor singing to his love, "Honey-Bun." My first order of business was to obtain a sailor uniform.

In a bittersweet and touching gesture, my grandmother, Mary Emma Parker, opened up the precious belongings of her oldest son and allowed me to use the hat from my uncle's faded navy uniform for the pageant. One of the more tragic events of my family involved the death of my father's older brother, Orion C. Parker, III; a navy seaman who died in an accident in the 1950's.

Wearing a sailor suit, and my uncle's hat cocked sideways on my head, a friend from school completed the show-stopping performance when he mimicked the character, *Luther Billis.* Dressed in a hula skirt wearing a bra made of coconut-halves laced together with twine, he proceeded to dance his way out on stage as I sassily sang the song …making the performance an absolute sensation.

At the part of the pageant when judges pose contestants a defining question, I couldn't believe the one selected for me. Almost as if peering into my soul, they asked: "Gracie, what do you first notice when you meet another person?"

Without hesitation, the obvious answer that flowed from my heart was, "I look into their eyes." Continuing on, I also added to the delight of the audience, "If someone doesn't look me in the eyes and they just look around, well, they're just ... crafty!"

The audience laughed and applauded even more, and Mom later chuckled while saying, "I've never even heard you use the word 'crafty,' Gracie."

I may have been an unlikely contestant, but I won ...and no one was more shocked than I was! Taking my walk to accept the title, I hadn't even practiced the customary "pageant wave" to the applauding crowd! While the crowd cheered, I strolled onstage wearing a vintage gown and waving like a little girl watching Santa ride by at the Christmas parade ...knowing my family laughed and rolled their eyes at my lack of preparation for such an event. I savored the moment. With her heart in her throat, Mom beamed with excitement and pride. Daddy makes his presence known at these kinds of events by "hootin' an' a hollerin'" (his Tennessee heritage shines through at such times), so, even though I couldn't see past the stage lights, I felt my father's pride and excitement when I heard what sounded like a Comanche war-cry echoing through the auditorium.

It was so much fun ...and I did it on my terms!!

As much as I enjoyed the pageant, high school in general grew increasingly monotonous so I sought to graduate early. Amply demonstrating my academic capabilities, I not only earned straight "A's," but the weighted advanced placement courses helped me even surpass that achievement ... and I earned a 4.2 grade point average. Each accomplishment helped nurture a desire for more challenges, and I grew eager to spread my wings and achieve successes in larger arenas. Having garnered a pageant title, great grades, musical accolades, and with a professional tour under my belt, I felt ready to take on the world. The summer following my junior year loomed ahead, and I planned to tour a second time with *The Continentals*; this time all over Europe and into Israel. Taking the plunge, I completed all my studies, and finished high school a year early; ranked seventh in a class of more than six hundred.

Singing replaced the eye problem as the defining characteristic of my life. Devouring classical, jazz, gospel, Italian, German; I performed virtually every type of music available. This little girl with crossed eyes found her voice ....and it helped her not only cope, but transcend the painful early memories of feeling ostracized. On the tour that summer, I gained experience as a soloist, and formed friendships and relationships that would be the basis of a music career.

Continuing my old habit, I often close my eyes when pouring out my feelings through music; losing myself, and my imperfections, when singing. My heart is unrestrained by perceived limits, and every note seems to contain a part of my soul; I don't feel defective when I sing. If the audience is blessed, then I am grateful; but it's a personal and private experience for me ... paradoxically one I've shared with tens of thousands of people. Opening my mouth to sing, people seem to look past my defectiveness, and amazingly enough, some may never notice it at all.

Chapter 3
Path of Purpose

A ship is safe in harbor, but that's not what ships are for.

—William Shedd

lthough raised in Florida, my Tennessee roots run deep and strong. Grandmother Parker's family traces back to founding members of the Volunteer State; in fact, I am a ninth-generation Tennessean. Hidden away (or as the locals say, "way up ahrr") in the northeast corner of Tennessee is the charming, small town of Elizabethton; the county seat of Carter County. Driving into Elizabethton is a step back into the pristine beauty and roots of our country. The town is actually named for my great, great, great, great, great grandmother …Elizabeth Carter. Her husband, General Landon Carter, and his father, Col. John Carter, a member of the Continental Congress, helped settle the area now known as the Tri–Cities (Johnson City, Kingsport, and Bristol).

In addition to physically settling Tennessee, my ancestors also helped shape the political landscape of the sixteenth state. So much so, that my grandmother's two great uncles,

Bob and Alf Taylor, pitted against each other in the race for Governor. Bob, the Democrat, was known for his wonderful fiddle playing as he gave speeches around the state. We have one of those violins at our home now; it was presented to him as a gift from the then adjutant general. At one point, Bob hid behind the barn while Alf practiced his speech …and then Bob stole the speech for a debate scheduled between the brothers later that night. Bob won the election, and Alf eventually went to the U.S. Congress. In the early 1920's Alf settled his unfinished business with the governor's office and eventually won ….becoming the oldest elected governor of Tennessee.

With so much Tennessee history in my heritage, it seemed only natural to honor the family by attending a college in the Volunteer State. From the moment I stood to sing at First Baptist Church in Fort Walton Beach, I knew I wanted to be a successful singer, so even in junior high, I set my sights on the music program at Nashville's Belmont College (now Belmont University). Grandmother Grace's mother, my maternal great-grandmother, attended Belmont in the early 1900's when it was an all girl's school known as Ward Belmont. In the 1950's, Belmont expanded to a co-ed school, and by 1983 featured one of only a handful of collegiate commercial music programs.

Belmont's music program attracted national attention, and it seemed the perfect place to launch my career. In recent years, Belmont has gained enormous exposure with *American Idol* contestants and the Presidential debate between now President Obama and Senator John McCain. With a view of the famous "Music Row" from Belmont's front entrance, Nashville seemed to bristle with all the excitement and adventure that a teenage girl with dreams of a music career could hope to experience.

Before my first tour with *The Continentals*, and while I wrestled with the decision to graduate early, Andrea accepted a marriage proposal from her long-time boyfriend, Bobby Killingsworth. Andrea not only honored me by asking me to serve as her maid of honor, but invited me to sing, as well. Witnessing Bobby and Andrea reciting their vows to each other, I reflected how quickly my family was changing.

Just two weeks prior to their wedding, we lost Grandmother Grace to cancer. A loving woman who seemed to never stop working, she stamped me with a sense of "stick-to-itive-ness." She helped shape so much of my young life, and her passing created a deep void, but left me with many treasured memories of long summers spent at her home in Plano, Texas.

Requesting and gaining permission from *The Continentals* ahead of time for Andrea's wedding, Grandmother Grace's funeral was an unexpected event, and I was not allowed to leave the tour for her funeral. Not having that closure weighed even more on me, and the day of her funeral, I could hardly do my job knowing my family was grieving together in Texas while I was on tour trying to summon the courage to put on a "happy face" and perform. Spending long hours in a tour bus traveling across the United States during that summer after her death, I found myself crying a good bit. Even with my new friends, seeing exciting places, and staying in the homes of wonderful people along the tour, the grief of losing Grandmother Grace lay heavily upon me.

With Andrea's wedding, Grandmother Grace's death, and the tour with *The Continentals*, a busy summer ended and I returned home to Fort Walton Beach. But there was a yearning that the coastal town couldn't seem to satisfy. With so many events in such a short time span, my emotions were all over the map, and I felt an eagerness to chart a new course. Fort Walton Beach seemed smaller somehow, and now that my only sibling had a new life without me, something outside seemed to beckon.

I enrolled at Belmont College for the 1983 fall semester …and then headed to Europe and the Middle East for my second tour with *The Con-*

tinentals. This time, instead of criss-crossing America, I traveled around Europe and experienced staying in youth hostels, spending nights in churches built before our country existed, and even lodging with families who didn't speak English.

Traveling through Budapest, Hungary I, along with a couple of other tour members, lodged with a family connected with an "underground church" in the then communist country. In honor of our being in their home, they invited numerous other fellow Christians from neighboring Romania, Yugoslavia, and even as far away as East Germany. The only problem was that few spoke a common language. Having an idea, I decided to use the universal language of music, so I sat at the piano and played "Jesus Loves Me." To my surprise and delight, the host family and all the guests joined in singing …each in their own language. It's hard to describe the feelings from that evening and the impact on my young life of those wonderful people who chose to trust Christ in a hostile environment. Although severe hardships plagued their lives, they possessed a faith which transcended their surroundings, and pointed them to *the Hope* that outshone the gloom and despair of communist oppression. Impressed by the courageous conviction of these families, I was inspired by their trust in Christ during harsh times.

Yet, although traveling through the Alps, Rome, and into Israel … seeing breathtaking landscapes and experiencing fascinating historical landmarks on seemingly every corner, I still found myself increasingly eager to start college and find the source of something that seemed to constantly beckon. Even from half-way across the world, I counted the days until starting a brand new adventure.

Arriving at Belmont three days late because of the tour, I found myself not only playing "catch-up" on sleep, but also in classes and college life. Mother and Daddy moved my belongings into my dorm room and even stood in line to register me for classes; so that I could literally dash into Nashville to launch my academic career. At Belmont, I jumped in quickly and threw myself full-throttle into classes, voice lessons, making new friends …and even managed to jog several miles a day. For as long as I can remember, I pushed myself towards the only life I knew: success and achievement. I was determined not to let a little fatigue stand in the way of accomplishment. That driven philosophy harkened back to hot summer days in Texas toiling away in Grandmother Grace's garden, listening to her often say, "I'll rest when I'm in Heaven."

Unfortunately, I took that phrase quite literally.

Exercising and running every day, I toned my body into the best physical shape of my life, and the fall semester uneventfully progressed with no medical issues whatsoever, other than a bout with Nashville allergies. That part of Music City is left off all the marketing brochures.

Although specifically asking for a non-smoking roommate, the people in charge of dorms inexplicably assigned me to share a room with a girl who incessantly smoked. With my hay fever and allergies, this arrangement clearly had no chance of turning out well …particularly for a vocal performance major. Another student in the dorm, Nancy Strode, suffered the same problem, so we prevailed on the dorm mother and resident advisor to allow us to room together. Swapping roommates, Nancy and I quickly and happily settled in together; launching a lifetime friendship.

As that freshman fall progressed, November brought a phone call from long-time friend and former voice teacher, Linda Dunshee; she wanted to try to get together and catch up. Linda lived in Dallas at the time, and through several phone calls we calculated how to meet. Negotiating a half-way mark between Nashville and Dallas, we agreed to spend the weekend in Little Rock, Arkansas. Both planning to leave Friday morning, November 18; each of us would make a five-hour trip.

On Thursday evening, November 17, 1983 …I chose to stay up entirely too late. Since arriving at Belmont, I maintained a frantic pace that left hardly any time for sleep, and topping it all off, the Tennessee autumn brought on a cold. Taking some Robitussin, I tried to punch through the fatigue and sniffles; studying while Nancy reluctantly helped me pack for the weekend trip. Noticing how tired I appeared, she strongly discouraged me from making the trip.

A friend from *The Continentals*, Mike Feller, asked me to join him for breakfast the next morning before heading out to meet Linda. Mike, an accomplished drummer from Los Angeles, took me on as a project to launch a music career. Mike's brother, Bob, served as director for my second tour with *The Continentals*, and Linda served as a "tour-mom," for a separate group during the previous summer …so we all felt like one big *Continental* family. Although breakfast did not fit with my schedule, Mike's relocating back to California that weekend did not offer much time to meet together, and so, waking up early after only a couple hours of sleep …I headed down the street and met Mike at one of Nashville's renowned establishments: the Pancake Pantry.

On any given day the line to get in stretches around the block. NFL players, music stars, nationally known comedians, and politicians are among the regulars who will stand in line for a seat at the table.

Waking up early in order to avoid the infamous line of waiting customers, Mike and I got a table and one of the servers bustled up to us and said, "Sugar, what would you like to drink this morning?"

Ingrained as it was in my taste buds from Carl's Café, I enthusiastically requested coffee …glad I wouldn't have to get on the countertop and sing for it! As the waitress rushed off, I felt the weariness of too little sleep, cold medicine, and nearly a solid year of running at full speed.

Chapter 3 Path of Purpose

"Should I go, Mike?" I asked while stifling a yawn. "I'm kind of tired, and I really don't feel well, but Linda already left Dallas, and is on the way to meet me in Arkansas."

"I don't know, Parker," Mike replied. He rarely called me "Gracie." For some unknown reason he simply liked referring to me by my last name. "I've got several music folks I want you to meet ...they're pretty interested in you, and I think it might be a good career move."

Thinking for a moment, he added, "But I don't want to mess up your weekend."

Settling the issue, I committed to go to Little Rock and meet Linda. Mike and I left the Pantry, ran some errands, and met with a few of Mike's friends anyway ... before I had to insist on leaving.

Even so, I didn't actually pull out of Nashville until nearly eleven o'clock in the morning. Mom and Dad called me twice to say I sounded too tired, and that I shouldn't go. Nancy also fussed at me, and said that I was in no shape to make this trip. Like many seventeen-year-olds, I suffered from the delusion of immortality, so I shunned their advice, told them I would be fine, and that I would pray for God's angels to watch over me.

Drinking a lot of coffee I rushed out of my dorm to the parking lot; vowing to Nancy that I would call the moment I arrived in Little Rock. Tossing my overnight bag into the trunk and opening the door of the petite green Honda Accord, I rested my right hand on the cold metal roof of the car, closed my eyes, and prayed a familiar prayer of protection; fulfilling my promise to my parents to ask for God's angels to watch over me as I traveled. Had I stayed in Fort Walton Beach, I would have been normally attending my senior year ...safe in the harbor of high school and near my family. The wind filled my sails, however, and life beckoned; I answered the summons ...regardless of the risks. Bending to slide into the car, I paused a moment longer and offered another prayer; not a prayer of protection, but rather one reflecting a desire to be molded into a woman who pleased God.

"Lord, continue making me into the woman you want me to be."

Not knowing I was climbing into my cute little Honda for the last time with an athletic, trim, pain-free body, I slipped behind the wheel, drove out of my college dorm parking lot, and journeyed toward the interstate. Navigating down Nashville's famous Music Row, I quickly wheeled on to Interstate 40 aiming west towards Little Rock, Arkansas. Another friend of mine made a tape of a tune he composed, and asked me to write some lyrics. Pushing the cassette into the tape player and listening to the melody, I allowed my mind to toy around with a few words. As good ideas came to me, I quickly jotted them down in a notebook lying haphazardly in the passenger seat. I settled into the trip, but somehow felt uneasy.

If only I didn't feel so sleepy.

Ninety Minutes Later

Lying trapped in the car with a broken, bleeding body …and staring into flames, it all came crashing down: hopes, dreams, ambitions, and even my much touted tenacity could not help me. Nothing I owned, nothing I could do, no one I knew…could save me. Helpless in a burning car somewhere in the middle of Tennessee, images of family, friends, classmates, and teachers tore through my mind; none of them aware that I lay by the side of the highway …dying and alone.

"It can't end this way," I thought as my heart broke with the knowledge that I was going to die …right there. What will happen to my family? How will they ever know? This can't be happening ...after all I've accomplished and survived. Oh, God, please no! Streaming from a cut just at the hairline, the blood freely flowing over my face now mingled with tears. With my thoughts growing increasingly murky, I summoned the last bit of energy to push back the darkness that seemed so close. Through bruised and bleeding lips, nearly glued shut from all the blood pouring from my scalp and down my cheeks and a mouth that seemed strangely difficult to open, I managed to speak out loud.

A resigned voice cried out from the twisted and burning car: "Jesus, only you can save me, now!"

Part II

Ordeal

You have some difficult trials to bear
but you need them since God has
allowed these events to happen.
He knows how to select them.
You could not have picked for yourself
what God brings into your life through the cross.

The cross that you would pick out
would build your self-will
instead of breaking it down.

—Fenelon
The Seeking Heart

Chapter 4

Aftermath

...This youth that you see here
I snatch'd one half out of the jaws of death...

—William Shakespeare
Twelfth Night, Act III, Sc. IV

ying in the burning wreckage of my car, the heartbroken cry to Jesus faded from my lips. As I expended what I thought was my last breath, the interstate above became a chaotic flurry of activity; bringing the traffic heading west to a standstill. Rippling east, the line of cars and trucks sat frozen for miles and miles. Reacting quickly and grabbing fire extinguishers while leaping from the cabs of their eighteen-wheelers now parked haphazardly along the interstate, a throng of trucker-drivers scrambled and half-slid down the ravine toward the burning car. Several truckers called for rescue workers on CB radios, and others sprayed fire smothering foam all over the burning engine ...littering the scene of the crash with used extinguishers.

Although remaining unconscious, the growing crowd of volunteers trying to save me kept peppering me with questions.

Apparently, I gave them my name …and even my parents' phone number, but later learned I mixed up the numbers. Helplessly waiting beside the wrecked car, the truckers did their best to keep me awake until paramedics arrived. Even the toughest of them felt knots of fear when peering into the smashed heap of the Honda.

"What is your name? What is your phone number? Don't go to sleep," a trucker named Ricky kept repeating to me. Driving the eighteen-wheeler directly behind me, he witnessed the whole wreck from the cab of his truck.

"Help's on the way, little girl," another said. "You just hold on, now," a third trucker echoed. "We're going to get you out of there," a fourth chimed in while choking back tears. Seeing me covered with blood, and my body twisted like a pretzel, most inwardly believed a young girl lay dying right before their eyes. Noticing my nearly severed right foot caused more than a few to grow nauseous.

"Hang in there young lady, you're going to be alright," they repeated, but with less conviction as they watched the floorboard of the car filling with dark pools of congealing blood. Tough, hardened men used to seeing tragedy on the road stood by with unabashed tears in their eyes while witnessing a life apparently slipping away. Not knowing what else to do, several brave men simply wrapped the foot dangling by a strip of skin in the only cloth they had, and fastened it loosely to my leg in order to keep it from being missed in the efforts to extract me.

Through the gruesome ordeal, one man kept reaching into the car to help re-start my heart. Again and again, leaning through the wreckage and administering CPR, he worked to keep me alive while continuing to clear away the blood filling my mouth and throat. All the truckers witnessed him repeatedly resuscitating me, but no one ever identified him … and he seemed to vanish as quickly as he appeared; we never heard from him again.

Chapter 4 Aftermath

For the record, I believe that God's angels actively work around us. Clearly familiar with archangels, cherubim, and seraphim often mentioned in the Bible, I've never actually read of "paramedic or truck driving angels" anywhere ...but who knows?

Within minutes (seemingly hours to the powerless onlookers), the sounds of several sirens split the air as rescue workers, highway patrol officers, and the sheriff's deputies raced to the scene. Reaching into the car, paramedics immediately started me on fluids while another team used the "jaws of life" to extract my broken, mangled body from what was left of the small sedan. Through the arduous process of just getting me out of the car, up the embankment, and into the ambulance, ninety minutes ticked by; everyone knew that time was now the enemy of this girl whose life was literally seeping away with each heartbeat. Once inside the ambulance, they wasted no time rushing me to the nearest hospital, now known as Camden General Hospital in Benton County, Tennessee.

The staff at the tiny community hospital quickly recognized the facility could not handle my level of trauma, and the closest hospital with adequate facilities and staff lay in either Memphis or Nashville. Making a split-second decision based upon the miles to Nashville versus Memphis, while calculating flight times to and from the nearest hospital with helicopter service ... they chose to put me back into the ambulance and return me to Nashville. By the time a Med-Evac helicopter could be contacted to fly to Benton County, the ambulance could be well on the way to Nashville ...and would probably beat the time of any summoned life-flight. Screaming east on Interstate 40, the racing ambulance carried me to Nashville's first major trauma facility closest to the interstate: St. Thomas Hospital.

Calling ahead to inform the emergency room staff of arrival time and patient condition, the triage team prepared for an MVA (motor vehicle accident) with massive trauma.

As the ambulance shrieked up to the emergency room entrance, a whole team of people took over from the paramedics, and rushed me straight into surgery. Holding IV bags, visually assessing me, and taking my blood pressure all at the same time, this seemingly frenzied group operated like a well-oiled machine. Expert eyes scanned me from head to toe, making mental and written notes of injuries, fluid levels, and breathing condition. In mere seconds, trained eyes knew enough, and nurses exchanged quick glances conveying pessimism. One yelled out a blood pressure of forty over twenty, and they all witnessed blood bubbles foaming from my mouth. In layman's terms, my lungs were filling with blood; I was bleeding to death from the enormous trauma ...externally and internally. My heart stopped four times that day, and many of the ER team inwardly feared the worst. On a gurney in the emergency room at St. Thomas Hospital, it appeared I truly was drawing my last breath.

Despite incredible odds however, and in the middle of what many call chaos, surgeons literally reached into my broken body; putting themselves between me and certain death. Without wasting a second, a team of highly skilled professionals shouldered the colossal task of saving my life.

The triage report was catastrophic: Every bone below my waist sustained some type of fracture (one resident later reported he counted nearly two hundred breaks), multiple compound fractures, numerous internal injuries including partial loss of spleen, appendix, and eventually gall bladder. Slamming against the steering wheel fractured my sternum, and the force of impact actually flattened the gold add-a-beads on the necklace I wore. The mashed jewelry ripped into my chest. The damage also included a frontal lobe concussion, numerous lacerations ...including the eighteen-inch gash left by the mile-marker post, severed right ankle held on only by skin, fractured pelvis, fractured jaw, and a crushed left foot along with a large portion of flesh the size of a man's hand ripped off my left shin that exposed the bone.

As the medical team worked tirelessly, but grimly ...the afternoon turned into evening. Not one unnecessary word passed between them. Hope was not discussed, and feelings were not shown; life and death were in every move of their hands. Emotions shelved; the years of training and skill took over. Without stopping, watching the clock, or even thinking of various other tasks in their lives that needed their time, the surgeons' only thoughts focused on what used to be a healthy young woman.

Furiously pumping blood into me to replace the amount flowing out of the massive number of wounds, nurses assisted the vascular surgeon as he performed an emergency exploratory surgery, opening me from abdomen to sternum ...working quickly to stop the massive internal bleeding. The transfusion count soared to two dozen units; more than three times the normal amount of blood in the bodies of most seventeen-year-old girls.

The orthopedic surgeon directed his eyes and hands to the wreck's most devastating injuries: my legs. Piecing together fragments, re-setting bones, and inserting a body shop's worth of metal to shore up the shattered bones, he did what "all the king's horses and all the king's men" couldn't do. The severed right ankle received a great deal of attention, and, using a Hoffman device, he re-attached the foot. The Hoffman device, an open tube-like apparatus, encompasses the limb ...and anchors multiple pins piercing through the skin and bone; holding everything together until the bone fuses. With my foot fastened in place, the surgeon suspended my leg in traction. The hours mounted, and still, they pushed on, driven by the calling on their lives ...and the desire to save and heal.

Finally, the exhausted team put down their tools and sent me to the critical care pods. Stabilized temporarily, my life lay in the hands of a greater physician.

Chapter 5

From Whence Cometh My Help?

God is our refuge and strength, a very present help in trouble.
Therefore we will not fear, though the earth should change
And though the mountains slip into the heart of the sea;
though its waters roar and foam,
Though the mountains quake at its swelling pride.

—Psalm 46:1-3 (NASB)

All afternoon, Nancy felt uneasy; impatiently waiting for the agreed upon phone call from me to let her know I had safely arrived in Little Rock. While literally standing guard over the dorm phone, she lunged for the receiver upon hearing the first ring ...only to discover her mother at the other end. Carolyn Strode, calling from her Nashville residence only minutes away from campus, told Nancy to come home immediately. Flatly refusing her mother, my distraught roommate exclaimed, "I'm not going anywhere Mother; not until Gracie calls me to let me know she made it to Little Rock!"

"Nancy," her mother said softly, "Gracie's not going to call you."

"What do you mean?" Nancy nearly yelled into the phone, approaching hysteria.

"Gracie's had an accident. You need to come home, and I'll tell you about it then."

Tearing out of the dorm, Nancy raced home as fast as she could, ignoring speed limits and stop signs. Rushing into her home, Nancy burst out, "What happened to Gracie?" Mrs. Strode tried unsuccessfully to get her now hysterical daughter to sit down, but Nancy adamantly refused. "Mother, just tell me!"

"Evidently, Gracie fell asleep at the wheel and is in serious condition at St. Thomas Hospital."

Through sobs, Nancy shrieked, "I told her not to go!"

Once Nancy and I moved in together, I filled out new local emergency contacts for Belmont and listed Nancy's parents, Dr. and Mrs. Wilborn Strode. Dr. Strode, a well-known and respected Nashville obstetrician, made the perfect choice for anyone to call in the unlikely event that anything ever happened to me ...or so I thought while filling out the paperwork and listing his office and home number. Unable to locate my parents, Belmont officials, who by now were fully briefed by the highway patrol officers who discovered my college ID, tried paging Dr. Strode after unsuccessfully trying to locate my parents, but he was delivering a baby at nearby Baptist Hospital ...so Mrs. Strode received the call at home.

Mrs. Strode made Nancy promise she would go back to the dorm to let my classmates know what happened, and Nancy agreed. She then got into her car, and headed straight to St. Thomas Hospital by herself. Both

Chapter 5 From Whence Cometh My Help?

Nancy and I seemed to have had a problem following directions from our parents that day.

Dashing into the critical-care waiting room, Nancy breathlessly sprinted to the visitor's desk to ask about Gracie Parker. Scrolling through her list of critical care patients, the volunteer stated, "We don't have a Gracie Parker."

Stunned for a moment, her heart nearly skipping a beat while fearing the worst, Nancy tried again, "Look up Mary Grace Parker."

"Yes, we have a Mary Grace Parker. Are you family?"

Without batting an eye, Nancy lied right through her teeth, "Yes, I'm family!" Inwardly justifying the lie with, *"I'm the only family she's got right now …and I will not leave her alone."*

"She's still in surgery; we'll call you when we have an update."

Nancy, not quite twenty years old, took a deep breath and turned to look at other families waiting beside her; each with their own trauma. Concerned only about me and wanting me not to be alone, Nancy now felt terribly alone herself…and very scared.

After surgeons sent me to the critical care pod following the initial round of surgeries, the nurses paged "family of Mary Grace Parker." Rushing up to the desk with her fingers mentally crossed behind her back, Nancy again announced herself as my sister.

"You can go up, now."

Heading to the elevator leading to the critical care pods, Nancy prepared herself for what she would see. With a childhood spent around doctors, hospitals, and nurses, Nancy felt ready for whatever lay on the floor above. Stepping off the elevator, a nurse approached her, and Nancy stated again that she was my sister.

"In Christ, I am her sister," she whispered to herself.

"Honey, are you up to seeing her like this?" the nurse asked pointedly.

"Oh yes, my father's a doctor and I can handle it." Nancy said with growing confidence.

"Okay," the nurse said reluctantly. "But some things you're going to see may look strange to you; difficult things you may not understand right now."

Nodding with feigned comprehension, Nancy followed the nurse into the pod and instantly realized her inability to handle what confronted her in the tiny room. Gazing at the carnage caused from a car accident that took only mere moments, Nancy's heart broke while looking at the wounds covering my body. Waves of nausea hit Nancy …so much so that the nurse quickly stepped closer and asked her if she was going to be alright. Taking a deep breath, steadying herself, and forcing her reeling senses to settle, she eased closer; taking off her shoes so as not to make any sound that could wake me.

Forcing her eyes to focus on my head first, Nancy noticed a large scratch under my chin, and a sizeable laceration along the hairline; except for the odd way my jaw looked, they seemed to be the only two noteworthy injuries to my face. Somewhere along the way, nurses or paramedics wiped the blood from my chin, forehead, and cheeks, but my hair still contained matted clumps of blood and tiny pieces of glass.

Painstakingly reaching to barely touch my hand, Nancy noted they were both undamaged, but nearly devoid of color …as if all the blood had drained from them. Feeling relief that my face, hands, and arms escaped mutilation, Nancy then allowed her eyes to shift towards the part of me that had not. The sight of my mangled legs caused her to turn nearly as white as my hands. Steeling herself for multiple lacerations, Nancy felt her own heart almost stop as she looked at my right leg lying completely exposed to the bone; the entire leg virtually peeled back. Continuously dripping blood flowing from the gaping maw of what only hours ago was a lithe, beautiful leg …trickled and gathered into a basin positioned beneath my suspended foot and ankle.

With tears rolling down her face, Nancy looked over my legs and couldn't help but remember watching me exercise in the dorm room. Toning my legs, I used to read a book while leaning against the wall in a seated position. Looking up from her studies while lying in her bed, Nancy would often laugh at my tenacity while shaking her head in amazement at my leg muscles twitching and shaking with the strain …as I calmly read my Bible or a textbook. Nancy knew those once beautiful and shapely legs would never be the same.

A severe frontal lobe concussion left me in an unconscious state, so I have no memory of anything after blacking out while still trapped in the car. Even while in this condition, however, I twitched, groaned and sometimes spoke. Astonished, Nancy saw my mouth moving and heard me whisper out, *"Goodness."*

When feeling the temptation to swear, I often used the word, "Goodness." In any other place, Nancy may have laughed at the outrageousness of the understatement. But laughter and smiles remain scarce in critical care pods. Leaning in closer, Nancy heard me say two more words: *"I hurt."*

Noticing the way I struggled to open my mouth, Nancy whispered forcefully to the nurse, indignantly pointing out the exposed leg and, evidently, a broken jaw. Calmly looking at Nancy, the gracious nurse motioned her to step outside the pod, and told the flustered and overwhelmed young woman, "You don't understand … they can't close her leg because of the swelling; it would just split wide open. They're not fixing everything right now, honey; they're just trying to keep her from dying in the next few hours."

Nancy's heart sank. Racing around for hours on nothing but adrenaline and fear, it all caught up with my roommate, and she felt her head swim. The thought of my dying, maybe even right there in front of her, felt like a kick in the stomach; and Nancy struggled to even keep a coherent thought. Recognizing the emotions, fatigue, and grief engulfing the young college student, the nurse reached out with compassion, put her arm around Nancy, and quietly said, "Honey, you need to understand, this little girl was hurt so bad, that if she lives …she will have a lifetime of surgery ahead of her. They will never be able to fix all that happened to her."

Crestfallen, Nancy went back over to the bed and whispered into my ear that she loved me; that I wasn't alone; she was there for me. Before leaving my bedside, Nancy heard me say something else. Breaking into sobs, she heard me whisper through a fractured jaw and pale, almost lifeless lips …

"Jesus, Jesus, Jesus."

Chapter 6
A Frantic Convergence

If you're going through Hell, keep going.

—Winston Churchill

Returning to the downstairs waiting room, Nancy met an anxious group of friends. The nurses refused to allow anyone else to visit me, so they all clamored around Nancy for information. At two o'clock in the morning, an exhausted and emotionally drained Nancy shared highlights with the group waiting, but didn't have the heart or even ability to relay the extent of the damage. Close friends seemed to breathe a sigh of relief, falsely thinking that I was merely "bumped up badly" and had a few broken bones. One even made an attempt at humor to lighten the mood.

Well-meaning smiles vanished as an officer in civilian clothes stepped up to the group asking questions about their knowledge of Mary Grace Parker. The entire group froze in shock as this unknown person authoritatively stated, "There appears to be a suicide note."

Jaime Work, now Dr. Jaime Work, served as the president of the Baptist Student Union at Belmont, and is one of the best preachers I've ever known. He was a pastor that night ...long before his ordination. Receiving the call from the Belmont administration, Jaime quickly headed over to St. Thomas with his fiancé, Dana. Upon hearing the report, Jaime, a quiet, soft-spoken man, hurriedly stepped forward and said there must be some sort of mistake.

A longtime childhood friend from Fort Walton Beach, Jayme Tidwell, along with her fiancé (and now husband for twenty-five years), fellow Belmont student, Cole Young, echoed the sentiments, and Nancy nearly came (more) unglued as she growled fiercely at the officer, "You don't know this girl, and you don't have any idea of what you're talking about."

Defensively, the officer read the words I scribbled while driving in an effort to write lyrics to my friend's song.

Father here I am seeking you once more,

Giving up to you these burdens, I've given up before.

Why must there be a constant struggle in me; a giving of myself?

Granted, they're not the best lyrics ever written, but certainly not a suicide note. Hearing the words read from my bloodstained notebook, longtime friend, Lyndon Wilson, hanging back behind the crowd, stepped forward in an effort to clear up the misunderstanding.

"That's the song we were working on together," he quietly said to the officer, now facing an angry mob of my friends. Lyndon's explanation temporarily diffusing the situation, the officer left. The issue, however, remained unresolved for some time, and for a while, added insult to injury; leaving all my friends and eventually family wondering *"Did Gracie try to kill herself?"*

As Nancy left me in the critical care pods, Mom and Dad, followed by Bobby and Andrea, raced north to Nashville. Hours earlier, using my driver's license, the Tennessee sheriff tracked down the sheriff in Fort Walton Beach who, thankfully, knew my family …and Andrea's in-laws. Calling Bobby's brother, Greg, they finally located Mom at my sister's apartment in Pensacola. Collecting all the information from the local authorities, Mom called the sheriff in Tennessee. Before making the call, Mom's information remained limited; her daughter had a wreck and was in a Nashville hospital. Minutes into the conversation with the Tennessee sheriff, Mom quickly realized the seriousness of the accident, and just as quickly recognized her inability to deal with this new reality. Unable to hold it together, Mom relinquished much of the information flow to Andrea. Between sobs and her own fears, Andrea tracked down Daddy and Bobby who were both deer hunting in lower Alabama.

Hastily throwing a change of clothes into the car, Andrea and Mom rushed to meet Dad and Bobby on Interstate 65, south of Montgomery. My sister, only twenty-one, had one eye on the road, and the other on our hysterical mother. For nearly three hours, Andrea sped along the back roads from Pensacola to the meeting point, gripping the wheel tightly while trying to keep her own emotions in check.

Finally meeting Bobby and Daddy, Andrea gratefully handed Mom over to our father, while nearly collapsing in her own husband's arms. Safe with Bobby, she finally allowed her grief and fear to come to the surface, and Bobby did his best to console my sister.

This was long before cell phones were common, so my family periodically stopped at rest areas and service stations and sprinted to the nearest pay phone. The hospital operator routed their calls straight into the operating room where a surgical nurse provided what few updates were available. With every call, the nurse on duty could only confirm I was still alive. At one point, the orthopedic surgeon, Leonard Marvin, MD*, talked to Daddy. All he could say to my now weeping father was that I clung to life. Abruptly ending the conversation to return to repairing my body, Dr. Marvin left my father staring at a pay phone somewhere in Alabama; feeling like his whole world was caving in on him. With his heart sinking deeper by the moment, Daddy called his longtime college friend, Bill Hillard, who lived north of Nashville and asked if he would go to the hospital to check on my status until my family could arrive.

At some point, Andrea contacted Linda's husband, Bob Dunshee, at their home in Dallas who then quickly called a frantic Linda at the hotel in Little Rock where we planned to stay for the weekend. Worried sick, Linda knew it was too late to start her own trip to Nashville, so she cried herself to sleep; determined to drive to Nashville the next morning.

Driving through the night, my parents somehow obtained directions to St. Thomas, and then rushed into the critical care waiting area. It was not quite dawn as they hurried past the by now dwindling group, and the staff ushered them straight to critical care. Riding in the elevator, Mom could no longer push this off as a bad dream. The elevator represented the ultimate reality to her; carrying her to one of a parent's worst nightmares. Glancing at Mom, and knowing how distraught she felt, Andrea, a licensed practical nurse (LPN), took the lead and said she'd go in first to see how things looked.

Name has been changed in keeping with HIPAA laws.

Chapter 6 A Frantic Convergence

Encountering the same scenario as my *pretend sister*, Nancy, did just hours earlier, my real sister returned to gather the rest of the family … and ushered them into the tiny pod. Andrea's nursing training helped her understand the seriousness of my condition. Later she confided that seeing everything hooked up to me, save only a trachea tube, clearly communicated my status; but she parsed out information carefully so as not to completely overwhelm our parents. Not knowing what to expect, they felt a slight twinge of hope when they saw my face and hands …I still looked like the daughter they sent off to school. With no apparent disfigurement, a brief flicker of relief hit them.

Peering around the sheet and dressings covering my lower body, they stared at my legs.

With tears rolling down their faces, the emotions bounced from horror to despair. Daddy, unable to contain his grief, kept repeating, "God, why would you allow this to happen to my baby girl? What has she ever done to deserve such a thing?"

Mom could hardly breathe while whispering over and over, "Oh Lord, this can't be happening!"

Approaching my exhausted family, the charge nurse provided a report. Hours earlier as the nurse was trying to learn medical history from my "sister," Nancy finally had to come clean and admit the truth to the nurse. Taking pity on her, the nurse let Nancy stay, but they still needed more information on my background. As the nurse continued, she mentioned my unresponsive left eye indicated possible brain damage to the triage team. Listening to the nurse relay the assessment, Mom quickly found the presence of mind to clear up the misdiagnosis and explained the eye problem. Resolving the question of brain damage eased breathing for everyone …just a bit.

Although wanting to know as much as possible, the fatigue and stress caused them to struggle to keep up with all that happened. Midway through the nurse's report, the orthopedic surgeon, Dr. Marvin, still in scrubs, approached the weary group and introduced himself. Having a key figure in charge provided a place to focus, and they gave him their full attention. Dr. Marvin, never one to use many words, economized the report into a few simple sentences. Nodding with understanding, they hung on his every word. In less than twenty-four hours, my family's life flipped upside-down; the only person on the scene able to lead them through this nightmare …was this stranger in whose hands now literally lay the life of one of their own.

Once again taking the lead, Andrea comprehended the news better than the rest. Filtering the surgeon's report through her training, Andrea knew the situation was bleak. Reeling from the sensory overload, Daddy tried to process all that he heard, but it quickly faded as only one question consumed him. Inspecting a few more things before leaving to treat other patients, Dr. Marvin turned to leave the pod.

"Just a minute, Doc," my father called out.

Turning back towards my weary family, the surgeon paused momentarily.

With his heart in his throat, and twisting his always familiar gray fedora in his hands, the question surged from the bottom of my father's soul, "Doc, is my daughter going to live?"

Hesitating just slightly, he looked Daddy square in the eyes and curtly said, "We don't know. We've done all we can do …you'll have to ask God."

Chapter 7

"We Gather Together"

"For I know the plans I have for you," declares the Lord,
"plans to prosper you and not to harm you,
plans to give you hope and a future."

—Jeremiah 29:11 (NIV)

Numbed by the shock of it all, my family struggled to make sense of how their lives had changed. Keeping vigil over the possible death of the youngest family member felt too surreal, and each of them wrestled with dark, disheartening thoughts while often blankly staring into space. Mom simply could not believe any of this was actually happening. In the waiting area, she felt space to breathe and denial offered a measure of emotional comfort. Stepping into the tiny elevator for the precious few visits allowed to the pods, Mom's heart froze with fear as reality, shoving all denial away, forced itself upon her bombarded senses.

Linda arrived around noon the following day, and spelled my family while they freshened up. Sitting with me fighting for life in critical care, Linda struggled with a flood of feelings. Since taking me on as a voice student six years earlier, Linda felt such love and motherly feelings for me, and her heart broke with guilt, horror, and an overwhelming sense of loss. As she gazed at the bandages covering so much of my body, Mike Feller appeared. Members of *The Continentals* attending Belmont tracked down Mike's brother Bob in Los Angeles, who called Mike as he packed for his move to California. Rushing over to the hospital, Mike walked into the critical care unit and nearly passed out upon seeing me. Linda's description was that the blood left his face and he looked as white as a ghost.

Leaving St. Thomas and driving to California the next day, Mike stopped by the scene of the wreck to take pictures, and then headed to the impound lot to see the car. With his jaw clenched tightly and his hands digging into his own steering wheel during the long drive west, Mike re-lived those last few hours we had together; repeatedly criticizing himself for not stopping me from making the trip.

Camping out in the family waiting room, Dad took the lead and at-tempted to organize their next steps, but strict critical care visiting hours, coupled with a fear of wandering too far from the waiting room in the event of a call, led them to simply sleep on the floor alongside other anx-ious families.

After a few days, Daddy and Bobby drove over to the impound lot in Benton county to gather my belongings from the wreck. The lot at-tendant led them to what remained of my car. Remembering buying the automobile, Daddy felt tears in his eyes again as he imagined his daugh-ter trapped inside the smashed vehicle. Examining the interior, the tears came even faster when he observed dried pools of blood on the floor-boards. Gathering my luggage and possessions, they soberly returned to Nashville on the same path I took in the ambulance just days earlier.

With no sign of any change in my condition, Bobby and Andrea, both in school with approaching exams, temporarily returned to Pensacola. My grandmother's cousin, Peggy, lived in an apartment across the street, and she provided a guest room where Mom and Dad could shower and catch up on some rest, but Mom adamantly refused to leave the hospital for anything more than a quick nap and shower.

Thanksgiving came two weeks into the nightmare, and Bobby and Andrea made the long drive back to Nashville while on their school break ...along with Grandmother Parker and Aunt Anne. A bittersweet re-union, they huddled around the table in the hospital cafeteria to eat an institutional Thanksgiving dinner ...while my life hung by a hair just one floor above them. Surviving the Great Depression, burying her oldest son, and then the death of her husband, Grandmother Parker knew the importance of pushing forward, and so she brought a few Thanksgiving decorations ...and even put a fold-out paper turkey on the table. Al-though acknowledging the gesture with a glimmer of appreciation, they all despondently picked at their food; feeling frustrated and heartbroken.

Critical care visiting hours dictated their lives; days and nights blend-ed together as the elevator transported them to and from the tiny pod that now occupied every thought. Along the way, more visitors appeared. A local church in Nashville, St. Bartholomew's, received a call from our church in Destin, asking if members would take time to visit the devas-tated family. Sending over several "hospital ministry" team members, Imogene (Gene) Stranch, Mrs. Tom Seckman (M.E. as she was known), and a new member of the church's hospital ministry team, Sam Clarke regularly showed up at St. Thomas to pray and spend time with my family who gratefully welcomed the friendly faces and warm hearts. Complete strangers one week prior, these dear people loved my family through those weeks, months, and even years ...particularly Mom. Dad traveled back and forth to Fort Walton Beach several times, but Mom never left the hospital. Gene, M.E. Seckman, and Sam prayed, talked, and served as a source of encouragement to my struggling mother for hours at a time ...nearly every day.

During all this time, I continued muttering, praying, quoting Bible verses, and even singing. Knowing the nature of my injuries and unconscious state, visitors were shocked when I spontaneously mumbled out hymns and scripture verses. Mistakenly convinced of gained awareness, they tried engaging me, but to no avail. I simply would not wake up.

While I fought for my life, the hospital billing staff was putting pressure on Daddy to start making arrangements for the massive costs accumulating every hour. With a cloud of suspicion surrounding the accident as an attempted suicide, approvals were slow in coming for the release of funds. The insurance company refused to provide authorization for the payments while the investigation remained open. Daddy called our family's insurance agent in Florida, John Hunnicutt, to enlist his help in convincing the insurance company that I had not attempted to take my life. Going way beyond the call of duty, Mr. Hunnicutt surprised my family by driving from Florida to Nashville the next day in order to meet with the billing office at St. Thomas. Firmly telling them to leave my parents alone and deal only with him, Mr. Hunnicutt worked behind the scenes and helped quickly to resolve the situation. Amazingly, the cassette tape of the song I was writing lyrics to remained intact, and that, along with the testimony of friends and family helped in clearing up all the misconceptions about the accident. The investigation was closed, and the insurance company began immediately authorizing payment for medical services. Everyone breathed a sigh of relief …and authorities even returned the blood-stained notebook with my scribbled lyrics that caused so much confusion.

Today, that notebook resides safely tucked away in my desk.

For three weeks, friends from school, family, tour friends from *The Continentals,* pastors, ministry teams from St. Bartholomew's and even strangers clung to hope and prayed for Gracie Parker to wake up. Each word or song passing from my mouth sparked new excitement in anyone who happened to be sitting close by, but as the words faded from cracked lips, the tiny hope also vanished.

During the precious few visiting hours, several friends from *The Continentals* who converged on the hospital rushed to fill up the tiny elevator preventing Andrea from her turn to visit me. My sister did not take that well, and a couple of angry looks from her sent them back to the crowded waiting room. Passing the time, many of them clustered in a separate family waiting area and held Bible studies, prayer vigils and generally struggled for weeks trying to understand God's will in all of this. Some of them later confided how this event tore down a lot of their theological ideas of God, suffering, and His sovereignty.

Although they had a sizeable head start ...it did for me, too.

At the end of the third week following my accident, my father sat alone with me reading his Bible and pouring out his heart to God during one of those precious visits. Interrupting his prayer, he heard me mumble. "Daddy, Daddy." Hearing my whimpers, he looked up from his Bible to see my lips moving again. Something seemed different in the way I spoke, so he stood up and leaned over my bed, holding his ear just above my face to listen to the faint sounds coming from my lips.

Holding his breath with hope, he whispered, "Daddy's here, Gracie. Daddy's here."

This time he heard me respond to his voice as I choked out again, "Daddy, Daddy."

Resting his hand gently on my head, he quietly repeated, "Daddy's here, Gracie, Daddy's here."

With tears streaming down his face while watching me struggle to regain consciousness, my father whispered a "thank-you" to God for allowing his daughter to awaken; *to live.*

Chapter 8

Daddy's Here

My God, my God, why hast thou forsaken me?

—King David of Israel, Psalm 22:1 (KJV)
Jesus of Nazareth, Matthew 27:46 (KJV)

The best prayers have often more groans than words.

—John Bunyan

Clawing my way back to awareness, I awoke to searing pain unlike anything I had ever experienced … and since that day, I have not had a conscious moment without hurting. Not simply stabbing from a specific location such as my legs; rather my whole body felt enveloped in a cocoon of agony. This had to be a nightmare; no reality could be this bad.

Struggling to focus my thoughts, it appeared I lay in some sort of dark room, chained flat to a hard table. A constant beeping noise kept stabbing into my brain, causing more confusion and agitation.

"Daddy, Daddy," I moaned, although the tearing feeling in my throat must have distorted the words. To my astonishment, I heard my father's deep and recognizable voice over me. "Daddy's here, Gracie, Daddy's here."

With the bed lowered to accommodate my legs in traction, Daddy leaned over and had his face directly above mine, whispering softly to me. The first thing that helped anchor me to reality was my father's voice. Dad was here, but I didn't even know where "here" was. Feeling his strong, work-gnarled hand on my forehead, I heard him whisper, "You had a terrible car accident, honey, and you're in St. Thomas Hospital in Nashville."

The memories of my trip flooded back, but everything seemed nebulous and hard to bring into focus. Somewhere in mid-thought I drifted back to sleep. Not the oblivious sleep I had just emerged from, but rather a fitful sleep filled with disturbing images and loud noises. Even in sleep, the pain crushed into my awareness, and I found myself floundering while struggling to grasp something real and tangible. Through the haze, pain, and disorientation, a slender life-line brushed past me, and I grasped it with all the strength I could muster. When waves of confusion and agony flooded over me, I heard the voice again.

"Daddy's here, Gracie. Daddy's here."

In a critical care pod at St. Thomas, I wrapped my mind around the only phrase penetrating the haze of anesthesia and the massive pain coursing through my body: *"Daddy's here, Gracie, Daddy's here."* The pain didn't subside; the nightmare worsened. But my father's words still echoed in my mind.

Within days of waking up, my thoughts grew clearer and I processed more information …but at the same time, horrific questions flooded my mind …questions my soul screamed to heaven. Louder than the pain now coursing over my body, and into my brain itself, everything in me seemed to shriek out with an agony I couldn't contain. Not wasting time asking family, friends, doctors, and pastors ...I threw my heartbreak, anguish, and grief straight to God.

Why have you allowed this?

How can I live like this?

What's going to happen to me?

What's the matter with me that you would not step in and stop this from happening?

Is there something wrong with me?

Lord, I told others I'd be OK because I belong to You ...and nothing would happen to me because of that. Why didn't you protect me?

The first of many times Heaven's heard those questions from me.

Each question went unanswered; not one issue resolved. In the faintest of sighs, however, seemingly from the depths of my heart, a new voice spoke; one much deeper than Jim Parker's voice as he comforted his youngest daughter. This voice seemed to brush against my very soul. Although ancient and vast beyond my understanding, the voice seemed new and so close that it almost whispered into my ear:

*"Daddy's here, Mary Grace. Daddy ...**is here.**"*

Chapter 9
Faith Worth Imitating

God, who foresaw your tribulation, has specially armed
you to go through it, not without pain but without stain.

—**C.S. Lewis,** *The Problem of Pain*

I struggled to process all the events I had missed during my three weeks of unconsciousness. Patiently recounting the previous month's occurrences, sometimes repeatedly, family and friends filled me in on the details …many of which I really didn't want to know. It's difficult to recall those initial weeks. Every day contained horrific pain, humiliation and embarrassment for being exposed, and revulsion at seeing my once athletic and beautiful legs … now twisted and misshapen with all manner of pins and tubes protruding from them. Even after nearly a month, my hair still had bits of glass and blood matted in it, and I looked awful. Long stays in hospitals often rob patients of "time-awareness"; days, weeks, and months all seemed to run together. Couple that with lying oblivious for twenty-one days, and a great deal of time passed before I "caught up with the clock." A month prior, my days revolved around sunrise and sunset, classes, appointments, and meals. Now, surgery, pain medicine, doctor visits, and bodily functions controlled my sense of time and replaced simple things like an alarm clock or a sunrise.

How many teenagers experience nightmares about standing up in front of the class in only their underwear? I know a worse one.

Critical care doesn't lend itself to modesty; maintaining any kind of decorum about personal space, bodily functions, or even wearing clothes. Over the years, I've witnessed countless numbers of senior citizens sprawled out in hospital beds, naked as jaybirds, and making all kinds of bodily noises …without seeming to notice or care. Maybe growing older lessens certain inhibitions, but at age seventeen, I found myself horrified to spend every day mostly naked while strangers (not to mention my friends) filed in. Bodily functions don't stop while in the hospital, quite the opposite, they often speed up …and *way too many* people express interest in them! Trapped in a web of pulleys and cords, IV lines, and monitors, I felt so exposed and embarrassed as my body performed normal functions without so much as asking permission.

Invariably, a nurse or tech stood close by …always eager for a report.

Sitting on a bedpan gave me nightmares, and I cried every time someone made me use one. Almost without fail, just as soon as the nurse settled me on the horrible device, someone new strolled in …and I felt mortified. The thing about bedpans is this …you need heels to help keep your bottom in place and out of the middle of the bedpan. At the time, my heels were in traction; making it impossible to maintain the proper position. I might as well have been using a diaper. It was horrendous!

I found that I could partly lift myself up using the trapeze bar suspended over the bed, and so Bobby and Daddy, and sometimes Mom and Andrea, would take turns positioning the bedpan while holding my body

in the air to, well, you know. It took a real servant's heart on their parts …
and I'm still humbled by their caring for me. But ohhhh, I hated bedpans.

Eventually doctors got around to tackling lesser injuries …like the unusual way my mouth looked. Mom took the lead on that issue, and unlike
the last time it was discussed, everyone knew by now that I would live …
and things such as jaws, and even matted hair still containing bits of glass
needed to be addressed. A call went out to an oral surgeon, and I once
again headed to surgery; this time to repair my jaw.

Wired jaws forced me to drink everything through a straw; even
blended turkey and gravy, stuffing, and pretty much all of Christmas dinner. After living on Jell-O for weeks, it tasted good. I lost so much
weight, that I was encouraged to drink a lot of milkshakes; I really love
milkshakes. Daddy, who evidently serves as the source of my "sweet-
tooth" seemed especially eager to run and get milkshakes for me. He always seemed to be licking his lips when he returned with my milkshake,
so I'm fairly certain he bought two!

Dr. Marvin visited every day; often two or three times. I met him
a month after my family did during that terrible first night. He seemed
courteous enough, but always stern and grim. We didn't speak much …
he had this horrible habit of showing up at five o'clock in the morning,
knocking loudly on the door while pushing it open. A man of few words,
his lack of talking, and my early morning grogginess, caused our first
couple of conversations to consist of a dozen words from him and a handful of grunts and groans from me.

One day after checking all of his work, as he was preparing to leave,
I summoned the nerve to float out a personal question. "Why don't you
ever smile?" I struggled to ask through wired jaws.

"I'll smile when you walk out of here," was his only response as he closed the door behind him.

That day, I determined to make him smile.

Nancy, staying nearly around the clock the first few days, eventually returned to class …and an empty dorm room. School clearly out of the picture for me, Nancy sadly helped my parents gather all my belongings from the room we shared.

Recently, Nancy met me in Florida and as we prepared to leave, she helped me pack a suitcase. While folding and placing my clothes, Nancy started crying, and I asked her what was the matter. "The last time I helped you pack, was the day of your car wreck," she sobbed. "Then I had to pack up your stuff from our room."

Even after a quarter-century, it still troubled her.

Although my friends from Belmont visited daily, particularly Lyndon and Nancy …Dad, Andrea and Bobby, had to return to Florida. Mom stayed and slept on a foam mattress on the floor next to me once the doctor finally transferred me to a regular room.

Some of my professors also joined the regular procession of classmates and friends to Ward 5 D at St. Thomas. John Arnn, who not only served as my professor, but accompanied me when I auditioned for the school of music was one of my regular visitors. My voice professor, Marjorie Halbert, and music theory professor, Kris Elsberry, not only visited, but also helped me with closing the books on my fall semester. Mike Feller returned from California and Linda Dunshee visited from Dallas. (Once after visiting hours, Mike hid in the shower hoping to stay longer …until my father firmly ushered him from the room.) Mike, a man of deep feelings, mistakenly felt responsible for not stopping me from making the trip; Linda and he both needlessly carried a great deal of guilt for many years.

Chapter 9 Faith Worth Imitating

But as wonderful as visitors were, Mom and I remained alone for most of the time. An excruciating period for both of us, the strain on Mom was enormous, and she felt as helpless as anyone would in this hateful reality. Recalling the sense of feeling overwhelmed when faced with my learning disability, Mom again felt thrust into a world beyond her ability to navigate ...except this time there was no teacher to mentor her; Mom and I had to blaze this trail on our own.

Self-doubt, fear, fatigue, anger, and just about every other negative emotion swirled through her heart as she dug down into the vast reservoir of courage she often overlooked. My car accident served as a harsh exclamation point to an extremely difficult period of time for Carol Parker; within eighteen months, her mother died, her oldest daughter married, and now her youngest daughter, barely out of the nest, clung to life ...and faced a lifetime of disability. I know Mom lay awake at night struggling to understand God's love and compassion as she took care of her daughter's shattered body, while her own broken heart still grieved over the loss of her mother. Sam Clarke and the tiny troop from St. Bartholomew's Episcopal still showed up virtually every day to sit with Mom and comfort her as she wearily tried to adjust to this new burden which seemed to mercilessly pound her to her knees.

Keeping busy seemed to be the only way to hold the pain at bay, so Mom became a whirlwind of activity. The tiny hospital room we shared remained spotless (even by the standards of the nuns who operated the hospital). Taking care of my hair, brushing my teeth, even putting lipstick on my pale lips, keeping a fresh supply of clean gowns nearby, managing the flowers, and all the other daily activities involved with long-term care, Mom threw herself into anything and everything in order to distract from the intense aching in her heart and soul.

Learning many of the problems for patients in traction, Mom determined she would never let me get bedsores or infections, and made sure the tiny room not only remained in pristine shape, but that my body was immaculately cleaned, as well. By doing so, it kept her mind off the hateful negative things, and gave her a positive task she could accomplish; she "...would keep her daughter as clean and healthy as any human being could." With fresh memories of her own mother dying after lying sick in a bed, Mom resolved to not let her daughter go the same way her mother went; she WOULD nurse me back to health.

Unlike so many of the well-meaning visitors who stopped by, Mom didn't offer flowing prayers ...or scriptures of comfort; she simply silently cried out to God every night from her small foam mattress with the only prayer she knew: "Lord, WHY?"

As the days stretched into weeks and months, a few lighter moments presented themselves. The best one I quietly shared with my sister when she whispered what her face so obviously showed; she was pregnant... confirmed by Nancy's father, Dr. Strode. In the midst of such pain and misery, God gave the gift of a new life. We didn't want to stress Mom (more), but we couldn't hide it from her for long. She grew wild eyed and couldn't catch her breath upon discovering the news. She was soon to be a grandmother.

A patient recuperating across the hall provided some comic relief at times. The young man, in traction like me, expressed his rage by often throwing items from his room into the hallway. In order to better hear us in case of emergencies, nurses left both of our doors open at times ... and so bedpans, phones, IV poles, and even portions of the angry man's bed often skidded into my room. Becoming a regular occurrence, I frequently graded the throws like an Olympic judge.

"That's about a five!" I'd yell out through wired jaws, as airborne hospital equipment sailed into my room.

But even the tiny bit of distraction offered by the catapulting patient across the hall didn't diminish the harshness of my new reality; running into each other, the days stretched on dismally.

If "dismal" described the days, then "horrific" serves as a perfect word for the nights. Sleep came sporadically; staring at the ceiling waiting for the next pain medicine injection served as the only activity. I lost count of how many times nurses and techs rolled me to surgery for debriding the wounds, adjusting the Hoffman device holding my severed right foot to my leg, and whatever other surgery I needed. Yearning to find any position of comfort, I resigned myself to never be anything other than truly miserable.

The nagging question that surfaced earlier erupted with a renewed anguish one night as I raged at the ceiling, "Why is this happening to me?!" I screamed silently at unmoving ceiling tiles. Hurling my hurt, rage, and despair at Heaven once more, the groaning, tears, and heartache flooded out of me. In the deluge of emotions, however, I heard another question in the farthest corner of my mind.

"Is Jesus your friend?"

"Huh?" I replied with bewilderment to the thick foreign accent.

Suddenly, I was six years old and meeting an elderly woman back in Fort Walton Beach. Riding in the back of Aunt Anne's car over to her friend's house, I swung my little legs while smoothing out my new dress. "Today Gracie," Aunt Anne told me, "You're going to meet a special lady who is spending the winter with a friend of mine …and you get to give her a Christmas present."

Holding the gift tightly in my hands, I offered it to an old woman sitting in a wheelchair. Feeling nervous under the intense gaze of the strange woman, I backed away somewhat …until she asked the oddest question about Jesus being my friend. Wearing a patch following the fourth operation to repair my eyes, I think the woman may have considered me mentally challenged since I didn't respond to the question.

"Is Jesus your friend?" She asked again more purposefully.

You know, looking back, I think she really thought I was "slow!"

> When our lives are filled with pain and despair, the Bible tells us to look back at those "leaders and superiors" who journeyed in faith before us ...and be encouraged that they too felt the same feelings, yet they pressed forward.

For several months prior to meeting this woman, I traveled from family to pastor asking how I could become a Christian; but everyone told me to wait until I was older. Yet here before me sat a strange old woman, with an even stranger accent, bluntly asking me if I was friends with Jesus.

"I want Him to be, but no one will tell me how!" I blurted out.

"It's very easy, dear." She responded with such kindness, and then told me in the most simplistic way about the reality of our sinful life, and that God made a way for us to be saved from sin by sending His Son, Jesus, to die in our place so that we could be free ...if we turned from our life of sin and trusted in Him. Looking at this woman, she clearly believed the words she spoke; as if nothing on this earth could shake her conviction. That day, I gave my heart to Christ. I believed the old woman with the strange accent. I believed God.

With legs in traction and my body in pain, I asked myself silently, "Do I still believe God; do I still believe He loves me?"

Chapter 9 Faith Worth Imitating

Struggling with those questions, I avoided sharing them out loud with others. Who did I even know who could credibly speak to the faith I previously thought strong ...but now seemed so fragile?

Remember your leaders and superiors in authority, [for it was they] who brought to you the Word of God. Observe attentively and consider their manner of living—the outcome of their well-spent lives— and imitate their faith [that is, their conviction that God exists and is the Creator and Ruler of all things, the Provider and Bestower of eternal salvation through Christ; and their leaning of the entire human personality on God in absolute trust and confidence in His power, wisdom and goodness].—HEBREWS 13:7, *THE AMPLIFIED BIBLE*

When our lives are filled with pain and despair, the Bible tells us to look back at those "leaders and superiors" who journeyed in faith before us ...and be encouraged that they too felt the same feelings, yet they pressed forward.

Many people talk a good talk ...and use a lot of churchy words and catchy motivational phrases, but I often wonder if they truly get it; would those nice words and inspirational slogans sustain them while in agony for days, weeks, months, years, and even *decades?*

Struggling to reconcile their own faith with the suffering they witnessed, even friends and family offered me platitudes and shallow observations reflecting their limited understanding of God's providence ... while I lay helpless in bed. Down the hall from the room where I lay writhing in pain, many of my visitors struggled in impromptu late night Bible studies; trying to wrap their minds around the theological implications of a level of suffering that once served as an academic discussion, but now was witnessed up close and in person.

We often are tempted to "adjust" or "compensate" for God in order to reconcile unpleasant circumstances with our belief about God and His actions towards pain and suffering in this world. One or two well-meaning, but sadly naïve, people even went so far as to question what I had done to deserve this. This type of mentality reflects such poor theology that an entire book could be written on that subject alone …in fact one has already been written: it's called THE BIBLE—I recommend it often. *[Sarcasm intended]*

When confronted with suffering, many of us want to grasp how a loving God could allow misery. "Since God is love, then the person suffering must have done something to offend the loving God …therefore it's the sufferer's fault." That logic and view of God is not consistent with scripture.

> God often does not reveal His purposes, but He does reveal Himself …and difficult as it may be, that revelation is usually through suffering.

I have encountered individuals who express an understanding of what and how God doles out what we deserve and don't deserve. I'm not qualified to speak for God …and I have found it's usually better to refer back to God speaking for Himself. When Job's friends threw out their suggestions as to why Job had to suffer, God's response was stern and shocking.

After GOD had finished addressing Job, he turned to Eliphaz the Temanite and said, "I've had it with you and your two friends. I'm fed up! You haven't been honest either with me or about me—not the way my friend Job has. So here's what you must do. Take seven bulls and seven rams, and go to my friend Job. Sacrifice a burnt offering on your own behalf. My friend Job will pray for you, and I will accept his prayer. He will ask me not to treat you as you deserve for talking nonsense about me, and for not being honest with me, as he has."
—JOB 42:7-8, *THE MESSAGE*

Chapter 9 Faith Worth Imitating

Reading the book of Job, it is worth noticing that God never explained to Job _why_ the suffering and loss, most of it horrendously brutal, was allowed in the first place. God often does not reveal His purposes, but He does reveal Himself …and difficult as it may be, that revelation is usually through suffering. Through that suffering, however, an individual's faith can be honed, chiseled, and purified to the point of becoming a powerful beacon of encouragement to others facing their own trials.

While lying in a hospital bed in agony …with scarce hope for a different reality, I knew positive thinking messages, encouraging sermons, motivational speeches, or even soul searching for blame offered no help. Friends' or family members' "theories" of God's faithfulness and love couldn't penetrate the wretchedness of my new life.

No, somewhere in my background, there had to be a faith, one of those unquestioned beacons ..._a life,_ worth imitating. Hebrews 13:7 clearly states to look to those _who brought the Word of the Lord_…implying a personal encounter. Considering pastors and teachers in my life, I mentally inventoried those who spoke the Word of God to me. Asking myself if I recalled any of them dealing with brutal realities eclipsing positive slogans and "feel-good theology"; I couldn't think of any.

In my heart, I also knew this _life of faith_ I rummaged for in the recesses of my mind would have to be a woman …with a credible understanding of personal suffering, loss, humiliation, and despair; a person who stood out as a beacon of God's faithfulness, who chose to trust God in the blackest of circumstances.

Who in my life met such a criteria?

"Is Jesus your friend?" I heard once more from the old woman in the wheelchair.

What I thought for years was a chance meeting now clearly illustrated God weaving a credible anchor of faith into my life; the strange-sounding old woman who looked at me with such intensity …had endured suffering, loss, and humiliation on a scale *far* surpassing mine. Traveling through some of the darkest pits conceivable while enduring terror on an unimaginable scale; this unusual woman emerged with a faith that literally reached around the world.

The most important meeting in my life, where I began a journey of faith in trusting Jesus Christ, was the encounter God arranged between a six-year-old little girl with a patch over her eye …and an old woman who chose to trust God through the horrors, degradation, loss, and unspeakable despair of the *Holocaust*. Of all the people I'd encountered in my life until that point, and even still today, *that woman* possessed a faith worth imitating.

Her name was *Corrie ten Boom.*

Chapter 10
The Cross Before Me

You may never know that JESUS is all you need,
until JESUS is all you have.

—Corrie ten Boom

Things that hurt, instruct.
—Benjamin Franklin

*I*n 1633 Saint Vincent de Paul and Saint Louise de Marillac trained local peasant women to care for the poor and sick. This initiative launched the Daughters of Charity as a mission from the Roman Catholic Church, which expanded to America. In 1898, the Daughters of Charity founded St. Thomas Hospital in Nashville, Tennessee.

Never noticing St. Thomas Hospital during my brief time at Belmont before the wreck, I knew nothing of the rich history, mission, or theology of the hospital now serving as my home. Without any opportunity to explore my surroundings, I interacted with the precious few things in my limited field of vision, but critical care is not known for spectacular views and scenic windows. Half of my body suspended in traction, I could only face straight ahead, and all there was to see on the wall before me was a ten-inch crucifix placed there dutifully by the Daughters of Charity.

Raised Baptist, I took issue with the crucifix. No matter that I was in excruciating pain *(the word excruciating is a Latin word invented by Roman soldiers to describe the horrific pain of the cross)*, I somehow found the wherewithal to have a theological argument with my new landlords, and implored my father to remove the crucifix.

Each time I succeeded in motivating Daddy to remove the crucifix, however, a tiny, ancient nun named Sister Euphemia almost instantly appeared to place it back on the wall. Her demeanor clearly communicated this was a non-negotiable issue, and she carried a presence about her that would likely cause trained soldiers to defer and back up.

In every waking moment, all I could see was a crucifix …just off to the side of my suspended right leg. That crucifix became the focal point of all my fear, anger, rage, and heartache. I suppose the crucifix remaining on the wall represented my inability to change, alter, or in any way exert control over my circumstances. I didn't want it there, I didn't like it …and there was absolutely nothing I could do about it.

After leaving critical care and transferring to a regular floor, I discovered the nuns of the Daughters of Charity dutifully displayed a crucifix in *every* hospital room. "Jesus rose from the dead, and is no longer on the cross, so take it down!" I often demanded through the clenched teeth of my wired mouth.

Sister Euphemia exercised free reign over the entire hospital, and so she took it upon herself to follow me from critical care to the regular floor. Able to do whatever she wished, while I remained stuck in a hospital bed, she chose to ignore the silly demands of a seventeen-year-old girl, and instead went about her self-appointed task of educating Mary

Chapter 10 The Cross Before Me

Grace Parker. Had Sister Euphemia been alive in 1633 (and I'm not to-
tally sure she wasn't), it's doubtful that Saint Vincent de Paul and Saint
Louise de Marillac would have achieved sainthood, much less start the
Daughters of Charity. Democracy was not an important word to Sister
Euphemia. She had rules; she liked rules. But *her* rules **ruled** everyone
else's rules.

Over the months of recovery, dozens of flowers often filled my room.
One day, Sister Euphemia pushed a cart into my room and loaded it with
many of the vases filled with beautiful arrangements. Mom worked hard
to carefully place the lovely flowers around the bed, bedside table, and
the shelf along the wall, and she cared for them every day. I couldn't
believe my eyes as I watched *a nun* of all people …pilfering them.

"What are you doing with my flowers?!" I helplessly implored from
my bed.

"Mary Grace, (oh, the sisters loved my full name), you have more
than enough, and there are others around you who have none."

So, off she went with a cart full of *my* flowers ….and a replaced crucifix on the wall. I could only fume in bed, while angrily staring at the
crucifix. Humming to herself while pushing the cart down the hall, Sister
Euphemia clearly ignored the pleas echoing from my room as she happily distributed MY flowers to other people. I never heard if she told the
other grateful patients the origin of the "donated" floral arrangements!

During one of many times I loudly complained while feeling sorry
for myself, she abruptly entered the room pushing a man in a wheelchair. Nashville hosts an expansive prison just 10 miles from St. Thomas
Hospital, and this man, up until getting a severe sinus infection that progressed into his brain, was serving life sentence at Riverbend Maximum
Security Institution. Part of his skull was removed following a radical
brain surgery. I later learned he died just ten yards from my room. As an

eighteen-year-old girl (my eighteenth birthday was two months after my wreck), I found the encounter with that man shocking and deeply disturbing. Sister Euphemia's only comment while replacing the crucifix on the wall was, "I thought it might have been good for you two to meet."

Her point was not lost. Suffering lay all around me, and I wasn't the only one struggling. My vast rage, heartache, self-pity, and overall misery …all collided with a tiny nun who refused to budge, compromise, or in any way give in to my outbursts, moods, or even pain.

Sister Euphemia was neither heartless nor cruel; quite the opposite. Looking back, I think she recognized the trauma to my body, and so she focused on my spirit. Her whole life spent in treating the sick and wounded, she could imagine the difficult future looming ahead for me. She clearly believed that for me to survive, I needed to learn to give out of my lack; even if it meant the precious few things I owned …like flowers. Living a life filled with pain causes many to retreat into themselves, rendering them ineffectual and sidelined from life. Introducing a well-to-do coed to a wretched, dying prisoner, Sister Euphemia recognized the need to startle me out of self-pity… and into living a life of purpose; embracing the heartache of others literally lying at my doorstep.

With all those things in mind, she threw herself into caring for me in the best way she knew how: she pointed me to Christ. More specifically, Sister Euphemia recognized my need to better understand the cross; to cultivate an awareness of what Jesus did for me on that cross ... so she made sure I focused on it *every* day.

The crucifix remained. In every room, surgical suite, holding room, post-op room, and x-ray room ...I witnessed a crucifix prominently displayed. The weeks turned into months, and the months became years as I journeyed back and forth to St. Thomas for lengthy follow-up stays and procedures. Often, I hallucinated while looking at the crucifix; snakes seem to writhe around it, and I woke up screaming. During many of those episodes, Sister Euphemia suddenly appeared to pray over me until I fell back asleep.

As pain remained my constant companion, the tiny image of Jesus on the cross filled my vision. While rage and heartache choked me, my eyes could only see the cross. Yelling, crying, and screaming; the crucifix silently hung on the wall offering no commentary.

Rods the size of my little finger pierced through my ankles, tibias and femurs ...of both legs. These metal rods protruded out either side of each leg and connected to cables running along the top of the orthopedic bar mounted to my bed. Various weights hung from those cables creating the appropriate tension on my crushed legs as they healed. Any adjustments to those weights caused such pain to course over my body that is impossible to describe with mere words. Only a patient care technician named Frank Drake, a legend at St. Thomas, could appropriately adjust the weights to relieve any of the anguish caused by the traction system. Screaming and begging for Frank to come in the middle of the night, the crucifix remained passively suspended in front of my tortured body.

In that position, having to do any restroom-type functions became nightmares of agony and humiliation. The crucifix hung on the wall as I moaned in shame and pain.

Over time, gazing day after day at the rods piercing my legs, the details of the crucifix grew clearer to my eyes, and my heart was flooded with awareness; He *truly* understood.

Slowly, I came to view the crucifix differently. I gradually accepted that Jesus endured the cross, and all that suffering and humiliation, on my behalf. I accepted Jesus as my savior years earlier in the encounter with Corrie ten Boom, and although failing to understand His purpose in my suffering, I made the decision in that very hospital room to continue trusting God. But I guess it never registered how much suffering He endured due to *my black heart.*

In an abstract way, I knew He died for the sins of the world …particularly because of people like Hitler, but lying in my bed at St. Thomas Hospital, the awful realization crept over me; He chose to die because of me. *Me personally*; not just all mankind lumped together. As He hung there, He knew *my name.*

Over time, gazing day after day at the rods piercing my legs, the details of the crucifix grew clearer to my eyes, and my heart was flooded with awareness; He truly understood.

Pondering that thought, I looked at my pierced, broken, and scarred legs hanging from ropes and pulleys lifted in the foreground …almost as if they were lifted up to the crucifix in the background.

Wiping the tears now rolling down my face onto the hospital gown and sheet; I couldn't even get to a box of Kleenex. It's hard to bow your head in a hospital bed, so fumbling with all the tubes and IV lines, I put my hands over my face …and sobbed. All I could do was simply say His name.

Chapter 10   The Cross Before Me

"Jesus, Jesus, Jesus."

Several years passed and finally, after dozens of surgeries and years of struggling, I made peace with the crucifix; thankfulness replaced my misguided anger and indignation. When confronted with the reality of Christ's sacrifice for me, gratitude floods my heart. Gratitude for the precious gift of salvation that God provided, gratitude for His own profound understanding of suffering, pain, and humiliation …and gratitude for a little nun who pointed me to Him.

Postscript

When a member of the Daughters of Charity passes away, a library containing photos, letters, publications, and a variety of other collected items is established to honor the member's life.

The Daughters of Charity placed this story in the library of Sister Euphemia Baschnagel.

Chapter 11
A Match Made
in Heaving

Politics doesn't make strange bedfellows—marriage does.

—Groucho Marx

After an initial stay of two-and-a-half months, I finally left St. Thomas Hospital at the end of January 1984 …but only relocated a few miles down the road. Mom and I stayed in an apartment just minutes from St. Thomas, and I traveled back and forth for extensive physical therapy. My friend Lyndon showed up nearly every day to assist the physical therapist in helping me work muscles and limbs which now seemed pitifully weak. Friends for years, Lyndon took the wreck harder than most, but focused his sorrow and grief into a positive outlet by serving as an encouraging voice and an effective "physical therapy assistant." Little by little, with the help of therapists and Lyndon, I started walking …albeit with a pronounced limp.

It was hard to look at my once beautiful legs; they looked so scarred and misshapen. Taking my eyes off my legs, however, I stared straight ahead while using the parallel bars and willed myself to walk the agonizing steps. Feeling the pain in each footfall, I inwardly cringed at the screaming nerves, but I pushed through the pain; forcing myself to stand and walk. With each exercise, I mercilessly forced my body to comply; determined to regain my independence and prior status as an able-bodied teenager.

Surprising many, I made great strides …so much so that Mom and I moved back to Florida. The gulf coast of Florida is beautiful, but hot and muggy. Always hot-natured, I found the humidity and heat now intensified the swelling and pain in my mangled limbs and joints. Believing I would "will" myself back to health, the searing pain exacerbated by the sweltering Florida climate nurtured a seed of doubt in my heart. Although outwardly brave, I secretly wondered if I would ever return to normal.

After several months of increased improvement, the restless feeling returned. In spite of my limp, I walked better and even ventured to drive. Sliding behind the wheel for the first time since my wreck caused significant apprehension. As memories of those awful moments of the accident flooded over me, I grabbed the steering wheel and forced myself to live in the present. One advantage, however, is that I did feel safer behind the wheel of my mother's car. After the wreck, Daddy had used the car insurance money to buy a new car; a large Cadillac Fleetwood Brougham. He bought it because of the enormous back seat that made it easier to transport me, encased in a body cast, back and forth to physical therapy for several months following my initial release from the hospital. Although much safer, it still was a big adjustment to go from driving a sporty Honda to what seemed like a limousine.

The swelling and pain continued in the rapidly warming Florida spring, and as May and June loomed, I seemed to be headed for a long and miserable summer. After much deliberation, a *Continental* friend stepped up and offered to let me stay with her in climate-friendly California, while we looked for a school to attend nearby. Understandably, I would be sent to California *without* a car!

Weary from the grueling experiences we had together, Mom agreed, and less than a year after my accident, I found myself living on the west coast with my friend, Sheri, and attending classes part-time at the University of California, Fresno in June and July of 1984. After summer classes, I enrolled at Westmont College in Santa Barbara and enjoyed a wonderful but painful fall semester in one of the most beautiful places in America. The campus of Westmont is hilly, so Daddy bought me a golf cart to get around the school in order to arrive at classes without being in too much pain from walking.

Arriving home for Christmas break, my parents noticed I suffered from dizziness and blurred vision. Right after New Year's Day, they set up an appointment with a doctor in Fort Walton Beach who mistakenly diagnosed me with a brain tumor. For the second time within a year, I had to withdraw from college. After a lengthy series of tests from a specialist in nearby Pensacola, we learned I had a small lump on the pituitary gland. The specialists assured my worried family that I was alright; the problem most likely a leftover from the frontal lobe concussion sustained in the wreck.

Although I was relieved to have good news, I now faced a long and boring semester at home. Surviving the car accident, learning to walk again, and resuming college all served as the type of goals needed for my strong-willed and eager-to-live-life personality. Since waking up from the wreck, I had pushed myself to survive and resume life. The thought of sitting on the sidelines, even in such a beautiful vacation spot as the Florida panhandle, seemed intolerable; I survived …and now I wanted to LIVE!

Learning I would not return to Westmont in Santa Barbara for the 1985 spring semester, Linda Dunshee offered for me to stay with her family for a couple of months at their home in West Germany. A colonel in the United States Air Force, Linda's husband had been transferred to Ramstein Air Force Base shortly after my car accident. Jumping at the chance, I left Fort Walton Beach for Europe. It took more than a year, long stays in the hospital, and a number of operations …but I finally kept my meeting with Linda!

This time, however, I took a plane.

Although in a great deal of pain, I enjoyed Linda and her family immensely, and loved Germany. While on tour with *The Continentals* two years earlier, a man named Matthias had traveled from Leipzig (then communist) to Budapest to attend one of our concerts. We became pen-pals and, upon learning I'd be spending time in Germany, I wrote him to see if we could meet. Eagerly writing back, we worked out the arrangements to meet in East Berlin.

Linda and I went across the border at the place known as "Check-point Charlie" into the communist country. Before we traveled across the border, however, security guards separated us, and Linda was whisked away to a different entry point. Her husband's connection with the U.S. Air Force and NATO evidently caused a different security protocol, so I walked the two-and-one-half miles across the checkpoints alone. By the time I put my swollen and misshapen feet on communist soil, I was in agony.

Matthias had asked for Bibles, so Linda and I, with a mixture of apprehension and excitement, smuggled them into East Germany in make-shift backpacks. When separated, fear gripped me. I worried that the guards would discover the Bibles, but no one bothered me. Delivering my precious cargo to Matthias and other members of the underground church in East Germany, my pain, though still intense, seemed to be put into perspective. Maybe the guards at the checkpoint thought a young girl with such a pronounced limp was not worth searching; who knows? Regardless, I accomplished an amazing feat that day, and something clicked in my brain: *"I can still serve God ...even with a broken body."*

While in Germany, I spent a great deal of time praying about my next steps. I really felt I should return to Belmont in Nashville, but Daddy and Mom disagreed. I wanted to go back to school, but not as far as California ...and through excessive air-conditioning, I could try to exist peaceably with the south's humidity. I asked my parents to pray about it as well, and they assured me they would ...however reluctant they felt about me returning to Tennessee. Sending me to California without a car seemed somehow less terrifying to them than my being in the state where my accident occurred.

Flying back to Fort Walton Beach after a wonderful time, I arrived late into the night. Weary, in pain, and irritable from traveling, I just wanted to go to sleep. Daddy, for some reason, kept going on and on about his "tomatoes." Not knowing Dad to be a farmer or gardener, I felt puzzled by his excessive "tomato talk" and kind of zoned out during the ride from the airport. Daddy, however, insisted that I see this one giant tomato in the backyard. "Gracie, you won't believe how big this thing is ...wait 'til you see it!"

"Can't it wait until tomorrow?" I pleaded with my way-too-tomato-happy father.

Assuring me it would only take a moment, he led me into the back-yard to see a beautiful, brand-new *tomato-red* Volvo sedan! With a catch in his throat, he nodded his head while stating, "I've been assured it's the safest car on the road." Hugging my parents, I knew that they put their hearts into this gift. I also knew that if possible, they would have bought me a Sherman Tank!

After much prayer and discussion, I was allowed to return to Belmont. Packing up my belongings, which Daddy had retrieved from my dorm room at Westmont, my parents helped me get an apartment near Belmont's campus so I wouldn't have to struggle in the dorm. The *Americans With Disability Act* still loomed several years in the future, so accessibility issues served as a big problem ...even parking. I have it on good authority that the first handicap parking space on Belmont's campus was put there for me, so my tomato-red Volvo became a familiar sight next to the school of music.

It felt great to be back in Nashville, and at the end of summer 1985, I started classes with a lot of enthusiasm. A number of my friends were still there, and several of them kept mentioning a transfer student from South Carolina name Peter Rosenberger.

All of them believed we belonged together, but I felt uncertain; he seemed too slick, had too much of a reputation for dating a LOT of girls, and just over all, well, too immature; I quickly decided I didn't want to like him. Thinking I'd put an end to the matchmaking, I determined to put Peter through the ringer and test him; and in doing so, prove all of our friends wrong.

Approaching him as he sat outside Belmont's student center with a bunch of our friends, I plopped in the chair next to him and pointedly asked to put my feet in his lap. My scarred and misshapen feet still swelled after only minutes of walking, and needed constant elevation. My first words to Peter were intended to challenge him while at the same time demand something from him; I felt this would be a good way to see what this guy had to him. Interestingly enough, that behavior still surfaces in our relationship. At the time, however, I felt pretty cocky and self-assured; confident in my ability to discern what makes guys tick.

Not Peter. In some ways, I'm still learning what makes Peter tick.

Looking puzzled at first, Peter agreed to my strange request, but as I propped my swollen feet on this young man's lap, he looked down at the scars on my ankles peeking out below my cropped jeans, and loudly exclaimed, "Good Lord, girl …what happened to you?!" Seeing my injuries should have made Peter feel uncomfortable, or at least a little more *sensitive* to me. Instead, he went the opposite way; he appeared comfortable, and not in the least shy about drawing *attention* to my injuries. The test wasn't going the way I wanted it to. "I had a really bad car accident!" I replied defensively.

After getting off to a rocky start, I still kept my feet in his lap, and we exchanged a few pleasantries …and for some reason, I gave him my phone number. Even after a phone call or two, I still tried to convince myself I didn't want to like him, but something about him nagged at me. After a great deal of pestering on his part, I finally agreed to let him take me out to dinner one night. To see how well he could afford to treat me, I put him to the test again and ordered an appetizer, an expensive meal, and dessert with coffee. (Peter jokes that he mentally calculated the bill, compared it against the thirty dollars in his wallet, and then ordered…*salt!*)

Later, I learned he spent all he had on me that night, and then went without food for the rest of the weekend. *Depleting himself while trying to meet my needs …would become a pattern.*

Attentive and contagiously funny at dinner, he gave no hint of inwardly freaking out …not only about starving later that weekend, but just worrying about getting out of the restaurant without washing dishes. (When his eyes widened at the bill, I did offer to leave the tip.) I had money, and wasn't about to let Peter be left in a lurch. But he didn't know that; he didn't think what I had was also available to him.

Things on the menu looked great to him, but he made sure I received what I wanted and resigned himself to accepting leftovers, scraps, or maybe one of the less expensive items ...leaving the dinner still feeling hungry.

Other than nervousness about the bill, I have to admit he was a lot of fun. I'd had many dates with different kinds of young men: serious, talented, smart, ambitious, wealthy ... Peter seemed to incorporate characteristics of all of them—except the wealthy part. But even with all that, I wasn't sold ...and kept telling myself that I didn't want to like him.

September 1985, 6:00 AM Nashville

"Hello?" The groggy voice answered.

"Peter?" I asked in my most pitiful voice. "This is Gracie Parker. I hate to call you, but I am in bad shape. I got sick in the middle of the night and have thrown up everywhere. Can you come over and help me?"

Although hearing a groan on the other end, I felt too bad to respond ...and too desperate to care.

"Mmmm, ok, I'll be over in a few minutes."

Within twenty minutes, Peter Rosenberger showed up at my apartment. Struggling to the door, I let him in, and then staggered back to bed while apologizing profusely for the mess in the hall, by my bed, in the bathroom, and wherever else it may be. I also grumbled out apologies for how I looked ...which was pretty bad.

The night before, I had taken Lyndon out for his birthday dinner. Growing up together, we became dear friends, and that companionship supported me through agonizing hours of learning to walk again, as well as strengthened my faltering heart as I struggled with my new reality. Upon my return to Belmont, our relationship grew, not romantically, but as a close friendship. Promising my parents he would look after me helped put their mind at ease when allowing me to go back to Nashville. Calling Lyndon first and receiving no answer, I desperately called Peter …this guy I met just weeks prior, and he didn't even hesitate to come over and clean up a gross mess he didn't create.

In many ways, that act defines Peter. He's willingly and knowingly volunteered to help clean a mess he didn't create …for more than two decades.

Donning dish gloves, Peter grabbed a bucket, mop, and rags …and went to work cleaning up a lot of vomit. As he cleaned up pile after pile throughout my apartment, I could almost hear the muttering, *"Honestly girl …have you ever heard of AIMING? The bathroom's down the hall … what's the matter with using the toilet? Heck, I would have settled for the bathtub …but the hall, the kitchen, the den? They should make a horror movie about this … 'The puke-o-nator!' I don't need a mop, I need the Barf-Master 2000 to clean this up!"*

Peter had a million one-liners he groused to himself while cleaning the apartment …literally on his hands and knees. Later he confessed his constant prayers begging for God to help him not throw up himself …but if he did, he went on to say, "I certainly would have made it to the bathroom!"

In all fairness, I was woozy and couldn't make it far, and when I failed to get to the bathroom, the kitchen sink seemed like a good idea.

I know, it wasn't!

I had legs then, too, so I couldn't even use that as an excuse; I guess I'm an explosive "heaver." The other night, I became sick again, but made it to the bathroom in my wheel chair while not wearing my pros- thetic limbs. There was no mess to clean up …and I was so proud (so

*was Peter). I challenge anyone to try throwing up from a wheelchair ...
without legs! I'm an experienced disabled "puker" and make it look
easy; but it's certainly not!*

After returning my apartment to pristine condition, Peter put a cool
compress on my head, returned to his dorm, and attended a full day
of classes.

That's how our relationship started. Not repelled by my scars, offering all he had to provide for me even if it meant going without himself, and dropping to his hands and knees to clean up an awful mess that
wasn't his; Peter clearly transcended my trivial tests, and made me appear petty for trying him in such a fashion. Peter's attentiveness, charm,
and humor all won me over, and I fell in love with this young man from
South Carolina who seemingly stepped out of nowhere into my life.

Although handsome, Peter looked terribly thin. Long after our first
date, I learned why. He simply went without, way too often. Accustomed
to dining out with my family, I failed to grasp how precious even thirty
dollars was to Peter. It's more than a little humbling to learn that this guy,
who barely knew me, spent all he had on me on our first date.

Peter asked me to marry him while we walked down Navarre Beach
at sunset. Looking out at the ocean, I turned around to see that Peter had
written "Marry Me" in huge letters in the sugar white sand bordering
what is called the Emerald Coast. Smiling and wrapping my arms around
him, I kissed him and said, "YES!"

Although he obtained the blessing of my father ...friends and family were stunned. But all of them seemed fond of Peter, and felt he was
capable (if not naïve) of doing what he set out to do. Before getting
married, family members grilled him to make sure he comprehended the
responsibilities involved in taking care of *Gracie Parker.* He assured
them he did, but how could he? With absolutely no reference; without

ever breaking a bone in his body or even possessing a noteworthy scar, he seized the helm of a medical nightmare. With his huge heart, he prepared to take on an immense task; understandably nervous, he still felt able to manage what he later learned to call, "the unmanageable."

Months before our wedding, I endured another surgery to help repair my damaged right ankle. This time, however, a new player joined my family at St. Thomas Hospital; the skinny young man from South Carolina. With every eye on Peter to see how he handled the pressure, he stepped into an alien world full of doctors, nurses, needles, blood, screaming, and everything else associated with my medical journey …all with nothing but love and sincerity to sustain him. When family members said there wasn't much he could do during the long hours, he took them at their word and went to see a movie and get some air.

Well, you should have heard the clicking of tongues and seen the heads shake with disapproval over Peter's apparent lack of ability to handle my medical issues. Even non-family members who happened to be visiting (actually in-laws of some of Peter's relatives) loudly proclaimed how disappointing it was to see Peter go to the theater in the middle of a crisis. Interestingly enough they all sat out in the waiting room talking about Peter …while doing nothing to help me, so I don't know what Peter actually missed, but they seemed to be worked into a froth.

The wife of Peter's then boss quietly listened to the comments about Peter, and later pulled him aside to provide a few pointers on how to integrate back into the group. Completely unaware he had in any way done something wrong, Peter was taken aback by the strong disapproval he received. That day, Peter learned that when someone stated "there was nothing he could do," they really meant he had to hover around and _look like_ he was doing something. It took years for him to properly revert back to his instinct; which was to get some fresh air in order to be rested and able to care for me when the situation demanded his full attention.

Mistakenly, he listened to the "gripers;" adding another layer of conviction to his already growing awareness that "Gracie was more important, and must be seen to first and always." It has taken years, and a lot of heartache, to reverse that belief and put us both back on equal footing in Peter's mind.

My family exerted a great deal of pressure on Peter to make him understand health insurance and my medical bills remained the priority; Peter, with barely any understanding of even going to the doctor, assumed the responsibility of my health insurance catastrophe. He laughingly recalls attending an employee meeting on "benefits" early in his professional life ... he honestly thought they meant "benefits" as in *longer lunches* and *better parking spaces.*

He's come a long way. Referring to the hapless singer whose horrible audition on *American Idol* made national headlines, Peter calls himself the *"William Huang of Healthcare,"* and mimics him perfectly saying, "I have had no formal training!"

We stood at the altar in Destin, Florida on August 16, 1986 and said our vows. Peter's father and my father officiated (Daddy's an ordained Baptist minister). To minimize my limp, Daddy walked me slowly down the aisle. I wore a beautiful gown that belonged to Aunt Anne. Ordered from New York for her wedding back in the fifties, this gown was truly breathtaking. Hand-sewn pearls and crystals adorned the body of the dress, and one couldn't help but feel special while wearing this gown. The story behind this garment, however, is even more precious to me than the dress. Anne's marriage didn't make it, and she suffered a particularly traumatic divorce. Never having children of her own, Anne has been incredibly generous with Andrea and me; her only two nieces. But the dress represented something even more than the lovely heirlooms she's given to us over the years. The beautiful dress of Anne's embodied

her broken heart, and I was honored to wear it. She did have one request, however; she asked if we would pray over the dress…she wanted
to make sure it was consecrated as a holy garment for me, and carried
nothing associated with her painful marriage. With a great deal of emotion, we obliged.

Holding on to Daddy's strong arm, while wearing the gown his sister
had worn in her wedding, I made my way to the altar to meet the man
I would entrust with my life, my love …and my broken body. Daddy,
before putting my hand in Peter's, asked the first part of the vows to me
and Peter. No longer was it a clergy member asking the questions, but
my father asking this young man, "Will you take this woman…." In a
transaction as old as time, my father placed my hand into the waiting
hand of Peter William Rosenberger, who then, for the rest of his life …
assumed responsibility for Mary Grace Parker.

Turning, we then faced Peter's father who performed the ceremony.
Everything went smoothly until I got to the part, "in sickness and health."
I choked up. Those words took on new meaning to me now …did Peter
understand this? How could he? Was I crazy to be doing this? Peter's father gently looked at me, and helped me through it. That would not be the
last time that Peter's dad helped me as I faltered. During communion, our
professor from Belmont, John Arnn, played a solo for us, and Anne also
sang an additional piece. The entire choir from the church showed up to
sing, and I must say …it was a fabulous and heart-driven wedding. With
my aunt Dottie's husband, Jim Dickson (also an ordained minister), and
two other ministers participating, Peter's dad kiddingly told us afterwards,
"Well, it took five pastors, but the knot's tied …and it's a strong knot!"

It would need to be.

Chapter 12

Guardian and Protector

Behold, he that keepeth Israel shall neither slumber nor sleep.

—Psalm 121:4 (KJV)

His eye is on the sparrow, and I know He watches me.

—Civilla Martin, *His Eye Is on the Sparrow*

©1905 Civilla Martin

"If you're thinking about having children, you should not wait too long," Peter and I heard while meeting with my doctor; just newlyweds, three years after my accident. Unclear if I could even conceive, the broken pelvis and other injuries cast serious doubts on carrying ...and delivering a child.

Right after our first anniversary, I learned the exciting news ...well, I felt excited. Few others, however, showed the excitement I wanted them to feel. It seemed nearly everyone felt fear rather than elation. Most all agreed pregnancy and bringing a child into the world would be hard on me, but it seemed their concern also carried a self-serving fear of how my difficulties might affect them.

I relate to "Steel Magnolias" and the reaction Sally Field's character displayed when Shelby (played by Julia Roberts) became pregnant. Painful to watch; painful to live. I sobbed so loudly in that movie, I had to leave …I was making too much of a scene and other viewers were growing uncomfortable.

Even Peter expressed similar sentiments. Still adjusting to familiarizing himself with a new wife and her extreme health issues, this fresh addition put him on an even more demanding path. To add to it all, I needed to finish my senior commercial vocal recital at Belmont that fall. Rising to the occasion, Peter, a music major himself, handled all the musical charts, band members, sound system, and even played in the band. Performing my forty-five-minute recital five-and-a-half months pregnant and wearing the cutest formal maternity dress Mom had bought me, the show went off without a hitch …I received an A! Belmont's School of Music may need to confirm, but I believe I remain their only student to publically admit performing a senior recital while pregnant.

Settling into the next several months, I grew increasingly excited, but could feel the pain in my legs also intensifying. Taking note of my hip and pelvic injuries, my obstetrician decided that I was to have a planned C-section.

For more than twenty years, Peter has repeated the tired joke that "…C-babies are just like other babies, except every time they leave the house, they go out through the window!"

On March 23, 1988, I checked into Baptist Hospital (often referred to by Nashvillians as the "baby factory" for the large number of babies born there) for the first surgery since my car accident that wasn't filled with dread. St. Thomas, my first choice of hospitals for a baby, chose not to have a maternity ward to avoid dealing with the abortion issues. In the mid-1990's they reinstated it, but it only lasted a few years, and they shut it down again.

For some reason, Baptist Hospital didn't allow video cameras in the delivery room back in 1988, but they allowed a tape recorder and a camera. So Peter, looking like a reporter from the *Associated Press*, tussled with a camera and tape recorder as he watched his first son enter the world. The surgery went fine, but there was a lot more pain than I expected. After what I experienced from the wreck, I thought this would seem like a walk in the park. Who knew Caesarean sections could hurt so badly?!

Trying to shift my mind off pain, I focused on the brand new life that emerged from my broken body. Other than the unanticipated discomfort, everything else seemed to go smoothly. Well, except for one nurse who failed to properly read my armband and attempted to give me a pain shot of Dilaudid (I'm fatally allergic to the painkiller). Still a watchful big sister, Andrea quickly stopped her before injecting the painkiller that could have easily killed me.

Using Peter's middle name and my maiden name, we named our son, William Parker Rosenberger. Both "William" and "Parker" incorporate the meanings of guardian and protector. Watching him grow, I witnessed his names integrate into his personality and character. From helping my parents care for the ranch they purchased in Montana, to watching over me for virtually his entire life, Parker remains one of the most responsible and noble men I've ever known. Caring for me …and literally carrying me on his back at times, Parker embodies everything a mother hopes for in a son, and I want everyone to know how greatly I love him.

Parker's arrival hastened a departure. He didn't cause it; rather he simply accelerated the inevitable. My right leg never recovered from the strain of carrying him. With the great joy I experienced in this precious gift of life, I also felt the grieving over what my heart knew must happen.

With all that in mind, however, I still chose to deny the reality of the condition of my right leg and pushed myself to ignore the pain and dysfunction. There comes a point, however, when denial collides with reality. Not yet twenty-five years old, I walked with a cane. Not just any cane, mind you ... Daddy made this cane for me from a cedar tree on his ranch. Daddy, a wonderful wood-worker, builds decks, shelving, and all sorts of things ...but as all who know him will agree, "durability" stands out as his work's finest characteristic. So when he, with deep emotion, presented me with the "mother of all canes," I knew the work and love he put into carving what looked like the sturdiest cane ...ever!

> There comes a point, however, when denial collides with reality.

Not yet accepting reality, I underwent a particularly painful operation known as a fusion surgery; one of many I endured in an attempt to save my right leg. The damaged joint in my right foot was removed and replaced with bone fragments from my hip. My surgeon literally drilled and chiseled into my hip. If you think it sounds painful ...

A great deal of the pain I live with now is due to this surgery, and many more like it, that I endured trying to save my legs.

As usual, post-operative pain management with me is extremely difficult. I react poorly, sometimes even traumatically, to most of the drugs for this level of pain, so my doctors spend a lot of time making adjustments while trying to finesse just the right medicine and dosage.

Sometimes it works. More often than not, however, it seems to result in serious problems.

Chapter 12 Guardian and Protector

Three days after the fusion surgery, I lay in my hospital bed in agony, while doctors worked tirelessly to give me some level of pain relief. With Parker, barely a toddler, at my parent's home in Florida, Peter stayed around the clock with me, but showed increasing signs of strain and fatigue. Quickly learning the ropes during the first three years of a marriage, he'd journeyed in and out of hospital experiences with me. That night in the hospital, however, would serve as a brutal exam for his new education path.

For most of the evening, I noticed a strange feeling; my mouth felt "cottony," and had a metallic taste I thought peculiar. Tossing back and forth in the bed, I just couldn't seem to find any place of comfort.

"What's the problem, now?" A bleary-eyed Peter sighed from the recliner next to my bed.

"Something just doesn't feel right, I'm thirsty all the time ...and I can't sleep or even get comfortable."

"It's two in the morning ...just try to be still and breathe slowly," was his brilliant and helpful suggestion.

Gritting my teeth to avoid snapping back, I tried a different approach.

"Would you pleeeeeease go get me some grape juice?"

Muttering under his breath, he pulled himself from the recliner and walked down the hall to the nurses' galley. Peter has made himself at home on hospital floors for more than two decades, and has cooked meals, made sweet iced tea for me (I am Southern, you know), and just generally moved in ...while ignoring signs and warnings from the staff about restricted areas. Not patient by nature, he learned many years ago where all the supplies are kept, and so when I needed an extra pillow, blanket, fan, or grape juice during my many hospital visits, Peter often disappeared and returned with things nurses and patient care technicians sometimes took two shifts to deliver.

In many hospital stays prior to this one, I made a terrible fuss about wanting to hold the grape juice myself. I hated feeling dependent upon others to help me drink or eat. Peter made just as strong an argument about why I should drink it out of a straw while he held the cup.

"You're too groggy, and will spill it," he's stated on dozens of occasions.

"No I won't," I replied with a jutted jaw.

Back and forth we argued until out of frustration and fatigue, he gave in ...and let me hold the grape juice myself. Thirty seconds later, I invariably fell asleep and tipped the purple liquid on to my gown. Startled awake, the juice, ice, and cup always dumped all over me. One-and-a half hours later, after a gown and sheet change, and a general melee of nurses, medicine changes, and the works ...we all tried to go back to sleep. Of course now, we added another ninety minutes to the sleep deficit. Sadly, this contest of wills became a regular event during my many hospital stays ...as did the faintly mumbled, "I told you so!" that floated from the ever present recliner next to my bed as we both tried to will ourselves back to sleep.

All too familiar with this scenario, Peter prepared himself for another "grape-juice baptism" while trudging down the hall to the nurses' galley. Stumbling back to the room holding the Styrofoam cup like a precious artifact; Peter opened the door and quickly recognized the fight over who holds the grape juice ...would **_not_** happen that night.

In the glow of monitors in the room, he noticed my body was rigid and flat, but shaking furiously. Rushing to the bed, the light from the doorway showed that my eyes were rolled back into my head as my body continued to thrash. Bursting out of the room, he yelled to the first nurse he noticed and she leapt into action ...giving Peter only seconds to jump out of her way as she charged into the room. Immediately, a team of nurses surrounded me, and they, along with Peter, struggled to keep me from throwing myself out of the bed. As my body continued flailing, I began screaming and vomiting over myself, the bed, the nurses, and Peter.

While the small team restrained me, one nurse quickly administered a push of the drug Narcan through the port of my IV line to counteract the effects of the narcotic in my system. Another worked to reduce the pump rate of the pain medicine traveling into my IV line. After several long and terrifying minutes, I blacked out and fell into a deep sleep.

Thankfully remembering nothing of the seizure, I woke up several hours later even feeling somewhat refreshed. Peter, on the other hand, remembers the event with clarity. In fact, he classifies that night as one of the more pivotal moments in his life.

In September 2008, I returned to St. Thomas for several nights following some tests, and Andrea's and Bobby's oldest daughter, Kerra Killingsworth Hicks, who had moved to Nashville to take a job, came to visit. Walking down the hall, Peter pointed out various places where her parents and grandparents spent time with me ...and because of me. He showed her this particular room on 5 D, and told the story again. After more than twenty years, the memory of this event still bothers him.

As the room quieted down, a visibly stunned Peter collapsed into a chair while watching the nurses clean up the aftermath. Covered with vomit himself, Peter stared blankly at my panting, filthy, and sweaty body while his head hung weakly. One of the nurses put her hand on his shoulder and asked if he was okay. Numbly, he nodded without even looking up. Peter's oldest brother, John, experienced several *gran mal* seizures as a teenager, but surprisingly, Peter never witnessed one of John's episodes. After virtually no sleep for more than forty-eight hours, while caring for me around the clock ...Peter received a harsh introduction.

Watching the nurses, he noticed they all took a deep breath, and immediately went to work restoring the room to normal. They washed me, changed the bed and my gown, and one even brushed my hair.

After cleaning me and the room, they wiped off their own uniforms …and somewhere in the bustle, the doctor appeared. The surgeon on call that night arrived with his hair sticking straight up and looking pretty rough himself. He immediately took charge of the situation, and worked quickly and efficiently with the nurses to regulate all the medicines.

It didn't register at the time, but Peter pondered that event for many years before grasping a greater truth. First off, the nurses didn't freak out. Their training took over, and they literally jumped into action. Not trying to fix me, they instead cared for me and kept me from hurting myself. However messy and repulsive, they didn't treat me poorly for my actions, but recognizing a reaction due to things beyond my control, they instead spoke calmly and compassionately while caring for me. Not worrying about "getting it on them"; they properly attired themselves for the job with easily washed uniforms. As the trauma subsided, they also turned their attention to the others affected.

More importantly, they didn't try to solve the problem, but instead called the physician …who in turn prescribed the proper treatment.

In thinking about the seizure and the caregivers' response, Peter observed a powerful picture of the church. We Christians often encounter others in explosive and messy traumas. Our role is to care for each other and assist in protecting each other from further trauma to the best of our abilities. While wearing the most effective stain-resistant clothing in the universe, *the righteousness of Christ*, we don't have to worry about it "getting on us." The only "stain" on Christ's righteousness is the precious stain of His own blood that paid for all of our messes, gross stuff, heartache, and traumas.

Chapter 12 Guardian and Protector

In any traumatic event, we always find collateral damage, and it's important to keep an eye on the wounded off to the side; they're sometimes overlooked in great crises. Often neglected, they deserve notice. Their trauma is different, but important …and their wounds may not always be treated conventionally, but can still become infected. A festering wound is ugly and messy …and often makes us all feel uncomfortable, but our mission should reflect Christ's mission for Himself: healing the brokenhearted and setting the captive free.

The Spirit of the Lord is upon me, because he hath anointed me to preach the gospel to the poor; he hath sent me to heal the brokenhearted, to preach deliverance to the captives, and recovering of sight to the blind, to set at liberty them that are bruised.—LUKE 4:18, *KJV*

Lastly, Peter also noticed the corollary when the nurses recognized that their job was not to "fix" me, but rather they called the physician. As we minister to one another, our charge is to also call THE physician. In the midst of traumas and difficulties, our Savior …whose eye is on the sparrow …calms the storms with a gentle wave of His hand. Ever present, even through the valley of the shadow of death, our God, *our Protector and Guardian*, neither slumbers nor sleeps.

Part III

Permitted

God permits what He hates to achieve what He loves.

—Joni Eareckson-Tada

When God Weeps © 1977 by Joni Eareckson-Tada and Steve Estes

Never doubt that God is totally for you in Christ.
If you trust him with your life, you are in Christ.
Never doubt that all the evil that befalls you—even if it takes your life—is
God's loving, purifying, saving, fatherly discipline.
It is not an expression of his punishment in wrath.
That fell on Jesus Christ our substitute.

—John Piper

By John Piper. © Desiring God. Website: desiringGod.org

Chapter 13

Life and Limb

*Just because you can't see or imagine
a good reason why God might allow something
to happen doesn't mean there can't be one.*

—Timothy Keller

The Reason for God © 2008 Timothy Keller

My legs were not taken from me, I relinquished them.

Owning those words helps provide closure to what otherwise may remain an open wound. Something taken by force, against your will …whether by accident or intent, requires learning to forgive, trust again, and function overall as a whole person. Like so many others, I understand the feelings generated when precious things are stripped away, and I also know the work required while struggling through the grueling and brutal process of reclaiming a sense of wholeness and stability …and learning to trust again.

Willingly relinquishing something, however, opens an entirely different path of healing.

"Voluntary amputation"; even the words sound painful and scary. What type of pain does one endure before directing someone to remove a limb? When does one quit trying to save the unsalvageable?

Most of the pain I live with now is a direct result of the experimental and sometimes desperate things we did to try and save my legs. Ironically, by holding on to something that had to go, I added as much (if not more) pain than the original injury.

> Willingly relinquishing something, however, opens an entirely different path of healing.

No surgeon wants a seventeen-year-old girl to wake up and find legs missing. My doctor literally used every piece of knowledge available to save my legs, and for a while I enjoyed a life of two legs; albeit a painful one. Two legs made taking a shower much easier. Walking into a closet and getting dressed didn't take an extra couple of minutes. Even with a misshapen right ankle and a severe limp, I still possessed legs; and bad legs are better than no legs ...right?

Recalling the nightly prayers for my eyes to be healed, I endured surgery after surgery believing in my heart that through those seemingly endless operations God was going to miraculously heal me, my legs, remove my scars ...and return the beautiful body I had before the wreck. I had the faith, I willed myself to believe ...and because of that; felt I didn't have to tell my husband or family about the severity of the pain.

The disappointments mounted, however; the pain increased, and the limp grew more pronounced.

Chapter 13 Life and Limb

The fusion surgery did little to help, and I still feel deep regret for allowing it (and others). Those "do anything to avoid amputation" type of operations I tried have caused me more heartache and physical pain than I can adequately describe.

Taking care of a small child, while hobbling on a cane, took a toll on me, Peter, and even Parker. Active and energetic, like every other toddler, I couldn't catch Parker. The pain increased to the point where, barely able to walk on my right leg, I crawled from room to room. Parker, watching me crawling with curiosity, often scampered away; thinking we played a game. Gripped by fear that he might run away and get hurt, I often scolded and yelled at him to stay close, but he couldn't understand my fearful reaction. How could he?

In our kitchen one day, Peter and I talked frankly about this mounting problem. Asking how I felt about it, I told him, "the pain of each day clouds the joys." Nodding to me, he seemed to make a mental note of the statement, and we changed the subject.

Still not willing to face such an awful decision, we tried even experimental procedures to keep the pain in check. We used everything medical science offered including nerve blocks (I've had so many I've lost count), and a high-tech device used to interrupt the pain signal. When discussing this new device, my surgeon seemed skeptical about the *Dorsal Column Stimulator* being helpful; he didn't think my pain fit the profile of the device's coverage. The idea of this machine was to implant a device into my body that has leads attached to key areas of my spinal cord. With a handheld unit, I could activate the device to send an electrical signal to "interrupt" the pain signal. It sounded good, and the pain specialist doing the procedure was convincing.

I have a different device now implanted that sends pain medicine to my spinal cord area. It's a much better system, but the technology wasn't available at the time. Nearly everything attempted, in efforts to avoid amputating the leg, actually made my pain today much worse.

After lengthy discussions, and desperate to not lose my leg, I chose to have the procedure. Sadly, I made the wrong decision. Not only did the stimulator not properly address the pain, but while implanting the device, the pain management anesthesiologist nicked the protective membrane around my spinal cord. Imagine the worst headache of your life …then quadruple it. CSF (Cerebral Spinal Fluid) leaking from the large puncture caused the sack around my brain to compress. Drawing blood from my arms and re-inserting it into my back to coagulate around the hole (called a "blood-patch"), the doctor tried several times to repair the hole. Lying in the recovery room on my side, he repeatedly inserted a large needle into my back, all while my head felt like exploding. On the third or fourth try, with Peter even assisting, he finally achieved a work-ing blood-patch.

Although infrequently, I still see that same doctor around town. He seems to feel badly about the whole thing. We're nice and pleasant to each other, but I don't send him a Christmas card.

My surgeon's doubts proved well-founded; the pain in my leg, unaf-fected by the *Dorsal Column Stimulator*, worsened. I kept hoping that maybe there was some kind of more powerful drug …or I could cart an IV bag full of morphine around for the rest of my life. No medicine could stem this problem, however; I had built up too much resistance to many of them, and had adverse reactions to all but just a few.

Staring at the appendage causing me so much grief, I often day-dreamed about just taking a knife and cutting it off, but then my brain kicked in to override the absurd idea that my body screamed. It seemed my body knew the answer, but my heart and mind needed to catch up.

Chapter 13 Life and Limb

Disheartened and out of options, I returned to my surgeon's office full of discouragement. "When it gets bad enough, call me ...and we'll go from there." He never used the word amputation. He didn't have to. He, nor the wreck, took my leg. The choice belonged to me. Before sending me home to make the decision, he made one recommendation. "I want you to go visit Jim McElhiney at Nashville Orthotics and Prosthetics."

Two weeks later, my friend, Dana Work, helped me put Parker in the car. Dana married Pastor Jaime Work, who rushed to St. Thomas the night of the wreck. Driving to downtown Nashville, we found Mr. McElhiney's office. With Dana holding Parker, I hobbled into a strange, new world. Waiting nervously, I looked through magazines, noticed pictures on the walls, and quickly lost all of my preconceived notions about prosthetic limbs. Expecting wooden legs and awkward devices, I marveled instead at sleek, high-tech limbs allowing amputees to run, ski, and live active lifestyles.

Hearing my name called, I turned my attention to the caller and caught my breath. Wearing a lab coat and sticking out his hand was probably the largest man I'd ever met in my life. Standing at least six-and-a-half-feet tall, he looked like a professional wrestler. A superb athlete, and without seemingly one ounce of fat on him, this bear of a man halfway frightened me. Swallowing hard, I took the hand (which completely engulfed mine) of this salt-and-pepper haired man with a beard to match, and embarked on not just a wild journey, but a dear friendship with James S. McElhiney, CPO *(Certified Prosthetist and Orthotist)* ...whose voice and even appearance uncannily resemble veteran character actor, Sam Elliot.

With gruffness matching his size, Jim's deep voice and Tennessee drawl commanded, "Lemme see you wawlk."

Wearing shorts and feeling *very* self-conscious, I hobbled up and down the hallway as his eyes expertly scanned every inch of my body; almost as if he could see my skeleton.

"So, Marvin sent you over here, huh?" He asked pausing for a moment.

"Yes sir," I said almost timidly. His eyebrows lifted a trace when he heard me call him "sir."

"You know you gonna lose that left leg, too ...doncha."

He wasn't asking a question, but making a statement of fact.

Jim's amazing professional reputation is known throughout the world; but it *does not* include the words "good bedside manner." His matter-of-fact statement felt like a blow to my stomach, but I managed to weakly stammer out, "Let's just focus on the right one for now."

Sitting in his exam room, my thoughts reeled while struggling to process the severe pronouncement he had spoken so casually. Sensing my discomfort, he softened a bit and looked at me with all the tenderness and wisdom any girl could hope to have from a daddy. "It's gonna be alright ...you're gonna get through this."

"With all due respect, sir, I don't think you have any clue as to what you're talking about." I finally regained a little courage and composure.

Now his eyebrows shot straight up, and a hint of a smile shown through his beard. A crippled young woman calling him "sir" just gave this giant of a man some sass, and his only reaction was humor.

Jim reached down and knocked on his left leg. Instead of flesh meeting flesh, I clearly heard the "thump" as his hand hit something that didn't sound like skin and bone.

Dubious, I accused him of trying to pull a fast one; of using a sales technique to sell more legs!

Without even trying to hide how much he enjoyed this, he rolled up his left pant leg to expose an artificial limb, and laughingly stated, "This ain't no sales pitch! I do know what you're going through."

Chapter 13 Life and Limb

As I looked at him with stunned amazement, Jim continued, "Lost it after gettin' hurt in the Navy thirty years 'go," he said without any emotion or embarrassment; as if the fact that he had an amputated leg didn't bother him at all. After his accident, his leg hurt him terribly, but he hung on to it for several years before finally directing doctors to take it off.

For the last thirty minutes, I observed Jim walking …and had absolutely no idea he wore a prosthesis! Clearly, the world of artificial limbs surpassed the wooden clunkers I thought of when discussing the possibility of me wearing one.

"You go on back to your doc, and y'all figure whatchu wonna do … and then let me know; I'll take good care of you."

Stunned, I hobbled out of Jim's office feeling fear, excitement, hope and amazement all swirling together. Jim seemed so casual about the whole thing. He clearly understood what I eventually would come to know: limbs don't define a person. To him, a prosthetic leg functioned like a big shoe. It no more characterized him than a watch, or a suit; he put it on and lived his life.

With the utmost confidence in his skills, Jim offered a doorway to a world previously unconsidered. Spending so much time trying to save my leg, it never occurred to me to willingly let it go; the thought of living without a limb seemed too terrifying, too ugly, too rash a decision. What kind of person makes the call to amputate their own limb—not in a life and death scenario, but simply *because of pain and function?*

Jim did …and his courage strengthened mine.

As my limb continued to consume my life, I reflected on how I learned to walk "dysfunctionally" with the damaged leg. Did I possess enough faith to believe I would walk functionally without one?

Chapter 14
Does It Really Hurt That Bad?

When peace, like a river, attendeth my way,
When sorrows like sea billows roll;
Whatever my lot, Thou has taught me to say,
It is well, it is well, with my soul.

—Horatio Spafford

Amputating a leg, no matter how damaged or how much pain it causes, is no easy choice. In my life, I've made three painful, gut-wrenching decisions. This was the first. Making this choice, however, required time and space to think; I also needed peace and quiet. Too many voices competed for my attention as I struggled to reach a decision. It seemed everyone with two good legs had an opinion on what I should do.

Calling a "time out" from listening to Peter, my family, friends, and even complete strangers, I made an appointment with our pastor at the time, Bob, and asked if I could meet with him. Sitting on a sofa in his office, Bob gave me a great gift ...he let me enjoy the silence. Some people grow nervous and uncomfortable during lengthy periods of silence. Bob's not one of them. He didn't feel the need to fill the air with useless words, but sat quietly while this young woman in his office wrestled with one of the most difficult decisions a person could make.

Watching me stare out his office window, he didn't busy himself with paperwork or writing notes, but sat still. Finally, after a lengthy period of time, he quietly said, "Up to this point, Gracie, all I've heard from you and others is what *they* feel you should do. Those voices are not permitted in this office." Pausing for a moment, he gently asked, "What do you think is the right decision for you?"

After a few motionless seconds, I simply said what my heart now knew was true, "I want to let it go."

Finally saying it out loud, I looked at Bob and stated, "I need to be allowed to let it go. I don't know what that means, I don't know if I can live with myself by doing that, but I do know that I cannot live like *this* anymore."

Fighting with this decision, with my pain screaming on one side, and a lifetime of disfigurement and seemingly failure on the other ...I felt myself being literally pulled apart. If I looked weird or different, I'd be teased and even rejected; years of dealing with my eye issues helped convince me of that reality, and I fought against it for a lifetime. Born with a defect shaped so much of how I felt accepted, or even how I was accepted.

What would my family think now? Would the first words spoken about me be resurrected with even greater force: "Here's little Mary Grace, her eyes, now her legs ...isn't her life sad?!" To me, enduring an amputation in many ways felt like being told, "Gracie, you're going to have to live with crossed-eyes for the rest of your life."

But the pain was really that bad …and the conflict within me raged relentlessly.

Some decisions require considering the feelings of others before making them; this was not one of those decisions. If I chose to have my leg amputated, I knew it must be done without considering how others would or would not respond. I would do this on a personal level for me, without anyone else having input. For my own survival, I needed to make that separation; others' approval or rejection could not drive a decision of this magnitude.

Nodding at me while taking my hand, we prayed together. Hobbling out of his office with my cane, no dove lit on my shoulder, the heavens didn't open and affirm my decision; I simply felt resolute. For the first time, I felt the liberty to gather all the other voices, put them in an airtight container, and deposit them in storage somewhere; they didn't have access to affect my thinking and feeling about myself.

With that in mind, I walked away resolved—not in necessarily amputating my leg, but rather freed from a bondage I had not acknowledged until then; the prison of accommodating the disapproval of others. No one else had license in my decision to have my leg amputated; *the path I now determined* to follow. And I didn't have to prove to anyone else why I made this decision.

Sure, a knot of fear remained in my heart; the whole thing just seemed surreal. But as is always the case, in those high drama moments of my life (I've had way too many!), a peace settles over me *when I know* I made the appropriate decision. This first of the three excruciating decisions of my life, represented a willingness to accept that I could not change a circumstance; I relinquished my control …and even the perception of control. At that moment, without the input of others, I completely and irrevocably placed my life into the hand of God.

God, in turn, provided what He always does when we trust Him: peace.

Be not anxious about anything, but in everything make your request known. And the peace of God, which transcends all understanding, shall guard your mind and your heart in Christ Jesus. —PHILIPPIANS 4:6-7, *NIV*

Peter, sober and scared, nodded his agreement; knowing as well as I did …the time had come. Calling the family together, I told them of my decision. Tears, questions, and choked "we love you's!" came from all of our family, and the church family rallied around us, with the exception of a few.

A couple of hyper-spiritual women unexpectedly called to admonish us by stating that we were "…in rebellion." Even though barely acquainted with these women, they remained convinced that God had spoken directly to them and "…was going to heal me in June" (the surgery was scheduled for March). That part of it seemed strange; as if my having the amputation would thwart Almighty God from causing the leg to grow back if He so chose.

Peter tried to talk with them, but gave up in exasperation. Arguing with a bunch of women with bad theology wasn't working too well for him at that point in his life, and so our pastor stepped in and directly told those individuals to back off.

Sadly, I've encountered poor theology about God's providence in suffering from pastors and church members across the country. From the first moments of opening my eyes as an infant, to having the wreck, to now making the decision to relinquish my leg, it seems that people with the same theological struggles stood on the sidelines of my life offering commentary. This time, however, I resolutely avoided listening to others' voices …however well-intentioned but misguided. I literally chose to die to myself and trust God to resurrect what He desired.

Calling my surgeon and Jim McElhiney, a plan formed and we set the date: Wednesday, March 27, 1991. The next few weeks blurred in preparation for this somber event. Fitfully trying to sleep while struggling with the impending brutal reality coming at me with full force; I often awoke to find Peter staying up late watching over me. One night in particular, he sat up in bed with a notepad scribbling. Patting my shoulder, he whispered for me to go back to sleep. When I told him that "turning the light off would help," he asked for just a few minutes more, as he continued writing. Recalling the words I spoke to him just weeks earlier, "Sometimes the pain of each day…clouds the joy" Peter, while watching me tossing and turning because of pain, penned a beautiful song entitled "The Love of Jesus."

Mom and Dad, once again, embarked on the long road from Fort Walton Beach back to Nashville, dreading every mile. The memories of the nightmare journey that occurred less than ten years prior grew clearer with each passing landmark. Dark thoughts settled over both of them as they struggled to understand God's purpose in so much suffering and loss.

Joining Peter's parents who arrived from South Carolina, Daddy remained for the surgery, but Mom drove our little preschooler back to Florida again to be with Bobby and Andrea and their three children, Drew, Kerra, and Emma. Mom pulled more than a yeoman's share at the beginning; a new team now helped carry the burden. Mom also knew that, for that moment, only she could provide our son with what he needed during this tumultuous time, and she took that task on in an amazing way. Instead of living the drama in Nashville, Parker spent a wonderful time with his young cousins, and even attended pre-school with my young niece, Kerra.

The night before the surgery, I chose not to sleep. Peter's mom, Mary, stayed up with me, and we both prayed and sang hymns throughout the night. At one point, Peter stumbled into the living room and blearily recommended we ought to call it a night, but sending him back to bed, we continued singing and reading scripture.

Well into the wee hours, I finally looked at my mother-in-law and stated, "I'm ready."

Soon after that, I must have dozed off, because the next thing I remember was waking to find Peter standing over me saying, "It's time, Gracie." Wanting to look nice for me, he wore a navy blazer and slacks; although appearing especially sad, he looked handsome.

Peter drove me to the hospital that morning, and Daddy rode with us …followed by Peter's parents. Singing and listening to hymns the whole way, I felt as ready as possible. Going straight to a holding room, a small crowd gathered into the tiny room until the surgeon showed up; asking everyone except Peter to leave.

Pulling up a chair, he looked at me intensely and said, "Gracie, I'm going to ask you one more time …is the pain that bad?"

Without tears, emotion, or even fear, I listened to only one voice, calmly nodded my head, and said, "Yes …take it off."

"Okay," he said while patting me on the hand. Standing from his chair, he turned and left the room. Pastor Bob came in, along with Peter's parents, and my father. Holding my hand, our pastor prayed, *Father God, as I hold the hand of this my sister, I feel the calluses caused by gripping her cane while she struggles with such pain. We do not understand your purposes in all this, but we trust your heart and your hand in this surgery. Guide the doctors and nurses, comfort Gracie and her family, and glorify yourself in this. We ask all this in the name of your son, Jesus Christ."*

Within moments, techs appeared at the door, and helped me onto the gurney. Wheeling down the hall, the sad procession followed me. My heart raced as the operating room door loomed closer. What lay on the other side? Did God see this? Would He, as He did when Abraham raised his blade against Isaac, stop the knife in time?

In mere minutes, my right leg would be cut off from my body. A thousand questions flooded my mind:

"What was I doing?"

"Are you CRAZY?! They're cutting off your leg!"

"Oh, Jesus ... are you really going to let this happen?"

Peter held my hand the whole way, as if sensing my feelings. Pausing for a moment, I looked at the lines on his face, knowing his own battle raged within him. Trusting him to God, I recalled the peace I experienced weeks earlier in Bob's office, and I breathed a bit slower.

Daddy's here, Mary Grace. Daddy is here.

I didn't know <u>what</u> was on the other side of the surgery suite door ... but I knew <u>WHO</u> waited for me in the cold and sterile room.

Daddy's here, Mary Grace. Daddy is here.

Abruptly, a particularly uncharacteristic Pastor Bob rushed to the gurney, and with tears openly filling his eyes, whispered something in my ear. That brief moment of pastoral encouragement stayed with me and I never shared what he said. Peter later encouraged me to keep it private; it was between Bob and me.

Reaching the end of the hallway, everyone except Peter had to turn back. Wheeling me into the holding area, a flurry of activity started around me, and it soon drew close to the time when even Peter needed to leave. With a final kiss and prayer, we parted …and he returned to my hospital room. Within moments, the medicine flowing through my IV caused me to grow sleepy.

Walking back into my room, Peter rejoined his parents as they waited with Daddy. His mother, watching him closely, let her eyes follow Peter as he walked over to the recliner by the bed and sat down. Evading eye contact with anyone, he picked up a crossword puzzle and started to fill in the blocks. Within seconds, he could no longer see the words or shapes through the tears in his eyes, and he looked up and met his mother's gaze.

Unable to hold it back any longer, it all gushed out of him and he sobbed so hard that his ribs hurt. His mother, crawling into the recliner with him, held her son, while years of pain, fear, frustration and heartache poured from my weeping husband. Daddy, reeling from his own sorrow, turned his tear-stained face and walked towards the door to allow Peter a moment with his parents. Stepping closer and placing a hand on his son's head, Peter's father gently said, "It's okay, son …just let it out. It's okay."

Ninety minutes later, the phone rang and the nurse on the other end stated that the surgeon would meet the family at one of the small rooms near the surgery suites. Weary from stress and crying, Peter got up from the chair and headed to the second floor. Arriving at the surgical suite area they all knew too well, Peter stood at the intersection of two long hallways traveling nearly the length and width of the hospital. Gazing down the hallway leading to the recovery room, Peter spotted my surgeon turning the corner and heading directly to him. His scrubs visible under his lab coat, and still wearing his hat from the operating room, he walked straight to Peter, looked him square in the eyes, and stated that the surgery went well, and "…she's doing fine."

My right leg had been amputated below the knee.

The reality of it fell upon Peter like a ton of bricks; and, sensing the change, the cluster of family and friends seemed to pull back from him. Standing alone in the hallway, Peter felt lost, unsteady, and uncertain about what to do next. Feeling a hand on his shoulder, our long time college friend, Dennis Disney, wrapped his arm around Peter and quietly walked him back towards the room.

Waking up in recovery, I discovered Peter sitting next to me …unclear of how he got there. Smiling at me, he looked tired …but peaceful.

"Hi," I managed through a scratchy throat. For more than twenty years, our first greeting to each other after any major event continues to be simply, "Hi."

"Hi," he replied in kind.

"How're you feeling?" Peter asked quietly.

"Okay, I guess." I tried a smile, but it didn't quite materialize.

Pausing for a moment, with my heart in my eyes and throat, I asked him, "Do you want to see?" With a tender smile and eyes glistening with tears, he said, "Sure."

Slowly pulling back the covers, we both looked at the thick bandage covering what remained of my right leg …amputated just below the knee. Time stood still, and the moment seemed protected by God Himself. The normally busy recovery room remained unusually quiet, and the two of us shared one of the most precious moments of our life together. Gently pulling the covers back over my leg, carefully avoiding catching the drainage tube sprouting from the bandages, Peter patted my hand and said, "It's fine, Gracie. Everything's going to be okay."

Somewhere in midsentence I drifted off to sleep.

Chapter 15

Take Up Your Leg and Walk

I'm sure that my whole life would waste away,
except for grace, by which I'm saved.
But nothing lasts, except the grace of God,
by which I stand, in Jesus.

—Keith Green

Grace By Which I Stand © 1981 Keith Green

After the anesthesia wore off, the first twenty-four hours of my new life as an amputee felt nearly as bad as waking up from my wreck. During the amputation surgery, Dr. Marvin also removed the *Dorsal Column Stimulator* implanted in me; including the line leading from the device into the epidural space of my spinal cord area. Delegating pain management to an anesthesiologist, this new player in my case attempted to place an epidural block in my lower back in order to numb me from the waist down …

the idea to keep the leg numb and erase the "pain print" embossed on my brain over the years; theoretically minimizing phantom limb pain.

Phantom limb pain refers to a condition where amputees can still feel painful sensations from the amputated limb.

As the general anesthesia wore off, something seemed terribly wrong. The pain in my leg grew increasingly severe, nearly sending me into shock. Experiencing raw amputation pain, I screamed and yelled repeatedly, and the anesthesiologist kept pushing more and more medicine into the epidural space. With all the force of my will I blasted out at the anesthesiologist that I was going into shock, but he kept telling me that I was "psyching myself out."

In my life, I've never feigned a physical symptom, and when I state that I'm hurting, I'm not kidding; and it's certainly not in my mind. Drawing upon the last bit of energy I had, I clearly communicated that fact through barred teeth to the by now incredibly flustered doctor.

Exasperated, he tried to push more pain medicine through the line; going even further than the hospital rules allowed, but Dr. Marvin stepped in at that moment, while I struggled to keep from passing out from the by now searing pain flowing from a freshly amputated leg …with no relief from any pain medicine.

With all the chaos swirling in the tiny ICU room, the frustrated young anesthesiologist defensively made a point of criticizing St. Thomas' policies on drug administration, stating loudly (and belligerently) that the policy remained out of date. A firm discussion could be heard outside my room in intensive care between Dr. Marvin and this anesthesiologist on the receiving end of a stern lecture.

Dismissing him from the case, my surgeon quickly called another anesthesiologist named Travis Brannon. A former fighter pilot, Travis is one cool customer, and he immediately discerned the stimulator had created a "scar tissue" blockage in my epidural space. None of the pain-killer the first anesthesiologist pushed in …even made it to the target area. His lack of understanding left me in some of the greatest pain I've ever experienced.

In an interesting twist, Peter recently underwent an operation at Baptist Hospital's outpatient surgical center, and his anesthesiologist was … the same unfortunate soul! I didn't see Peter until afterwards, and he told me about the man who immediately made the connection when he saw Peter's name on the chart. Almost twenty years later, he said he remembered the event like it was yesterday; and apologized profusely to Peter for all the pain I endured. After nearly two decades, he still felt badly about the whole thing; I guess we can bury the hatchet. Just not in the epidural space!

Moving a little higher on my back, Travis inserted a spinal intrathecal line, properly numbed my right leg, and within ten minutes, I fell asleep; not under anesthesia, but finally out of pain …following hours of misery. From that moment on, C. Travis Brannon, MD made the list of my favorite people in the whole world. To this day Travis, who no longer regularly practices in surgery at St. Thomas, still serves as a consultant for virtually every procedure performed on me.

Jim McElhiney came by a few days after the surgery, and made a cast mold of my stump, and returned to his shop to make my first prosthetic limb. Known as an "initial leg," amputees wear these devices first …due to the rapid reduction of swelling occurring within weeks of the surgery. Following the amputation, the stump swells massively, but then, after a matter of weeks, starts to shrink. Noticing the size of the cast mold Jim just made, I certainly hoped the stump would shrink; it looked HUGE!

After subduing the pain, things smoothed over quite a bit …physically. Emotionally, however, I floundered. Arriving in a regular room after leaving intensive care, I lay in my hospital bed, and wondered, "Okay, now what?"

Remembering the sting of disapproval from those women following the surgery I endured just before we married, Peter dutifully stayed around the clock with me. A psychiatrist friend of ours who specialized in family therapy stopped by the hospital and noticed we were getting frayed. (Peter often states, *"...We've been raised by a pack of thera-pists!"*) Looking at Peter, Keith said, "You go see a movie and get out of here for a while!"

Turning to me, Keith then stated, "You relax and let him go with your blessings; he'll come back rested, refreshed, and able to care for you better."

Good advice; could have saved a lot of misery.

Clearing his head somewhat, Peter returned to the hospital and noticed my normal, "I've got to get up and get going" attitude seemed ... well, off. Food, television, or visitors had little impact, and I mostly just stared out the window. One young man, an amputee himself, found out about my surgery and took it upon himself to show up as an unofficial member of the "let's bring joy and cheer to an amputee" club. Making an effort to help ease the stigma, he proudly showed me his own prosthetic limb, and I nearly choked in horror. The gaping holes in his foot looked like it served as target practice for a shotgun, and the leg itself looked like it had been dragged behind a car. With my visitor beaming with pride as he sincerely thought he was cheering me up, I cried while picturing myself wearing such a device.

Jim McElhiney, however, clearly understood how to get patients back into life, and better still ...with a much more attractive limb. Jim returned two days later with my first prosthesis. Learning most amputees start walking within days of their surgery surprises people, but getting the patient vertical as soon as possible helps with acceptance and "getting back into life." In my case, the limb lacked open wounds prior to the surgery, unlike some patients who lose their limb due to ulcerating sores, poor circulation, or disease. In addition, the pressure from the limb fitting into the socket is not necessarily on the incision site, but is distributed around the entire lower limb …and by utilizing a walker, the limb benefitted from additional support.

Heading down the hall in a wheelchair, Peter pushed me to the same rehab room where, somewhat ironically, I re-learned to walk following my accident just eight years earlier. Asking for the shoes I needed for my first walk, Jim rolled his eyes when Peter and I both held up our hands admitting our forgetfulness. Taking off the worn Nike's that served as his "hospital shoes," Peter let Jim put one on my new artificial foot, while he placed the other on my left foot. Only a couple of sizes bigger than mine, the shoes stayed relatively secure on both feet. For our purposes that day, we only needed level shoes with good support.

Reaching into his bag, Jim pulled out several cloth items. Holding them up, he identified them as prosthetic socks that every amputee wears at one time or another. If the limb swells too much, you take off a sock; when it shrinks, usually at the end of the day, then you add a sock or two.

Showing me how to put one on, I slid a cotton cone-shaped cloth over my stump, followed by a heavier wool one. Kneeling down in front of me, like a shoe-salesman, Jim fit the large, white socket over my leg, and wrapped the attached belt around my waist.

"Arhhhhight, Gracie, we're gonna take this slow …you've been layin' down all week, so you might get *dizzy*." Jim always seems to emphasize the last word of every sentence.

With Peter and Jim helping, I grabbed the walker in front of me and stood. Just that quickly; I was standing. Spots circled in front of my eyes, as the dizziness Jim warned about slowly dissipated. Holding the walker with all my might, I swung my left foot out, afraid to trust my new right leg. Balancing myself on the walker and my remaining leg, Jim instructed me to go ahead and swing my right leg.

Literally taking a step of faith, I flexed my thigh muscles, swung my knee and watched an artificial foot respond to my movements. As the heel of the foot hit the ground, I "felt" the vibration. An odd feeling, I now understood more of what Jim meant when he said in his office, "… it's like a big shoe." To me, it sort of recalled the sensation of walking in ski boots. Growing up skiing in North Carolina, a tiny thought popped into my mind, "Wonder if I'll ever ski again." Choosing instead to focus on the path in front me, I pushed skiing out of my mind and continued to walk my first steps as an amputee.

Beaming with pride at the important milestone, I felt a surge of hope for the first time in months; maybe years. "You can do this," I told myself. "You're going to get through this; you're going to walk."

Except for another mild seizure two days later, the next week passed uneventfully. I don't remember the seizure, but Peter does …just as much as he remembered the other one a few years prior. I was given too much Demerol, and so, after backing it down somewhat, everything leveled out and I finally went home.

Peter helped me into our kitchen, and I rested my crutches against the counter. Only able to wear my new leg for short spurts during the day, I sat on a stool and carefully propped my stump against another stool to keep it elevated, watching Peter while he brought my suitcases into the house. Wanting a lot of light in the house to make it seem cheery, I quickly stepped out to flip the light switch on; temporarily failing to remember the absence of my right leg.

Chapter 15 Take Up Your Leg and Walk

Feeling myself fall, I instinctively kept trying to regain my balance with my legs, but crashed in a heap on the floor, almost landing directly on my stump. Dropping what he had in his arms, Peter crawled down on the floor and held me while I sobbed and moaned repeatedly, "I forgot I didn't have a leg."

One of many to come, my first fall served as a clear reminder of the difficult journey that lay ahead. Tempering my optimism just a bit, I knew caution must guide every decision made when standing or walking. Silently, I promised myself to keep crutches close by at all times until I became more proficient in my new status as an amputee.

Ten days after my amputation, Peter drove me to a recording studio where we recorded the song he wrote that night while watching me try to sleep. Standing with the help of my crutches, singing the lyrics my life inspired, I poured my soul into the song. Opting against penning a song offering solutions to problems, Peter instead wrote about a greater source of comfort when facing painful circumstances.

The Love of Jesus

Sometimes the hurt we carry seems too hard to bear.
Sometimes the pain each day can bring
Clouds the joy that's there
But I know in my heart there is a hope
Though at times is hard to see
I know a Love beyond other loves
And it won't let go of me.

The love of Jesus
Melts the hardest heart
The love of Jesus
Reaches the deepest part
I know it's never failing, never ending
Greater than any love can be
The love of Jesus for you and me.

You may not think there could be relief
For the hurt you feel.
You may believe an answer for you
Could not possibly be real
But deep in your heart
I believe
You know this love is true
You felt this love beyond other loves
And it won't let go of you.

Chapter 16

Less Gracie, More Grace

He is no fool who gives up what he cannot keep...
in order to gain what he cannot lose.

—Jim Elliot

(Missionary martyred in South America)

Shadow of the Almighty © 1958 Elisabeth Elliot

few falls notwithstanding, relinquishing my right leg truly became a blessing. The surgery successful, my pain levels slowly decreased. With each step, however, I recalled a warning from Jim that seemed to echo in my mind.

"Now that you've lost that right leg, you're gonna find out how bad that left one is!"

Nevertheless, I lived my life as fully and enthusiastically as possible. Once the swelling reduced, Jim fabricated a "definitive leg"; often called a "permanent." Showing me my new right foot, he called it a "Flex-Foot."

"This is a new product, and you're gonna like this foot a lot, Gracie." Describing the foot, he went on to tell me, "It's a carbon-fiber foot; it stores energy. So when you walk, it helps push you forward, while cushioning your back a little."

Sure enough, it did. Jim also had his technician, Pat, put a cosmetic covering over the leg, and fashioned the ankle and foot to be beautifully shaped. For the first time in more than eight years, my right ankle looked normal.

Months after this amputation, I visited Peter's parents in South Carolina. One evening, I mentioned to my sister-in-law, Liz, that I didn't feel too well. Looking at me with wide eyes, Liz asked if I might be pregnant. Stopping for a moment, I replied, "Well, according to all my doctors, it's highly unlikely, but I guess I could be."

Liz drove me to the only drug store open at that time of night to get a pregnancy test, but feeling nauseous, I stayed in the car while Liz went into the store. This required a great deal of spunk for Liz, only sixteen at the time; the drug store sat right across the street from her high school. After protesting profusely, she timidly walked into the store and purchased a pregnancy test.

Later I discovered the news; I was having another baby. Only Liz and I knew this, and I asked her if she felt we needed to get a second test to be sure. She nearly lost it begging me not to make her repeat the process.

"Grace, *(Liz is the only person who always calls me Grace)*, this is a small town, my dad's a well-known pastor …and everyone knows my family; pleeeeeease don't make me do this again!!!!"

Chapter 16 Less Gracie, More Grace

Going to a local doctor, the test confirmed …I was pregnant, but the doctor proceeded to advise me to take a special test so that I could make the "proper choice."

Due to the types and amount of prescription drugs flowing through my body, this doctor indicated the possibility of having a deformed child …maybe even one with no limbs, or an undeveloped brain or heart. With no question whatsoever, I shut him down, and took myself off every pain-killer and prescription drug …cold turkey. Brutally hard, I willed my body into submission; protecting the gift of life growing inside me.

Appalled that this doctor, and later one of my OWN doctors in Nash-ville, shared this belief; that an abortion was even a possibility, I recoiled in disgust and indignation. This was not one of the three difficult choices of my life; there was *no* "choice." God granted another gift of life into my broken body, and I simply trusted Him; the only "choice" belonged to God. He made the choice to give me this precious gift. After being told how difficult it would be for me to conceive, after all the loss, after all the injuries, for me to even GET pregnant was an amazing event.

Sharing this with my in-laws, they felt so excited for me following all of the loss we'd experienced. They were the only ones. Hovering near the phone with Liz and my mother-in-law, we waited nervously while my father-in-law called Peter in Nashville. He didn't take it so well. Peter struggled terribly during this time. The doctor's words scared him senseless; the thought of a deformed child on top of all the other issues weighed incredibly heavy on him.

Eventually, Peter rallied, and we started planning for our new addi-tion. Although brittle and tense, he tried to be supportive and helpful. Adding more pressure, we moved closer into Nashville during this time. Although surrounded by concerned family, I felt terribly alone during my second pregnancy, and look back at a long and painful period made more

difficult due to the lack of acceptance by those I desired it from the most. ***I paid*** the price physically for all of this, so I had a difficult time understanding why so many failed to rejoice in the new life God created. If the baby arrived with deformities, God's grace would be sufficient. If the baby died, God's grace would still be sufficient. My heart broke when I realized that others around me failed to share that belief. I understand the fear Peter felt. I felt afraid, too. But fear is no excuse for quitting early; that's what abortion is "…terminating *prematurely**."

Every day, while watching my belly swell, I trusted God more and more; virtually alone. Isn't that often the case, however, when we accept God's invitation to travel on a journey of faith? Sometimes others choose not to participate …but our Lord never abandons us.

Our second son arrived on January 29, 1992 with every body part, including what the world would learn years later …an extremely well-developed brain! Combining names as in Parker's case, this time we used a derivative of my name, as well as Peter's …and named him Peter Grayson Rosenberger. Grayson, literally a son of Grace, or Gray as he is often called, lives up to his names as well. The name "Peter" means "rock" and Grayson truly demonstrates such strength on every level. A tender heart of grace, however, tempers his impressive might, and similar to his brother, my heart overflows with love for Grayson. Even as a teenager, Grayson's powerful arms often gently support me while I transfer into my wheelchair …and many times, he's picked me up and carried me to the car or up the stairs on his back.

God graciously bestowed on me two exceptionally strong, yet sensitive sons. Strikingly handsome, they often take my breath away just looking at them. Both of them are living miracles and cherished gifts that God allowed to come from my mangled body. More than just being

* Webster's Seventh *New Collegiate Dictionary*.

140

a proud mother, I am a *convinced* mother; convinced that both of their precious lives are direct gifts from God.

At Grayson's birth, I rejoiced. Most everyone else breathed a sigh of relief; that a bullet was somehow dodged. Sadly, they missed the opportunity to celebrate God's provision during the journey. That's what faith is; *the evidence of things not seen.* During my pregnancy with Grayson, God granted me evidence of something I did not yet see; His enduring faithfulness.

I will praise Thee; for I am fearfully and wonderfully made: marvelous are Thy works—PSALM 139:14, *KJV*

As with Parker four years earlier, Grayson's arrival also signaled the demise of a leg. Jim McElhiney's words rang true, and the absence of my right leg clearly helped me notice the massive trauma of my left leg. Learning from mistakes, however, I took a different path and opted for only one fusion surgery in the ankle area to help stem the pain. If successful, the operation hopefully could buy me a few more years with the leg. If not …then the leg needed to go.

The surgery proved unsuccessful.

St. Thomas Hospital, June 13, 1995 (approximately eighteen months following the fusion surgery on my left leg)

That morning, I pulled the sheets back and saw the ultimate result of my car accident so many years ago: both legs amputated below the knee. Amputation is not commonly recommended for pain control; my case simply called for the radical action(s). Looking at what was left of my once beautiful legs, I mournfully reflected on how I would now live my life, *for the rest of my life on this earth,* with both of my legs abruptly ending below the knees. Familiar with the old statement, "I used to complain about not having shoes until I met someone without feet," I contemplated on how **I** was that *"someone."*

I felt like a freak.

"I'm just going to lie down for a minute," I told Peter. Preparing for the day, I somehow managed to pull on shorts under the hospital gown while avoiding staring at the new dressing covering what remained of my left leg. The right stump looked so small next to the swollen misshapen mass of the newly amputated left leg. With four years of experience as an amputee, I knew the swelling would go down, but it didn't make me feel any better.

Somehow while I still had one leg, I felt whole and independent. Now, waves of panic, disgust, and sorrow seemed to wash over me as I silently cried out, "Dear God, what have I done?"

As with my right leg, this decision was mine alone. No one took my legs from me; I relinquished them. As before, the surgeon met with Peter and me. There was no crying, hysteria, or even much emotion.

Unlike losing the right leg four years earlier, this time the entourage dwindled to just a few close friends and family members. Hoping to keep the event somewhat calmer, we cut down the visitors and maintained a lower profile. Still terrifying like the first experience, a little glimmer of hope shone in this event: I knew amputation helped the pain. Even so, another painful and scary journey awaited me.

Although knowing the inevitability of this decision, no one wanted to take the final step. Certainly no one could do it until I was ready. Sitting quietly in the hospital room, we repeated the scenario from the first amputation.

"Does it hurt that bad, Gracie."

Less than a week later, while lying in the hospital bed following the surgery, I remembered making my second excruciating choice. At the time, I *felt* ready …but now looking at the empty space where my feet used to be, well, I admit my heart faltered.

Reading a book, Peter sat next to me, and the room remained calm and quiet. Missing my boys who were once again with grandparents, I wondered what they might feel when they saw their Mommy now. Every few minutes I pushed the delivery button of the pain pump whirring beside my bed, and received a new infusion of narcotic. With the humming of the machine sending the pain killer into my veins, I lay still and tried to turn my brain off; I wanted to be numb and not face this new reality.

Sighing, I recalled the gripping fear once again as the gurney pushed through the holding room doors. Walking next to me the whole way, I studied Peter's face and noticed he looked older and sadder. Only thirty-two, his eyes looked weary and distant, and more gray hairs streaked across his head than were present at the first amputation. Kissing and praying with me one more time, Peter slipped out of the pre-op area. Amputations weren't the only operations I endured, and in less than ten years of marriage, he'd made the walk with me *dozens and dozens* of times.

> Unlike family and friends, God doesn't have to wait outside the operating room.

Never losing faith, I still needed to hear *"Daddy's here, Mary Grace"* from my heavenly Father. Bible verse after Bible verse raced through my mind as the gurney rolled closer to the surgical suite. Taking a deep breath, I yet again completely placed myself in God's hands as the gurney pushed through the doors. With Dr. Brannon leading the charge on anesthesia, the team expertly prepared me within minutes; I felt a great deal safer.

Unlike family and friends, God doesn't have to wait outside the operating room. My surgeon and I had an agreement to pray just before surgery, and lying on the table in the operating room, I stopped the team as they prepared to put me under. Propping up on my elbows, I loudly proclaimed to Dr. Marvin while he looked at x-rays, "We had a deal!"

Turning towards me, he stated, "You're right."

Walking over to the gurney, he took my hand and directed everyone in the room to bow their heads. A puzzled, but respectful surgical staff quietly lowered their heads as he prayed for wisdom and God's direction while he worked. After his prayer, he motioned to Dr. Brannon to put me to sleep.

Although Dr. Brannon did a great job of managing the pain post-operatively, it still hurt. As the fog of anesthesia slowly lifted, I felt the movement of the gurney in transit, heading to intensive care. Although the pain shooting from the amputation site increased with each passing moment of awareness, something else felt different as well. Despite what those well intentioned, but misguided, hyper-spiritual women said four years ago, I knew I wasn't disobeying God. Even in the haze following surgery, something anchored me in trusting God's purpose through all of this. So, while being wheeled to intensive care, Peter watched me, still groggy, come through the door with my hands raised and singing the "Doxology." Based upon Psalm 100, this familiar hymn echoed in the hallways of St. Thomas Hospital:

Praise God from Whom all blessings flow
Praise Him ye creatures here below
Praise Him above ye heavenly host
Praise Father, Son, and Holy Ghost.

Singing a hymn of praise to God may sound odd after an amputation surgery, but even semi-unconscious, my soul still remembered my chief purpose: *To glorify God and enjoy Him forever.* Scripture never qualifies our glorifying God during good times exclusively; or praising Him only for blessings defined by our finite understanding. Maybe losing my legs served as a blessing in disguise. At the time I remained unable to process that thought, but simply obeyed; offering praise to God while nurses wheeled me into intensive care.

> Scripture never qualifies our glorifying God during good times exclusively; or praising Him only for blessings defined by our finite understanding.

With praises lifting to God as the gurney entered the tiny room, a crucifix hung silently on the wall. Although long since gone from St. Thomas and living in a retirement center, Sister Euphemia would have been pleased.

I will bless the Lord at all times: his praise shall continually be in my mouth.—PSALM 34:1, *NASB*

Chapter 17

Ten Small Steps Today

Quit chur whinin'.

—James S. McElhiney

$\mathcal{E}$vidently falling asleep while recalling the events that led up to my second amputation, a loud banging on the hospital room door startled me awake. Without waiting for an answer to his jarring knock, in barged Jim McElhiney.

"Get your butt outta bed!" His booming voice echoed off the tiled room. *(I don't use that term … it's common, and I say that to Jim!)*

Jerking awake from what seemed like only seconds of sleep, I groaned out, "It's still early! Go away!"

Unaffected, he groused, "Hurry up, I ain't got all day."

Four years of hearing this sort of thing helped me grow accustomed to Jim's less than gentle bedside demeanor.

"We've gotta do this another day; there is no way I'm up for this." I pleaded with him. "It's still bleeding and swollen …

and my stitches aren't even out yet! I can't get up or anything. I know my body!"

Softening a little, he said to me, "I knew you were thinking this, but why don't we give it a shot and see?"

Sighing, I opened my eyes one at a time, and reached out to grab the trapeze bar hanging from the frame over the bed. Pulling myself up to a sitting position, I noticed Jim unpacking my new leg out of a bag he carried over his shoulder. Unlike four years ago, I felt no curiosity as to what the new limb looked like. The only feeling was apprehension as to whether or not I could actually do this.

Peter handed me my right prosthesis, and helped me put it on. This time, we brought proper shoes in order to avoid using Peter's like I did four years earlier. Jim knelt down and helped me put on my new leg, while Peter positioned the walker. A week earlier, I didn't require a walker …even with the intense pain and one artificial limb. Now, only twenty-nine, I felt like an old, decrepit woman. Rearranging all the IV lines and monitor leads; I positioned myself for another brand new chapter in life.

Perched on the side of the bed, I grabbed the walker, and with Peter's help …I stood up.

Standing vertical, with no feet of my own, still amazes me as a singularly unusual sensation. Blood quickly shifting around in my body after long days of lying flat caused a wave of dizziness, and while weaving, I felt Peter's arms around me. As the spots in front of my eyes cleared, Jim came into focus. Standing on the other side of the room, he beckoned me to walk to him.

"Quit chur whinin', and get your butt over here!" *(Peter insisted I quote Jim accurately …I still think that word is common!)*

Chapter 17 Ten Small Steps Today

Using a walker and balancing on my right artificial leg was not a new experience for me. While recuperating from the fusion surgery on my left ankle a year earlier, I couldn't bear weight at all on my remaining leg; I had to learn to hop with my right prosthetic leg while using a walker. So my first step as double-amputee was familiar.

My second was not.

Balancing myself on the walker and my "good leg," I tightened all the muscles in my left thigh and swung my new leg forward. I "felt" it make contact with the ground, and for a brief moment, I was balanced on my freshly amputated left leg. Holding on to the walker with all my might, sweat began pouring down my face, and I could feel it trickling down my neck and back. With every fiber in me, I grasped the walker and could feel the strain going up and down my arms and into my shoulders. My jaw was so tight, I thought my teeth would break; and the pain shooting up my leg was nearly overpowering. Just the week prior, even with a bad left leg, I compensated for my right artificial leg too many times …the brain just naturally wants to go with the remaining limb. Walking on two artificial legs, however, allowed for no compensation; the weight needed equal distribution, and the process required more fortitude than just about anything else I ever experienced.

Reminding myself to breathe, I eased forward …almost in slow motion. While I focused on his face, Jim looked intently at my legs and hips. Never looking down, I stepped forward just inches at a time, until I was standing directly in front of Jim. So intent on my legs, he jerked his head back in surprise when I nearly bumped into him. With tears rolling down my face, I threw my arms around Jim's neck and hugged him. Weeping, I could only whisper, "Thank you!" Peter, watching from across the room wiped a tear away, and, although he'd never admit it …so did Jim.

That day, I walked ten small, painful steps. Reaching the other side of that room became my only reality. I wasn't thinking of Peter, my boys, bills, milkshakes, coffee, or singing; I *existed* to get across the room. I knew I had to make that journey. Whatever God had in store for me was on the other side of those ten steps; they represented more than a physical distance.

Would I coddle myself? Would I feel sorry for myself? Would fear hold me hostage in a wheelchair or worse ...a bed? With each step, I answered every question (and more) with a resounding NO!

I was a victim of an accident ...but I refused to be victimized by my circumstances. If I had to live my life without legs, well then *by God*, I was going to live life to the absolute max that I could.

I *would* walk.

Peter helped me to my bed, and we slipped the new leg off. My muscles seem to deflate after the intense strain, and I felt my body go limp. Lying down, my hospital gown clung to me, drenched with sweat ...not perspiration or glistening, I was foaming like a horse that just ran the Kentucky Derby!

Still panting while resting my amputated limbs upon a pillow, I didn't mind the sweat ...or even the increased bloody drainage oozing from my left leg; that day *I accomplished something important!* With no idea where my artificial feet might take me, I clearly recognized the first steps of a momentous journey.

After walking on two prosthetic limbs for the first time, I lay alone in my hospital bed reflecting on the strides made that morning. Both Peter and

Chapter 17 Ten Small Steps Today

Jim had left hours earlier, and even the nurses seemed to leave me alone with my thoughts.

It brought to mind the apostle Peter getting out of the boat after Jesus beckoned him to do the impossible. Walking on water, Peter stared at Jesus …and as long as he kept his eyes on Jesus, it really didn't matter what he [Peter] stood on. He only faltered when he looked away from Christ.

The adrenaline from taking my first steps long gone, the pain in my left stump reminded me of my new status as a double-amputee. The car wreck seemed a lifetime ago, and yet I now felt a sense of completion to that horrible event that so shaped my life. Although affected for life with pain, and more operations, relinquishing my legs seemed to signify the end of one part of my life, while opening the door to a life beyond comprehension.

Resting my head on the pillow, I stared out the hospital window and wondered what lay ahead. Still "Gracie," I somehow felt different. No longer a seventeen-year-old girl hanging on to life, with people gathered around mourning over what could have been. I was now a wife and mother of two …who finally let go of the future I had dreamed of for my life.

Needing a distraction for a few moments, I surfed through the limited television channels available. A documentary caught my eye, and my heart. Watching the images on the screen, I lay mesmerized at the timing of seeing such a show at this moment of my life.

The film detailed Princess Diana's work with amputees in southeast Asia. Seeing images flashing across the screen of people *who I now* resembled, my eyes filled with tears. Working with various relief agencies, Diana helped bring prosthetic limbs to land-mine victims throughout Vietnam, Cambodia, Laos, and other countries. With eyes glued to the screen, I found myself barely able to breathe while watching men, women, and children, putting on limbs that looked somewhat similar to mine.

As the show ended, the room grew even more still, as if poised for an event. Finally able to let out my breath, I drew in another deep one and pulled the sheets back. Looking down at my amputated limbs, seeing the fresh dressing with just a hint of bloody drainage seeping through, I lifted my hands to heaven and offered my broken and maimed body to Christ. Somehow, I knew in my heart that the documentary I just witnessed reflected the path awaiting me.

> For twelve years, my mangled legs seemed to direct the course of my life; now, ironically, their absence would do the same.

Later that evening, I shared my epiphany with Peter. With a wild look in his eyes, he suggested I hit the button and get another dose of morphine ...and sleep it off. Muttering to himself about the clear impossibility of launching an artificial leg ministry, he rolled his eyes and busied himself straightening the room.

Undaunted by Peter's response, I knew better. The vision placed in my heart belonged to God; and now served as a compass.

For twelve years, my mangled legs seemed to direct the course of my life; now, ironically, their absence would do the same.

This day, I began a new life with ten steps. The next day ...I took more.

Chapter 18

A Path in the Storm

For He commands and raises the stormy wind,
Which lifts up the waves of the sea.
They mount up to the heavens,
They go down again to the depths;
Their soul melts because of trouble.
They reel to and fro, and stagger like a drunken man,
And are at their wits' end.
Then they cry out to the LORD in their trouble,
And He brings them out of their distresses.
He calms the storm, so that its waves are still.

—Psalm 107:25-29 (NKJV)

eaving St. Thomas Hospital following my second amputation, I found myself walking sooner than expected, without crutches or a walker. Although the shattered bones from the wreck caused permanent alignment issues resulting in what Jim calls my "waddling walking gait," I discovered that while wearing pants, few people I met knew I wore prostheses. I often returned to my car parked in a handicap parking space to find notes left on my windshield chastising me for using a space clearly reserved for people with disabilities; those notes serve as a badge of honor for me.

Within a matter of months, I enjoyed a level of independence that, until amputations, seemed all but gone. Reclaiming a new piece of ground every day, I welcomed the challenges. The hand controls for my car, purchased after the first amputation, offered even more freedom, and within a short amount of time I picked up the boys after school, went grocery shopping, and participated in all kinds of things.

There were setbacks. The wreck so damaged my limbs that scars literally covered my body from the waist down ...externally and internally. So, when the limbs were amputated, the skin used to form the "pad" for the stumps contained a substantial amount of scar tissue. Wearing prosthetic limbs often contributes to scars breaking down, and so I underwent several revision surgeries ...on both legs; with both an orthopedic and plastic surgeon working hard to find healthy tissue in order to avoid amputating my knees.

Just recently I had another revision of my left stump. The prediction about my having surgery for the rest of my life spoken to Nancy by that nurse in critical care so long ago ...came true.

Words kill, words give life; they're either poison or fruit—you choose.—PROVERBS 18:21, *THE MESSAGE*

That passage leads me to be careful about what I say ...and what I allow to be said around me.

Following one particular revision of my left stump, I spent time recovering at my parent's home in Florida. While there, a hurricane made landfall right in Fort Walton Beach and Navarre. As the mandatory evacuation went into effect, we all prepared to head north; safely away from the approaching storm.

Before leaving, however, while sitting in my wheelchair due to the inability to wear my prostheses, I wheeled out onto my parent's deck perched upon a bluff. As Mom and Dad worked frantically to pack things up, I knew I'd only be in the way ...so I used this time to stare at an approaching hurricane.

Huge waves crashed onto the shore of the inter-coastal waterway adjacent to my parent's home, and looking across the normally calm channel often peppered with passing barges, I made out the rapidly churning Gulf of Mexico on the other side of the Navarre Beach as the hurricane barreled toward northwest Florida. Feeling the wind whipping my hair, I sat for a moment; amazed at the power of the storm. The spray from the water blew wildly, and the smell of sea water filled my nostrils as I simply took in what has to be one of the most awe-inspiring sights on this earth: the face of a hurricane.

Then he got in the boat, his disciples with him. The next thing they knew, they were in a severe storm. Waves were crashing into the boat—and he was sound asleep! They roused him, pleading, "Master, save us! We're going down!"

Jesus reprimanded them. "Why are you such cowards, such faint-hearts?" Then he stood up and told the wind to be silent, the sea to quiet down: "Silence!" The sea became smooth as glass. The men rubbed their eyes, astonished. "What's going on here? Wind and sea come to heel at his command!" MATTHEW 8:23-27, *THE MESSAGE*

Jesus did not recklessly choose to nap in that boat; He never did anything in a reckless or haphazard manner. Clearly understanding His mission on earth was to die, Jesus just as clearly knew that His death would not be in a boat on the Sea of Galilee. Safe in the knowledge of His

Father's will, Jesus, fully human, felt comfortable resting in the middle of the storm.

Looking at the choppy waters in front of me, I tried to picture a small boat full of scared disciples bouncing upon those waves. Would I, like Peter, John, Matthew, and the others ...have panicked and frantically woken Jesus up? Feeling the daily, non-stop pain coursing through my body, while looking at what was left of my legs, I thought about the storms. Did I feel any stronger in my faith? Could I ride out the storm while resting in my Father's will ...even if it meant living another forty or fifty years without legs while in severe pain?

Although never liking the heartache, loss, and oftentimes devastation that seem to follow every storm, I do, however, crave and love the deepening relationship my Savior beckons me to pursue ...*through* the storm. When I hear thunder and see lightning, I am reminded that He is close, and I look for Him in those wild and turbulent times. Praying with Joni Tada recently, both of us dealing with severe pain, I heard her quietly petition God, "Lord, if pain is what it takes for us to see our sin ...and your redemption and glory, then we welcome it!"

Anyone else but Joni, and I would have thought them foolish for such a prayer and posturing to look spiritual. Joni, in a wheelchair for more than forty years following the diving accident that left her paralyzed ... doesn't posture, and she is certainly not foolish. When a woman who has endured quadriplegia for four decades prays like that, all of heaven takes note.

In my distress I called upon the LORD, and cried to my God for help; He heard my voice out of His temple, and my cry for help before Him came into His ears.—PSALM 18:6, *NASB*

I do not ask for storms or trials in my life; I don't want them. But the desire to see and experience my Savior is so powerful, that I will welcome them for just one moment with Him. Over these decades, I've learned that painful experiences usually precede and follow meaningful experiences in God's grace and presence. Taking my cue from the Apostle Paul, I've learned to view those experiences as glimpses of what awaits us in eternity.

For I consider that the sufferings of this present time (this present life) are not worth being compared with the glory that is about to be revealed to us and in us and for us and conferred on us!

We are assured and know that [God being a partner in their labor] all things work together and are [fitting into a plan] for good to and for those who love God and are called according to [His] design and purpose.—ROMANS 8:28, *THE AMPLIFIED BIBLE*

This passage of scripture is quoted from *The Amplified Bible*; Peter and I own a treasured copy given to Peter's mom by her loving husband and six children as a Christmas gift in 1975. Inside the cover an inscription reads, *"May God's word be a lamp unto you and guide to your steps. We all love you as wife and mother."* The red cover is faded, and the pages are bent, crinkled, and some are barely attached. The name on the front is barely legible, but you can still see the fading embossed gold text of my mother-in-law's name: *"Mary Emma Rosenberger."*

<u>*My*</u> name is *Mary Grace Rosenberger.*

I love this Bible, particularly the expansion of the text and the way it helps bring a larger meaning to even the smallest passages. This specific Bible, however, contains unique qualities extending beyond its translation and style. First, it possesses an inscription inside the cover with the names of my Rosenberger family. Peter, along with his four brothers and baby sister, all signed it with wobbly pre-teen and teenager signatures (Liz was not even three, but she scribbled in it, as well).

Flipping carefully through just a few pages, notes begin to appear; not from the *Mary Rosenberger* currently using this Bible, but from the first one. Even more poignant than the notes are the inscribed dates. Most of the dates jotted by passages correspond to the heartache my mother-in-law felt as she struggled with the extreme suffering and eventual death of her brother, Lee. Shortly before Lee died, Mary's mother also passed away …and both deaths were accompanied by other harsh realities Peter's mother experienced during those times. While my mother-in-law faced her own hurricane of suffering, she took the time to make notes in margins of the old, red Bible. She also underlined particularly meaningful passages offering comfort and wisdom; verses that often served as a lighthouse to her while tossed around by painful storms of despair, suffering, and watching loved ones die.

Unbeknownst to the first *Mary Rosenberger,* this other future *Mary Rosenberger* was fighting for her life, during many of those same moments; dates Peter's mother sprinkled through the tattered Bible corresponded with my car accident, surgeries, horrific nights of pain, and days bringing more heartache and struggles. Peter told me about the times he covered his mother with a blanket when he often found her asleep in the recliner with that same red Bible opened in her lap; providing him the unique experience of covering two sleeping *Mary Rosenbergers* with blankets, after they struggled with the same scriptures …from the same tattered red Bible.

I would like it to be said that neither "Mary Rosenberger" has found complete answers to all their questions. Nor does either of us find total relief from the deep throb of heartache and loss. But our parallel journey through those dates, passages, and long nights continues to bring healing and hope not only to each of us, but also to many more. When she stayed up with me all night before my first amputation, it's because she'd faced the storms …and knew how to seek God even as the wind howled and the thunder crashed.

Holding that tattered, red Bible, even in those painfully slow moments when morning seems to never arrive …I feel connected to something much larger; I'm not alone while looking for the hand of God. While my husband's parents looked at their own hurricanes directly in the face, my father-in-law helped point the first Mary Rosenberger to a deeper relationship with God. And because of that, a trail was left for this Mary Rosenberger. My heavenly Father waits for me there, and shows me that another "Mary Rosenberger" is also with Him, offering a joy and comfort through "company" at the foot of the cross.

As the hurricane grew closer to the Florida coast, I reluctantly wheeled away from my parent's dock …feeling that I somehow "missed out" on seeing the storm make landfall. Safety remains just as important to me as anyone, but I suppose the brutalities of my life helped me see the impending hurricane as something awe-inspiring and majestic. As big as that storm was …and it was a *Level 3*, it fit easily in the palm of my Heavenly Father's hand. I am comforted to know that if a massive hurricane bends to His will, then His sovereignty over my storms remains intact.

Chapter 19

"Look Mom...
No Legs!"

Security is mostly a superstition.
It does not exist in nature, nor do the children
of men as a whole experience it. Avoiding danger is
no safer in the long run than outright exposure.
Life is either a daring adventure, or nothing.

—Helen Keller

With my legs now absent, why not try different things? Sitting on the sidelines for so long, I felt eager to participate in any and every activity possible. With two extremely active sons, I often heard the question, "Hey Mom, do you think you can do this?"

This first time that question presented itself was from Parker who, while in grade school, went to a birthday party at a local rock-climbing gym and thought it might be cool for me to climb a rock wall. Hooking me up to ropes and a harness, I stepped into the world of rock climbing. With lots of safety precautions, I actually scaled rock walls.

In my parents' vacation home in Montana, they own several ATV's. I love zipping around on those machines with Peter, Parker, and Grayson. Dad also has several horses, and after begging Peter and the boys, they saddled up horses, and I played cowgirl …well, sort of. Here's a tiny tidbit that movies like *City Slickers* failed to mention: "When riding horseback, make sure you properly secure your artificial limbs to your body with duct tape!"

Let me share why this is an important fact to remember.

Peter and the boys are excellent riders, and handle horses like pros. Admittedly, I am a novice rider, but an enthusiastic one. The day we saddled up, I wore a great pair of jeans; perfect for hanging around a barn and getting dirty. Excellent in every way …except that they were *straight-leg jeans.* Normally not a problem for able-bodied people with legs, I, however, experienced an unusual setback. At the time, my prosthetic limbs featured a "pin-lock" system which consists of a liner on my stump with a protruding pin at the bottom clipping into a lock built into the bottom of the prosthesis' socket. Little release buttons were laminated into the wall of the socket …located where the inside of my calf *would be* on each limb.

While cantering on the horse, the legs bumped against the saddle, and the pressure hit those release buttons, and, well …the legs came off. They didn't FALL off, however, they simultaneously SLIPPED down my STRAIGHT LEG jeans and stopped; the top of the socket was caught in the tight cuff of the jean. With TWO artificial legs flopping loosely and beating against the terribly confused horse, he simply did what seemed natural; he started running.

Chapter 19 "Look Mom... No Legs!"

Screaming loudly, I held on for dear life while my now wildly flailing prosthetic legs smacked the horse even more. Peter and Parker quickly raced to my aid and slowed the panting and confused horse; puzzled for only doing what he was told. Unable to strip down and re-attach my legs, I settled for Peter twisting them out of the jeans and leading the horse back to the barn. Parker, grumbling and rolling his eyes, rode behind us…carrying one leg in his arms, while sliding the other into the rifle scabbard hanging on the saddle.

Another great activity I regularly enjoy involves snowmobiles. The cool thing about snowmobiles is that I can go just as fast as anyone while I'm riding. The first time I rode one, however, I experienced a minor problem. Without calf muscles to force my legs into place, the heavy snow boots I wore kept sliding off the runners; leaving me feeling frustrated and off-balance for most of the trip.

Thinking about it overnight, I tried something new the next day; I wore tennis shoes.

Well, it's not like my feet get cold!

Settling on the sleds, we headed into the national forest that my parents' home borders, and hit some wonderful trails. This time, my feet stayed on the runners easily and I felt much more in control while skimming along the deep snow covering the Montana Rockies.

Miles into the forest, an ancient, decrepit cabin serves as an informal rest stop for many snowmobilers, cross-country skiers, and hikers. In the winter time, the snow often nearly covers the door, so a path has to be cleared using the shovel hanging on a hook by the door. Once inside, the fireplace is usually ready to be lit; the code of the mountain for stranded hikers and sledders. We usually pack a picnic lunch with a thermos of hot chocolate; and take a break at the cabin. Gliding into the meadow where the dilapidated cabin has stood for more than one hundred years, we noticed a bunch of other riders had the same idea.

This group, from nearby Bozeman, looked like they stepped out of an ESPN show on snowmobile racing. Gleaming black helmets matched jet black snow-suits and sparkling new snowmobiles. We could almost hear the rock music soundtrack playing as they slowly pulled their helmets off.

Striking up a conversation, Peter noticed one of the riders sneaking glances at my snow covered shoes. At only ten degrees above zero, with nearly five feet of snow on the ground, I admit it did look odd to see a woman out in that climate wearing only sneakers. With the snow-suit covering the tops of my shoes, there was no way for the exceptionally perplexed man to know the truth about my legs.

Finally working up the courage to pry, he timidly asked Peter, "Where are you guys from?"

Clearly knowing what must be going through the poor man's mind, Peter, with his thickest southern accent looked at the confused local and drawled, "We from TENNA- SEEE!"

Never telling the alarmed man differently, the news confirmed the worst: "People in the south only have one pair of shoes!" To this day, that man is probably still telling the story of the crazy southerners who snowmobile in tennis shoes. I suppose it's a good thing I wasn't wearing overalls or cut-off blue jeans to make the stereotype complete.

Of all the things I tried following the amputations, I suppose snow-skiing has to be the ultimate challenge. Although even Peter felt it wasn't a good idea, I started a little investigative work into organizations that help people with disabilities learn to ski. Wouldn't sliding down a snow-covered mountain on metal legs attached to skis …be the ultimate trump card over the wreck that stole so much from me?

Breaking an ankle no longer an issue, well, if I did, I had spares ... I contacted one of those organizations in Bozeman, and signed up for training. Driving into the parking lot at Bridger Bowl, a public ski area just outside of Bozeman, we headed to the lodge and pulled into a familiarly blue-signed space. A handicap parking space for skiers is kind of a mind-bender in itself, but I'm glad it was there; just walking in the snow on two artificial limbs is no easy trick.

As they unloaded the gear, I left Peter and the boys and slowly walked to the lodge to meet my trainer, Barb. A registered nurse, Barb volunteered with Eagle Mount, a Montana organization that helps disabled people snow ski (as well as other exciting activities like white-water rafting!). Conventional wisdom, disapproving family members and friends, and a host of others all tried to convince me downhill skiing was a casualty of the car accident. Barb would help me prove them wrong.

While Peter and the boys purchased lift tickets and registered Grayson for ski school, Barb helped me slip my artificial feet into ski boots. Recalling the ski trip I'd taken the winter before my accident, I wryly thought about wearing two pairs of socks on that trip to keep my feet warm; today I wouldn't need any.

Peter and Parker returned a few minutes later. "Gray's in ski school and we're ready to head out," Peter reported. "You doing okay?" I could tell by their eyes they were eager to hit the slopes.

"Oh sure," I answered, trying to conceal my nervousness. After promising to check on me later, they raced off to the slopes sparkling under a vast Montana sky.

Barb rested her hand on my shoulder. "You ready, Gracie?"

The bravado that carried me to the slopes seemed far away ...and I didn't feel ready, but this was what I came to do. Droplets of sweat trickled down my face, and inside my snow-suit, my back felt soaked with perspiration from the warm air inside the ski shop; I exhaled slowly and answered, "Let's go."

Stepping outside the toasty lodge, the cold mountain air felt great and the frigid temperature provided a new burst of energy. As Barb helped me place my boots properly in the binders of my skis, I heard the familiar click recalled from days long past when I skied as an able-bodied teenager. I grabbed my outriggers and, straining with my arms, pushed myself forward to head to the lift. Outriggers are basically crutches with small skis mounted on the end. Although my outriggers looked odd, with my ski-suit on, no one watching would have dreamed I was doing this on two artificial limbs.

We slowly made our way over to the lift and Barb motioned for the operator to reduce the speed of the lift. I panicked just for a moment when I saw the lift chair making the circle around to me, but forced myself to concentrate on Barb's gentle instructions.

"Just hold your outriggers out straight, and bend your knees, Gracie."

Before I knew it, the chair touched the back of my knees and scooped me up to carry me to the top of the run.

My excitement was tempered slightly when I glanced over at Barb and saw to my surprise that she was holding onto me because I was sitting cockeyed and at risk of sliding off. After scooting around to sit more securely I gazed in wonder at the breathtaking Montana scenery. The weather was perfectly clear, the snow below glistening in the bright morning sun. Bringing me back to reality, Barb interrupted my sightseeing to tell me what to expect next.

"When we get closer to the end, the lift will slow down to let you off." She remarked nonchalantly ...almost as if having a woman with no legs slide off a ski lift was an everyday occurrence.

Chapter 19 "Look Mom... No Legs!"

For Barb ...it was.

Fear gripped me again as we approached the end of the lift. Sensing my anxiety, Barb again gently guided me through the process.

"Keep your ski tips up, hold your outriggers out ...and let the chair push you off."

And just that simply, I skied for the first time since my accident ... on two artificial limbs. Sure, I only made it to the end of the ramp before coming to a stop, but even skiing ten feet, just like the first ten steps I took in the hospital on two artificial limbs, represented a HUGE milestone for me. Barb, however, took me much further than ten steps. Pushing off, we started down the slope, and I felt the cold air rushing against my face ...and a thrill of excitement flowing through my body! I was SKIING!!

At the end of the day, although tired and in a lot of pain, I beamed with pride the entire trip home. Barb (and others) trained me over several seasons, but eventually my skiing grew smooth and confident ...and I pushed myself to tackle more challenging slopes. Once, while standing in the lift line for an advanced run, a group of people asked why I used those weird ski poles. I admit feeling a great deal of delight in seeing the astonished look on their faces when I told them I was a double amputee.

Of course, a few mishaps occurred along the way in this activity, as well. I use the word "few" loosely. Experience taught me to duct-tape the sleeves holding the prosthetic legs to my body. Long past using cumbersome belts to keep the legs on or even the pin-lock system, I used gel liners and sleeves that formed a suction seal. Extremely comfortable to wear, the liner/sleeve system allowed me tremendous ease and freedom in walking. The company that makes those products, Alps South, used me as an inspiration when making their tapered liners and sleeves back in the nineties.

As great as the sleeves and liners are, they have one drawback when skiing; while riding a chair lift, the weight of the ski boot attached to the ski …pulled at the sleeves and reduced the suction. Duct tape securely anchors the leg in place.

Again, how do I know this?

Well, one day while riding the lift with my instructor, I felt the suction release from the socket and my leg. Thinking it would hold, I didn't become too alarmed … until the suction let go of my prosthesis completely. Squeezing what little calf muscle I still have in an effort to keep it on for the rest of the lift ride, it wasn't enough …and then it was…GONE!

Picture this if you will: a family enjoying a day of skiing together; children laughing, couples smiling, and then running for cover when a ski nearly crashes on their heads. Not just any ski, mind you; this one still had the boot attached …and a leg sticking straight up out of the boot!

Calmly taking charge of the potential disaster, my trainer motioned to the operator to slow the lift down *(I screamed for them to stop it all together)*. Working with the lift operator, the ski, boot, and leg (still protruding from the boot), were all reclaimed. Wearing snow pants that day, I quickly unzipped the pants up the side of the leg, and, minutes later, everything returned to normal. Well, normal for me anyway; certainly a day to remember for those skiers who witnessed the debacle. *(We probably should have tracked them down and offered to help pay for the counseling needed after such an event.)*

Years later I had another mishap that caused some bystanders to gasp. Missing a tight turn on a particular run, I halfway flipped sideways, and felt my leg come loose while sliding in the snow for several yards. An accomplished skier by that time, I no longer needed an instructor to join me; Barb successfully trained Peter to be my "buddy-skier." Grayson, only six at the time, skied along with us for that run. Not seeing me fall,

Chapter 19 "Look Mom... No Legs!"

Grayson kept going on by himself, and Peter, abruptly skidding to a stop halfway between me and Grayson ...kept switching his gaze back and forth wondering who to take care of first. Seeing a ski patrol heading towards me, I motioned for Peter to chase after Grayson.

Other than the daily, ever present pain I always live with, only my pride was hurt. As the young ski-patrol member quickly approached, the blood seemed to drain from his face. Staring at my right leg, he looked as if he might throw up.

"Ma'am, I've ordered a skimobile with a stretcher ...they'll be here in just a minute!" He urgently said; almost crying.

Puzzled, I also looked at my right leg and had to laugh. Twisting off in the fall, the limb caught in my snowsuit, and had turned almost 180 degrees. The heel faced up, and the toes faced backwards. Resembling NFL quarterback Joe Theisman's horrific, career-ending leg injury repeatedly shown by sadistic sportscasters and at the beginning of the movie, *The Blind Side*, the position of my leg convinced the poor ski-patrol boy that he had a major disaster on his hands.

The whole thing got me so tickled, that I couldn't stop laughing.

"Ma'am," the young man said seriously, "I don't think this is a laughing matter."

"It will be when I catch my breath and explain." I choked out, while trying to find a comfortable spot in the snow.

Finally gaining my composure, I looked up at this exceedingly worried member of the ski patrol and said, "It's okay, honey; it's an artificial leg."

"Help me get to someplace, even an outhouse, so I can take this suit off and pop this thing back on!" I asked him while struggling to twist around.

I later learned that the ski patrol kept tabs on my whereabouts every time I skied, but although the staff mentioned to the patrols on duty that I was disabled, the fact that I was an amputee evidently wasn't always communicated.

Clueless about what I was saying, it took several attempts to bring him up to speed on how amputees re-attach prosthetic limbs that come off while wearing a snowsuit (I made a mental note to wear snow pants after that event). The look of relief on his face was priceless. I did feel a bit bruised that night, but after putting the leg back on securely, and meeting up with Peter and Grayson who by now returned up the mountain, I finished out the day with some great runs ...and some great laughs.

Now when we go skiing, Peter and I stay mostly on the advanced slopes. I've even once tackled an expert slope. I went slowly, but all the way down without falling! It started with Barb's training, continued with plenty of practice, and now the result is that the fear is gone. At first I was afraid of falling off the lift (and with good reason), yet now I can negotiate challenging slopes successfully and ski with my entire family. Sure, they're all faster than me, but not much.

Like Barb taught him to, Peter skis ahead of me, and I follow his trail. A particularly good skier, Peter's job is to take me down the safest, best path ...so that I enjoy the journey, feel the exhilaration, but avoid mishaps. How is that different from our Christian walk? Following Christ is a great deal more challenging than skiing, and the path often looks terrifying. Trusting him with amputated limbs, marriages, children, careers ...is a lot more difficult for me than skiing down a "blue" slope in Montana. But through His word, He trains and prepares me ...and not only leads me on the best and safest path, He also calmly helps me handle calamities along the way.

Chapter 19   "Look Mom... No Legs!"

On steep runs, Peter always looks back at me to motion the turns I need to take; often while removing any small rocks or twigs in my path. Imagine how much more our Savior does the same. Through car wrecks, surgeries, and even amputations, I often look at the runs ahead of me and gulp: *"What are you thinking? Are you nuts?"*

Those (and more) are familiar questions I find myself asking while facing terrifying events. Peter knows my limitations on the slopes, and protects me from taking runs I can't handle. The difference with Christ, however, is that He not only knows my abilities ...He knows HIS abilities. He doesn't ask me to go it alone; He leads, He equips, He carries.

I *can do all* things through Christ who strengthens me.—PHILIP-PIANS 4:13, *NKJV (Emphasis added)*

Staring down the gulley of amputations, looking at the face of a hurricane ...the terror that gripped me eased when seeing the Savior beckoning me to come, and trust Him. Helping me face howling storms and the two most excruciating decisions of my life, that same Savior soon beckoned me again...to also trust Him for the third.

Chapter 20
Laughing Until I Cry

Laughter is the closest distance between two people.

—Victor Borge

eter, in many ways, is a walking paradox. One moment he appears as a joking, "smart-alec" kind of guy, but then he humbly cleans up unpleasant messes like he modeled so well in my apartment that morning I threw-up everywhere. You think he's full of hot air, but then he speaks with amazing depth and understanding. Working hard to convince audiences he's a dumb redneck, he then astounds people with his intellect. In the midst of some of the most painful moments of my life, Peter often wisecracks things so funny, that even doctors and nurses bending over my hospital bed will start to chuckle while trying to treat me. He is one of the most caring individuals I've ever known, but has caused some of the greatest pain I've ever felt.

As a gifted and trained pianist, he exclusively accompanies me and our children. At age five, he asked God to grant him the gift of music so he could play the piano. Almost immediately,

Peter started playing, and continued learning on his own until turning down his family's traditional new bicycle for a tenth birthday ...instead asking that the money be used to pay for piano lessons. Throughout junior high school, Peter helped supplement the bill for his piano lessons by mowing grass, cleaning horse stalls, and whatever other odd jobs he found. Maintaining his musical studies following high school, Peter eventually obtained a music degree from Belmont University.

So much of what Peter does now is apart from the piano, I think it surprises people to discover he plays. I push him hard, and make him jump through many musical hoops ...like transposing songs for me on sight, sometimes right before performing on live television. Although moaning and whining about changing song arrangements for me on the spot, I think it's an act; he wants to make me feel like he's struggling on my behalf.

In all seriousness, he's that good. He can play virtually every song we perform in any key...almost instantly. He's always felt embarrassed about his rhythm (or lack thereof), saying he suffers from "terminal Caucasian-ness," and refers to himself as *"Indiana Peter and the **Tempo** of Doom."* But we've performed in places where his playing is so touching, that sometimes I want to stop singing and just listen to him myself. As a singer, I know Peter is there for me on every note, with every phrase. Like a safety net for a tightrope walker, Peter supports every song I perform. Although he's not a bad singer, he limits his musical performances to the piano and never sings in public; well, except once.

While performing at a church one evening, I whispered over to Peter and asked if he would finish the song for me. Wild-eyed, he did, and I simply stood on stage with my eyes closed. He did a nice job, and we finished the event that night. Later in the car he asked what happened.

"You seemed to be choked up, and I just assumed the song got to you!" He said as we drove home.

Sheepishly grinning, I said, "No …I just forgot the lyrics."

My confession elicited a few sarcastic grumblings. From then on, I never had to worry about having lyric sheets in front of me; Peter provided them in abundance, and kept copies on his laptop, phone, and even on his *iPod.* I guess he really doesn't want to sing in public again.

A producer in Nashville once provided one of the highest compliments we've ever received when he commented about how "in sync" we were, and it seemed as if we read each other's mind while performing. We've learned to communicate that way on stage. Grayson once saw us lose our place on a song in mid-performance (the audience didn't know …at least I hope not!) and he told us later that we were "fighting with our eyes" while performing. I guess when you play and sing together as much and as long as we have, you blend …and learn to communicate without words.

Over the years, our story has attracted quite a bit of media, and during his first interview on camera years ago, Peter found his "zone." He loves live TV and radio, and I call him the "bullet man" due to his ability to speak concisely on air. While on TV sets, as the floor director counts the seconds to a break, Peter can encapsulate the whole message into two quick sentences to smoothly communicate his points …almost as if scripted. I can't "button it up" like that, and it's really frustrating to me, the interviewer, the crew, and especially to Peter! Musically, I can find the groove of any song, but Peter finds the groove in interview situations. His command of the facts of whatever he's speaking about is astounding, and he can switch gears and segue into topics as smoothly as an anchorman on the evening news. On air, Peter stays perfectly in-synch with the clock and the camera crew …but one-on-one, away from microphones, he will talk your ear off!

His sharp mind has also helped him become a walking encyclopedia of my medical chart. He knows more about events, dates, and medical data than I do, and my doctors often rely on him for historical information when it comes to treating me. He goes with me to every doctor visit, and during operations, he pushes the gurney nearly all the way to the surgical suite. I (and my doctors) have to remind him, however, that he's *not* a doctor, and doesn't even play one on TV!

While in a medical office recently, Peter kept questioning the doctor's technique as he changed the dressing for a wound on my left stump that had been slow to heal. Interrupting Peter's intrusion into the conversation, I told him that he didn't have an "MD" after his name. Before Peter could respond, the doctor wisecracked, "Yeah, but he's got an 'I DO' after his ...that trumps everyone!"

I think he wants to be "Dr. Rosenberger" so badly, that it just irks him. He tells people he's a *cranial proctologist*. When they look at him with bewilderment, he says with a straight face that he, "...helps extract heads from rears!"

While I dreaded standardized tests of any kind, Peter loves them. Constantly working puzzles, brain teasers, Sudoku, and all the above, he also often immerses himself in three different books at the same time. Why he didn't apply himself academically in high school and college is a mystery to me. Growing up, he consistently scored in the high ninetieth percentile on every academic standardized test, but would often show up to class without even taking a textbook. While I graduated high school *summa cum laude*; Peter will laughingly tell you that he graduated *"Thank you Lawdy!"*

From commonplace events or difficult situations (and we've had them), Peter's mind just seems to grab those moments and shove them through his warped sense of humor; he has no fear when it comes to saying the craziest things. After my most recent operation, Joni Eareckson-Tada happened to be in town speaking, and asked to come over and visit with me. Since I was just out of surgery, Peter played host. Offering various things to Joni and her assistants, one of them mentioned Joni loves seedless grapes. Peter took a bowl from the kitchen into our bedroom where Joni and I were visiting and offered them to her.

Patiently instructing Peter on how to help feed someone with quadriplegia, Joni asked Peter to give her one grape at a time …slowly. Most people would be quite moved and understandably nervous at such an event. Not Peter. With a cocked-eyebrow, he said to this saint of a woman:

"Joni, when I feed grapes to Gracie like this, she normally makes me take my shirt off and rub oil all over my chest …but I don't want to make you feel uncomfortable!"

Nearly choking on a grape, Joni threw her head back and burst out laughing …loudly! Only Peter could say such a thing and get away with it!

The night before we appeared on NBC's TODAY show, NBC sent us to see the *Little Mermaid* on Broadway. The next morning, hosts Kathie Lee Gifford and Hoda Kotb asked us what we thought. Peter surprised everyone with a serious look on his face and replied, "Not good!"

Somewhat startled and alarmed, they all asked (on live television), "What happened?"

With exaggerated concern, Peter replied, "You know that little mermaid (Ariel) who kept singing, 'I want some legs, I want some legs?' Well, Gracie lobbed hers up on the stage and yelled out, 'Here you go little fish girl …now quit your whining!!'"

As Kathie Lee and Hoda, along with the whole production crew exploded with laughter, Peter kept going.

"Evidently, Broadway frowns on that sort of thing, and it really created a problem; the Port Authority was called in …Disney banned us for life. It was just a huge mess!"

Kathie Lee later quipped with Peter, "I guess you're not a leg man, huh?" Without missing a beat, Peter looked at her and said, "Sure I am! She pops those suckers off every night, hands them over and says 'Knock yourself out, big boy!'"

Kathie Lee howled with laughter. "You married him because he makes you laugh, didn't you?" She asked me, while wiping the tears from her eyes.

Peter just sees comedy in virtually every circumstance. While trying on a bunch of clothes with the help of my sisters-in-law, I stepped out of the dressing room in a fabulous skirt …but one that had an excessively high slit up the side. Twirling around in front of Peter, his sister Liz, and his sister-in-law Courtenay, Peter slyly winked at me and, while imitating Barry White's smooth bass voice said, "Oooh baby …you're showing a little prosthetic!!!" Courtenay and Liz (and a couple of salesladies) fell out laughing at the absurdity of the whole thing.

But as quick as his comedic insights are, his tears are usually not far behind. His own journey through pain parallels mine. He doesn't have the same sensations, understandings, and afflictions that I do …nor do I share his hurt. We simply both carry great scars and heartache, as well as a mutual growing understanding of God's redemption.

With a minister father who modeled caring for others, Peter, even at an early age, seemed to gravitate towards connecting with people …particularly those in pain. His uncle, Lee, suffered terribly from the horrible disease *neurofibromatosis*, and Peter's mother struggled enormously while watching her brother die. Of all of the children in Peter's family, Lee requested Peter's company the most during his final days. While Lee lay dying, fighting for nearly every breath, he and Peter swapped jokes. Between tears and laughter, they enjoyed each other immensely. Whispering to Peter, just weeks before his death, Lee asked him to play a love song for his wife, Diane, at the funeral everyone knew loomed close. With his eyes brimming with tears, Peter obliged. During the funeral service, Peter walked to the piano and played Lee and Diane's song: the love theme from *Dr. Zhivago*. Winking at his aunt while playing the last note of the song, the two of them shared an unusual moment: almost as if one caregiver handed the torch to a future one. Peter and his aunt still share a deep connection that doesn't require words for them to express their thoughts on the journey. They both simply understand all the feelings involved in helplessly watching the suffering of a loved one.

Peter's dad often called upon his son's piano skills, and so Peter frequently found himself playing for funerals his father conducted at the church he pastored. In doing so, Peter, alongside his father, also ministered to the grieving. Although not ordained, Peter has the soul of a pastor, and even the best of face usually fails to conceal a broken heart from Peter's keen eyes.

A young man at our church, recently slopping through a messy divorce, sat alone at a table during a Wednesday night dinner. Peter joined him and, without feeling self-conscious at all, simply asked the young man to share his heart.

Like so long ago when looking at my scarred legs plopped in his lap, Peter didn't shy away from the wounds or the mess. Asking piercing questions known only by those who have honestly dealt with their own wounds, Peter listened to the pain and built-up heartache from this man, who, unbeknownst to Peter, had ached for another man to be willing to just talk about the "elephant in the room." The young man later shared his stunned amazement and gratitude for Peter with one of the pastors at the church we attend.

"He asked what no one would ...and seemed so comfortable talking about pain and the mess in my life," the recently divorced man told the minister.

Knowing Peter better than most, our pastor understood why.

While I was recuperating following the car accident in 1984, Peter transferred to Belmont from a college near his hometown in South Carolina. Peter's father, Dr. Beryl Rosenberger, served most of his fifty plus years as a pastor in that same small town of Anderson; in the northwest corner of the Palmetto State ...where he and Peter's mother, Mary, raised their five sons and one daughter.

After our initial encounter at Belmont's student center, Peter said it was love at first sight. He also said in an interview *on live television*, "Gracie stalked me, and I had to call the police." As the television host exploded with laughter at the unexpected comment, Peter, with complete deadpan, bore in unmercifully: "It was all very sad and uncomfortable ...really kind of pitiful the way she threw herself at me," he said with an exaggerated sigh while raising his hands helplessly.

Even I laughed while shaking my head as the camera crew tried to regain composure.

Peter is the only man I seriously dated who didn't know me prior to the wreck. All the other guys in my life were friends with me through that nightmare, and maybe their prior perceptions of me carried some of that journey. Perhaps they still looked at me as the same person, but with new challenges. However others looked at me, only Peter knew me always as a woman with a disability. I find it interesting to discover what compels a man to love a woman in pain.

It was so apparent that God would use him in a powerful way, I fell in love with what I believe God showed me he would become ...and I suppose, like most women, felt confident in my ability to shape what didn't belong. God didn't clue me into the timeline, however, of how long it would take for Peter to transform into the wise, caring, compassionate, and focused man of God he is today.

A pre-disposed heart for ministry, coupled with a desire to "swoop in and rescue," certainly played a part in Peter's initial attraction to me. Although I acted fiercely independent and strong-willed, maybe Peter sensed the deep insecurities beneath the self-reliant shell I worked so hard to maintain. Since I've known him, he's always demonstrated a sense for that sort of thing, so perhaps, without consciously thinking about it, he felt the neediness in my heart, and simply responded.

With a mischievous grin, he frequently comments, "I wasn't thinking that deep, I just thought she was a 'babe!'"

For many years, Peter used humor to avoid acknowledging the deep anguish in his heart, but harsh circumstances can silence even the sharpest wit. The seizure I experienced in 1989, just three years after we married, served as one of those events for Peter. That night he grabbed my chart out of the nurses' station and, for the first time, read the complete story of what had happened to me on the interstate highway back in 1983. Until that point, the nurses convinced him that the chart remained a "top-secret" document only medical people could read. Peter threw rules to the wind, grabbed the huge stack and started reading.

While I slept soundly for the first time in days, Peter with vomit still on his clothes from my seizure only hours prior, remained hunched over volumes of medical data until nearly dawn. Not even my parents or sister knew all the details Peter now poured through. Doctors and hospitals keep detailed records, but only specific to *that* doctor, and *that* hospital. I've been treated by more than thirty specialists in six different hospitals; a veritable mountain of records. Every couple of years, Peter and one of those doctors compiled a summary sheet of my procedures; sitting down together and mapping it out. Peter has read virtually all of my records, and to this day, remains the only person to read my ENTIRE chart.

He said he would have rather waited for the movie.

The night of that awful seizure, Peter began spiraling into a despair that lasted more than a dozen years. Everyone told him about the car wreck, he knew about my pain and limitations, and he clearly noticed my scars, but with all that knowledge, he still didn't have an understanding of what happened to me years earlier on that dreary November day. For hours he scanned lab reports, doctors' notes, nurses' notes, and other chart information. Smart enough to understand it, and experienced enough by then to appreciate it, Peter felt a sickening feeling in his soul. That night, he felt fear, panic, and despondency grip him in a powerful way ...and struggled to understand how to process this new awareness of something he clearly remained powerless to change.

Parker having been recently born, we'd already started down the road of growing our family together. Pouring over my chart, Peter felt trapped for the first time in his life. He truly wanted to care for me, but an awareness grew in his heart; he knew he wasn't up to the task.

Clearly, I can be a demanding person. Probably at that confession a loud chorus of "Amen's," would echo throughout our families. Embracing me with no injuries and a healthy body tested several young men's nerve and fortitude when they dated me before my accident. Admittedly, I treated a few guys poorly, and really hurt their hearts. Often referring to me as a "force of nature," Peter laughs while saying that I did them a favor.

"Somebody would have ended up in a body bag," he once chuckled sarcastically.

My immense needs, however, even surpass an "over the top" personality. Combine fierce intensity with massive trauma, and the relationship can expect some rough roads ahead.

Chapter 20

Trying to emulate his father, the greatest model of caring in his life, Peter thought he could accomplish what simply could not be done. Merely wanting to love and care for someone does not guarantee the ability to do so. Using every skill and talent in his arsenal, committing each brain cell in his head, Peter misguidedly attempted the task belonging only to God. He never seemed to ask if God wanted him to manage this, he simply assumed it was his to do.

> Merely wanting to love and care for someone does not guarantee the ability to do so.

Placing my medical and insurance needs above his ambitions and career goals, Peter chose to work at companies with large enough insurance policies to cover me. Every day he trudged to a job he didn't like, to perform a task he cared little or nothing about. Instead of using his mind to solve problems, create wealth, or advance his own career goals, he simply put it in neutral and did the best he could to fit into the surroundings where he found himself spending his days.

Along the way, he achieved successes, won the admiration and friendship of co-workers and clients, and made a good name for himself; but none of it satisfied him. Like he did on our first date, Peter spent all he had insuring (literally) my needs were met, and resigned himself to going without …again; leaving the table still hungry.

All that notwithstanding, his accomplishments are nothing short of astounding; he practically memorized my medical history, learned to speak intelligently on complicated medical matters with doctors and nurses, and worked tirelessly with insurance companies. Of the nearly nine million dollars in health care costs (that we can estimate), our total debt is currently less than $1,000.00 (from charges this year). Peter regularly follows up with my health insurance company to ensure every bill is properly and timely paid; he's even caught mistakes in billing …saving the insurance company money (they loved that!).

Since taking responsibility for my health needs more than two decades ago, he's never lost an appeal with any health insurance company, and continues to achieve amazing successes navigating America's healthcare system. Although considered "uninsurable," we've changed policies for me at least six times, and, thanks to Peter, never experienced even *an hour gap* in coverage.

While pregnant with Grayson, I suffered extreme complications, and was bed-ridden for six months. During that time, a wonderful, middle-aged woman came to our home to work every week day. She cleaned the house, washed the clothes, cooked dinner and, thanks to an amazing effort by Peter, our medical insurance company willingly picked up the tab! Pretty spectacular work for anyone; a staggering achievement, however, for someone with no prior education or training in healthcare or insurance.

He tells others that he's still waiting on political leaders to call him and seek his advice on how to manage our country's healthcare system …but, so far, the call hasn't come.

As a caregiver, Peter is off the chart and has no peer. As a husband, Peter is all I could ask for …now. But for more than half of our marriage, Peter spent everything he had on care-giving, and put the relationship lower on the priority list.

Identifying with the men who lowered the paralytic through the roof to get him to Jesus, Peter accepted the role of "roof-demolisher" and "pulley system for the needy"; often struggling to carry me to Jesus, but failing to see the path for himself. Echoing back to that first surgery before our wedding, my demandingness, coupled with a demanding body, as well as the opinions of others, all helped push Peter closer to what he already seemed to believe: "Gracie's more important than me, and God should address her needs before mine."

When I think back on our life, it's sad to me that he spent so much time willing to believe God's concern and love for me, but somehow failing to recognize God's love for him. Part of that is also due to the fact that when people see Peter, they rarely ask about him. So many people in our life ignoring his needs and pain ...reinforced his belief in his lack of importance.

I'm struck by how our first date charted so much of our marriage. It never occurred to Peter that God's love for him *equals* His love for me, and all of us. Likewise, he somehow didn't grasp God's desire to meet *both of our needs*. His heart cried out for the things he saw others receive from God, but it seemed as if he kept looking at his wallet and accepting his fate of doing without. He couldn't seem to wrap his mind around the fact that there was enough Jesus for all of us ...at the same time.

Desperately longing to experience the fellowship with God that so many others openly discussed; Peter assumed he wasn't worthy. He *wasn't* worthy ...*none of us are.* It's called grace. Peter needed and wanted to experience grace in a way never before known to him.

Looking at the menu of life, Peter desired acceptance, rest, fellowship, intimacy with God, forgiveness, cleansing; he wanted *love*. But he thought that even if he did somehow receive it, just like on our first date, he feared having to "wash dishes" to experience it. Continuing to look at his own resources, perceived worth ... and despairing over his lack, Peter failed to look to Christ; he failed to rejoice in His abundance. Unknown to Peter, God prepared a meal just for him; a meal of love and grace exceeding his deepest desires.

It's difficult to experience and appreciate grace, however, until one recognizes and admits the need for it; but that journey often includes great pain and heartache.

Jesus said, "And I say unto you, Ask, and it shall be given you; seek, and ye shall find; knock, and it shall be opened unto you." —LUKE 11:9, *ASV*

Chapter 21

The Third Time

"Simon, Simon, behold, Satan has demanded permission to sift you like wheat; but I have prayed for you, that your faith may not fail; and you, when once you have turned again, strengthen your brothers." But he said to Him, "Lord, with You I am ready to go both to prison and to death!" And He said, "I say to you, Peter, the rooster will not crow today until you have denied three times that you know Me."

—Jesus to the Apostle, Peter
Luke 22:31-34 (NASV)

Gifted men often rely and live in their gifts instead of developing their whole heart. My husband, like so many other gifted men, chose to obtain favor, affirmation, and acceptance through his talents and abilities ...but failed to see how God loved him as a unique person. Peter would be the first to tell you how hard he worked to earn acceptance. Using his personality, musical ability, humor, intellect, or whatever he had in his armory, Peter worked feverishly to achieve success as *he defined it:* money, fame, affirmation ...or skillfully handling my medical needs.

The strain of managing the by now screaming needs of my body, drove Peter without mercy. Such was the burden on him that looking at his back, I almost half-way expect to see scars from a whip. Of all the people in his life, only his Aunt Diane can understand Peter's reality from her long years of caring for her ailing husband, but even she once told Peter, "I don't know how you do it."

"Lee and I had an end in sight," she once shared with him. "We knew death lay just around the corner; although a lousy end, it still represented an end."

No end lay in sight for Peter or me. I certainly didn't want to die, and he did not want to divorce me and just leave ...but we never knew *what* was coming around the corner. A broken body is not a terminal disease, so we live on the edge of whatever crisis happens to hit us each day. One of Peter's favorite comedians, Steven Wright, once quipped, "You know that feeling you get when leaning back in your chair on two legs ...and then you catch yourself before falling? Well, I feel like that all the time."

Steven's statement serves as a good description of our life. How do you live with this level of uncertainty for years, and even decades? Even money would not solve our issues. Peter looked across the table once and muttered, "If someone wrote a check to me today for a million dollars ...it still wouldn't make this stuff go away." Although possessing great abilities, the strain of our life's unpredictability mounted on Peter ...nearly driving him insane with impotent fury and rage.

The pressure on our relationship intensified, and the cracks grew wider. Arguments seemed to be the communication method of choice, and the brittleness of our hearts turned even the most innocuous event into a major ordeal. It seemed we could get through amputations and life-threatening surgeries, but would lose it arguing over such stupid things as the time and channel of a television show. After a particularly unpleasant fight once, Peter rummaged through the kitchen looking for ingredients to hurriedly prepare a dinner long overdue as a result of several medical appointments. When I offered to help fix the meal, Peter slammed a cabinet door closed while barking, "No, I'll do it …I have to be in control of something!"

After a lackluster meal full of tension and heated words, he later found himself alone racing in his car at nearly 100 mph, screaming at God. Finally bringing the car to a stop in some unknown parking lot, he put his head on the steering wheel and just sobbed. Begging God for relief, Peter heard only silence. He didn't even have a crucifix placed by Sister Euphemia to help point his eyes to the cross. With everything in him, he wanted to believe in a loving God who cared, but the screams piercing his brain seemed to crush his soul; he felt utterly lost.

Hardships make us hateful and, in order to avoid suffering, we will inflict pain on ourselves and flail out at others. When that happens, suffering makes us worse than we were. Affliction doesn't teach us about ourselves from a textbook, it uses the stuff inside us.
—JONI EARECKSON-TADA, *WHEN GOD WEEPS*

It's heartbreaking to recall these events, and even more so that they were not isolated. We were truly coming apart at the seams. Who could I sit down with and share the intimate details of my pain, suffering, and loss? I am not likely to meet many people who have had my kind of journey. Peter is the same way; even the best of intentioned friends still couldn't connect to the deep anguish Peter felt daily. If they tried, they often found themselves lost in the maze of his paradoxically engaging, but evasive (and increasingly fragmented) personality.

According to statistics I learned from Joni, the divorce rate in couples living with a disability in the family is approaching 90%. Peter and I

Relationship and
self-awareness issues
normally dealt with
over a lifetime,
are crammed into
tiny time frames
of a few years, or
even months with
a disability.

are both in agreement that it's not the disability *per se* that causes so many marriages to fail. Rather, it's the constant strain of the disability (or chronic pain), that quickly reveals "cracks" in the emotional makeup of the individuals in the relationship; cracks inherent in everyone, but a chronic disability accelerates the exposing of each flaw. Relationship and self-awareness issues normally dealt with over a lifetime, are crammed into tiny time frames of a few years, or even months with a disability.

Often the care-giving spouse, particularly men, feel the burden to fix, manage, or control the crises; only to eventually discover the impossibility of the task. The more capable the man, the longer it takes for him to deplete himself and learn the truth. Discovering the hopelessness of achieving success, usually results in a great deal of emotional and spiritual trauma to the caregiver, which often leads to abandonment.

Deserting the relationship is the most common ripcord pulled by husbands and fathers in a family with a disability. Too many mothers find themselves struggling with not only a disabled child, but then the added heartache and strain of losing a husband. Women desert as well, leaving men just as rejected, but men seem to bail in greater numbers. Individuals living with the burden of a chronic disability find an already well-developed sense of rejection amplified ...when a spouse leaves them in their great neediness.

I suppose it is all part of the original fall that started in the Garden of Eden and the curse attached; men must toil through thistles. The thing about working through weeds and thorns ... is that you never win. That's the harshest part of the curse; you can't beat it. The part of a man designed in the image of God feels responsible and assumes the role of caretaker. The part of the man cursed by sin collides with the original design, and he tries to fix what cannot be fixed; he tries to BE God ...for himself and the woman. He _will_ fail. The only variables to this universal truth are how long it takes each man to discover this tragic reality; and how much damage he will cause while learning the futility of his efforts.

A disability, particularly when constant crises and chronic pain are involved, will squeeze individuals without mercy; bubbling to the surface the gunk that's in their soul. As men travel down the self-destructive path of trying to manage the unmanageable, desertion (which assumes many forms and can often be camouflaged in a medicating behavior) becomes an increasingly attractive escape; deceptively promising a relief from the trauma of the disability ...as well as the avoidance of facing internal flaws.

The intensity of a chronic crisis forces so much pressure on a person (and a relationship) that the character flaws, self-preservation instincts, and selfishness are exposed in near volcano-like emotional and spiritual turbulence. With waves of this level of tumult cascading over the soul of individuals, some will often do the unthinkable in an effort to stop feeling the pain.

Peter chose to do the unthinkable; he chose unfaithfulness in order to escape the screaming that filled his ears. Sadly, he didn't understand that the screams he heard were not simply coming from my struggle with physical pain ...or even my own considerable demandingness; the shrieking also erupted from the massive agony in his own soul. The treachery of sin is that it promises relief, but instead provides anguish and death ... while simultaneously trapping individuals into a life of bondage. Peter's choices heaped even more misery on his already tortured heart.

Those that have long served God, and been kept from gross sins, have a great deal to be humbly thankful for, but nothing proudly to boast of.—MATTHEW HENRY

It's not easy to write about things like this, but you have to understand that we regularly encounter people in similar trauma even when visiting the grocery store. How can we not share our journey? Others did it for us. As you read this, maybe you're dealing with hurts like this; hurts so close to the surface, that it's hard to catch your breath at times. If so, please know that we include this part of our story for you.

Many people who have watched us on television, or even go to church with us may be shocked and disappointed ...and maybe even treat us, or at least Peter, differently. We'll deal with that as best as we can, but after a great deal of prayer and soul-searching, and the advice of trusted family members and friends, we feel it's important to share this exceptionally personal part of our story.

I didn't catch Peter. Although I suspected and confronted, he convincingly covered it with lies (adultery and lies are inextricably linked) ...and so we moved on. But Peter remained fragmented, and carried deep guilt and shame that nearly drove him crazy. Like a vaudeville performer spinning plates, Peter raced around at top speed; consumed with fear of the plates falling and exposing him as a failure and fraud. Every day he awoke to managing millions of dollars in health care costs, caring for our children, learning to cook meals, running the house, and working full time; all the while maintaining the façade that daily showed new cracks and fault lines.

Finally, Peter no longer wanted to spin plates. He quit pretending, stopped running, sat down ...and let it all crash. Unlike so many we see on the evening news, no one hauled Peter unwillingly into the light; he chose to step out of the shadows. The guilt, shame, and a splintered life carried for years, was simply too much for him …and he no longer wanted to pretend.

Our pastors constantly preach the Gospel …that Christ's sacrifice on the cross paid the penalty owed by our sin to God's justice. Every Sunday, Peter heard about this fabulous grace that "covered a multitude of sins." While the congregation sang hymns; I often saw him clutching the hymnal to his chest, sometimes gently beating it over his heart, as tears rolled down his eyes. When that happened, my heart broke for what could be causing him so much torment.

Listening to our pastors, Peter could almost taste it, and his heart begged for just one crumb. How he missed this growing up in the home of such an amazing minister, is a testament to how fragmented Peter became.

He couldn't carry the guilt anymore; he couldn't carry me anymore. Sitting in the church pew listening to that message every Sunday, Peter slowly, inch by painful inch, made his way to the foot of the cross. He wanted acceptance, forgiveness, and grace so badly, but knowing nothing could be made right if kept in the dark, Peter realized the need to step into the light, no matter the cost. Looking for the opportunity, Peter seized the moment, and took the ultimate step of faith by choosing to believe the grace of Jesus Christ …extended to him.

While watching a television show late one night, the subject of betrayal and adultery unfolded in the show's plot. Feeling something in my gut, I, for the third time in our life together, questioned Peter about this topic.

In his heart, Peter felt he heard a voice clearly tell him that this was THE opportunity for him to "come clean."

As I did long ago, Peter sat in his own twisted and burning wreck and clearly saw his helplessness. He too …looked into the fires and realized his inability to save himself. With one last, pitiful cry, Peter also prayed "Jesus, only you can save me," and stepped out of the shadows.

A broken and a contrite heart—These, O God, You will not despise.—PSALM 51:17, *NKJV*

What I did physically during the span of twelve years, Peter did in a matter of minutes. He relinquished everything. Putting our marriage and family, his career and reputation, and every other part of his life on the table, he literally lay down his life and resigned himself completely to the mercy of God. Often comparing it to what Harrison Ford's character must have felt in *Indiana Jones and the Last Crusade*, when he put his hand over his heart and stepped out across what he thought was a bottomless chasm, Peter stepped off a cliff …and into the hands of God.

To hear him say what he did was more painful than my car wreck; the account of his broken vows to me felt worse than amputations. The details are known to the ones who need to know …including our sons who provided unanimous support of this chapter being written.

My heart was broken.

I look back at those first months in amazement that neither of us jumped off a building or put a bullet through our head. Recalling the moments before my car accident,

Bending to slide into the car, I paused a moment longer and prayed another prayer; not a prayer of protection, but rather one reflecting a desire to be molded into a woman who pleased God.

"Lord, continue making me into the woman you want me to be."

It felt like I was re-living hitting that abutment and facing those flames …without having gone into shock; instead feeling the full impact …over and over again. Like the aftermath of losing my right leg without receiving any painkiller, I felt myself screaming for relief that never came.

Chapter 21 The Third Time

"God would never let something like this happen to me …would He?" A thousand images and voices flooded my mind. Growing up as a little girl looking forward to wearing a white wedding dress … and knowing something like this would never happen to me. He's my "daddy"; how could my daddy allow me to not only live without legs in unbearable pain …but now this? Mistakenly thinking amputations represented the apex of my brutal decisions, I now faced something eclipsing even those challenges.

Am I defective?

Jesus, Jesus, Jesus.

Is Jesus Your Friend?

Sister Euphemia pointing me to the cross.

Praise God from Whom All Blessings Flow

I can do ALL things through Christ who strengthens me.

A hurricane making landfall.

Down the treacherous path, the Savior beckons me to come …and trust Him.

I could hardly draw a breath, as the images, questions, and lessons of a lifetime of trusting God cascaded over me. Would I …*how would I* … continue to trust God? My third painful choice surpassed everything I had experienced until this point. Cutting through the confusion, heartache, disbelief, fear, and doubt all swirling to a climax, one voice again penetrated the fog of my anguish:

Daddy's here, Mary Grace …Daddy's here.

As long ago while in critical care, following the chaos of waking up to a new life of pain and disability, my heart heard the assurance of my Heavenly Father's presence. Now, more than at any other time, I needed to know that God Himself witnessed my heartache, and had not abandoned me.

Daddy's here, Mary Grace ...Daddy's here.

Sobbing, nearly in the fetal position, I listened to the still, small voice following the tornado that so cruelly ripped apart my life. In the shower, I sat on the bench I use when my legs are off, and just moaned. Way beyond tears, I wrapped my arms around me and groaned; too wounded for words.

Daddy's here, Mary Grace ...Daddy's here.

With absolutely no idea of how this would play out, I stood at the edge of a cliff and knew I would either crash on the rocks below ...or fly. Growing up on the coast in Florida, I've witnessed the carnage from a hurricane, and the stunned look on people's faces when viewing the damage. I now shared that look, and stood in disbelief at the devastation.

Daddy's here, Mary Grace ...Daddy's here.

Listening to that voice ...and no other ...I, for the third time, slipped my scared hands into the scarred hands of our Savior. I chose to trust Him with this new chapter of pain.

There will come a time

when you believe everything is finished.

That will be the beginning.

—Louis L'Amour, *Lonely on the Mountain*

Chapter 22

Mourning into Dancing

*How many husbands have thought themselves
so strong, so capable of leading a family—and being
a leader, husband, and father; trying to fix everything
...and in so doing simply prove how weak they
really are? It's crucially important that we know how
weak we are. Not how strong we are; nor how capable,
nor how gifted, nor how persuasive. We need to look
deep into our hearts, and see how much we need Him
...and see how big that cross is.*

—S. James Bachmann, Jr.

lthough even family members suggested otherwise, I chose to trust God with Peter and observed something in him that convinced me to stay: real repentance. Clinging to what Fanny Crosby stated in one of Peter's favorite hymns, "the vilest offender, who truly believes …that moment from Jesus a pardon receives" *(To God Be the Glory)*. Peter's belief in the pardon received from Christ permeated literally every part of him.

He wasn't merely remorseful or sorry; he truly repented and turned 180 degrees in every aspect of his life. Although emotions played a role in the journey, and still do, I'd have to say that Peter's repentance reflected "resolve" more than "feelings." He continues to feel sorry for his sin, but surpassing regret, Peter's resolute, single-minded purpose is to more closely know this Jesus who cleansed his soul.

Humbling ourselves means returning our gaze to Christ… where it belongs; groveling to an offended spouse, in an effort to atone, is still looking to ourselves, or each other, to lessen the pain.

He didn't keep his reputation foremost in his mind …but rather his desire for restitution. So many men, particularly public figures, spend a great deal of time "spinning" the situation to salvage some form of an image and "get back to normal." Peter, literally, found himself regenerated as a new man in Christ, so he wasn't interested in preserving something he considered dead. He hated his "normal" …and craved something new.

Throwing himself into this new walk, Peter humbled himself in ways few men have. Some men allow their scorned wives to debase them in order to placate and, through a self-determined penance, make peace. That's not humbling one's self, that's just appeasing; wallowing in shame and guilt. Both Peter and I often struggle with those respective roles traditionally assumed by couples in this scenario, but Peter consistently leads us out of that quagmire, refusing to linger in the pit of my demeaning him …or Peter demeaning himself, but instead appropriately elevates the tremendous work of Christ. Humbling ourselves means returning our gaze to Christ …where it belongs; groveling to an offended spouse, in an effort to atone, is still looking to ourselves, or each other, to lessen the pain.

Peter taught me that.

Our senior pastor affirmed to us that it was "… a rare thing we were doing," and he, along with the other pastors marveled at the explosion of grace God was pouring into our relationship. We worked hard, and it was costly in every way. The counseling bill added up to thousands of dollars. Every week we dutifully showed up to meet with our counselor (sometimes twice a week), often without knowing where the money would come from, but it always came.

At times, we used an equity line of credit; borrowing against our house, and instead investing in our home. We've both often wondered what Dave Ramsey, the financial guru and radio host, would say to the way we've handled our life. But honestly, there's really no one out there saying, "OK, your marriage is on the rocks, you've had millions of dollars in health care costs, you don't know how to get through the day without crawling under the bed and sobbing …so, here's how to spend your *money*!"

We simply did the best we could, with what we had. Instead of living day to day, we lived hour to hour. The consequences of Peter's choices cost us on every level …but we are still together. The consequences of **my** choices cost us on every level …but we are still together.

Like Peter did so many years ago, I "grabbed a mop and bucket, put on gloves," and helped clean up some gross stuff …praying, just as he did, that I wouldn't lose it myself. Rarely are things as easy as they appear on the surface, so, as Peter did when he poured through my chart that night so long ago, covered with my vomit …I now had the same opportunity to delve into Peter's life and learn the whole story of this deeply flawed man who chose to love a woman in pain. I journeyed with Peter into the basement of his soul as he disclosed every failure in his entire life …and together we worked to mend what could be repaired; and surrender what couldn't. Along the way, I re-discovered the man I love and experienced more of this unique individual who assumed responsibility for a problem he didn't create …and then assumed responsibility for a problem he did.

Almost immediately, Peter, like parched soil receiving rain, soaked in the grace and love offered to him by our Savior. For seemingly the first time in his life, he allowed scriptures, hymns, and sermons to saturate him. Hanging on every word spoken by his father, our pastors, sermons on tapes, and more importantly the Word of God, Peter immersed himself in the grace and love he'd desired for decades.

Months into this journey, Peter quit his job, without even giving notice. He simply walked in, got his belongings and told his boss good-bye. He's still friends with his former boss, and surprisingly, he knew Peter was doing the right thing. Without over-thinking it, Peter clearly felt in his heart that the Lord called him out. He relinquished his ability to manage things on his own, and irrevocably placed himself and our family in the hands of God.

With a stellar reputation at his work, they'd still be throwing good-bye parties for him, he was that well-thought of and liked. Avoiding all of it, however, Peter, packing up the few items he kept at work, slipped out the service elevator, and simply vanished. Alone in the elevator, holding a box of meager belongings, Peter quietly sang what I sang years ago after relinquishing my left leg, *"Praise God from Whom all blessings flow."*

Chapter 22 Mourning into Dancing

Arriving home, he told me that he left his job, and I reached up with both hands to hold his sweet face and said, "Whatever happens, baby, you will never work for health insurance again!"

People, including family members, thought he'd lost his mind. Just like me when I relinquished my legs, he received criticism, but he knew he had a calling on the other side of surrendering his ability to manage his life (and mine). He simply no longer wanted to try and figure it out; he didn't want to *manage the unmanageable* with his paltry efforts. I didn't know what was on the other side of the operating room door, but I knew WHO was waiting for me there. Peter didn't know what lay ahead for him after walking away from his job, but he knew WHO did.

The sturdy cane my father made for me years ago is in the foyer of our house collecting dust. It only served me when I walked on dysfunctional legs. (In fact, the cane's too short; I asked for taller legs when I became a double amputee.) The awards and recognition Peter received from working at places in his efforts to *manage the unmanageable* are tucked away in a closet. Viewing them as hollow achievements, Peter feels they serve only to remind him of a life spent caring for me on his terms. His office is now crammed with much better awards and recognitions; testimonials reflecting his trusting God for direction and provision …instead of himself. Those awards possess eternal significance.

For the following three weeks, Peter sat in a rocking chair in our bedroom and read through most of the Old Testament …in three different translations! I have never witnessed anyone devour the Word of God as he did. Almost as if he held a menu given to him from the hand of God Himself, Peter eagerly ordered and ordered and ordered. After a lifetime of leftovers, he wanted everything on the menu.

Ken, our counselor, mentioned on more than one occasion that of all the people he treated, he had never seen anyone work as hard …and be as effective as Peter Rosenberger. With his sense of humor still intact, Peter often winked and boasted to me that of all of Ken's "crazies," he was number one! I had to laugh.

It felt good to laugh again.

Psalm 51 (NKJV)

Have mercy upon me, O God,
According to Your lovingkindness;
According to the multitude of Your tender mercies,
Blot out my transgressions.
Wash me thoroughly from my iniquity,
And cleanse me from my sin.

For I acknowledge my transgressions,
And my sin is always before me.
Against You, You only, have I sinned,
And done this evil in Your sight—
That You may be found just when You speak,
And blameless when You judge.

Behold, I was brought forth in iniquity,
And in sin my mother conceived me.
Behold, You desire truth in the inward parts,
And in the hidden part You will make me to know wisdom.
Purge me with hyssop, and I shall be clean;
Wash me, and I shall be whiter than snow.
Make me hear joy and gladness,
That the bones You have broken may rejoice.
Hide Your face from my sins,
And blot out all my iniquities.

Create in me a clean heart, O God,
And renew a steadfast spirit within me.
Do not cast me away from Your presence,
And do not take Your Holy Spirit from me.

Restore to me the joy of Your salvation,
And uphold me by Your generous Spirit.
Then I will teach transgressors Your ways,
And sinners shall be converted to You.
Deliver me from the guilt of bloodshed, O God,
The God of my salvation,
And my tongue shall sing aloud of Your righteousness.
O Lord, open my lips,
And my mouth shall show forth Your praise.
For You do not desire sacrifice, or else I would give it;
You do not delight in burnt offering.
The sacrifices of God are a broken spirit,
A broken and a contrite heart—
These, O God, You will not despise.

Do good in Your good pleasure to Zion;
Build the walls of Jerusalem.
Then You shall be pleased with the sacrifices of righteousness,
With burnt offering and whole burnt offering;
Then they shall offer bulls on Your altar.

Chapter 23

An Exceptional Man

*The psychology of why I turned aside will
have to be left to another book—and another time.
The point I must make here is that because of
a prior commitment to God through Jesus Christ,
when I did fall I was not utterly cast down.*

—Jamie Buckingham
Where Eagles Soar

I once heard a sermon about King David in which the pastor mentioned that David was an exceptional man …and that exceptional men have really high "highs" and really low "lows." Their successes are exceptional, and their failures are equally exceptional.

Peter is an exceptional man.

His journey mirrors so much of mine. Both of us lived a life of self-determination. Both of us slammed into something and saw our inability to get out of it on our own, and we both married someone with no clue as to how to deal with the other's dysfunction or disability.

God has a way of bringing interesting people into our lives to help us prior to, or during, difficult ordeals; individuals who help anchor us with greater truths when intense realities confront us. With me, it had to be someone who suffered in a way I could respect. With Peter, it needed to be someone with abilities he could respect, but someone who let his gifts flow from his heart.

Seven months into this chapter of our life, our first public appearance together was with comedian Jeff Foxworthy. Jeff had no idea of all that was transpiring, but came down to our hotel room and stayed until nearly two in the morning ...eating sunflower seeds, spitting into a cup, and sharing his heart. Peter absorbed the whole experience; only God could have scripted such an encounter. Here was a personal hero of Peter's, opening his heart to him at a critical time in Peter's growth and learning.

From Jeff, Peter learned that he could be funny, real, and heart-driven ...all at the same time. He didn't have to work at it, but could let it flow from a heart no longer fragmented. By affirming Peter's humor and heart, Jeff helped Peter bridge the gap that *performance*, even in a medical nightmare, could be a genuine expression of a heart condition ... not something that has to be "put on." Iron sharpens iron, and Jeff spent many phone calls and e-mails with Peter, never knowing what Peter had done, but simply pointing him to the same Jesus that he himself trusted. Not able to fully hear the message from his own minister/father ...a redneck comedian spitting sunflower seeds finally succeeded in helping Peter wrap another arm around the cross of Christ.

From that moment on, Peter's humor changed. Onstage he grew increasingly funnier, but no longer appeared fractured. Easily shifting from outrageously hilarious stories to poignant insights, audiences saw a growth and depth to Peter that he'd never possessed before. Learning from Jeff, Peter didn't try to be funny ...he simply WAS funny. With shame and guilt removed, his realness and authenticity surfaced. Others found themselves embraced by Peter's heart, as well as his humor and wit; building not only meaningful friendships, but also a growing list of people who follow his writings.

Peter often states that the "Peter Rosenberger" who made such sinful choices is dead ...and we didn't even mark the grave. I believe him, and he has the track record to prove it. He literally risked losing everything: me, our sons, social standing, and career; he threw *everything* down in the hope that he could be loved as a whole person. First Peter 3:1 discusses wives winning over their husbands with godly behavior ...without preaching at them or even saying anything. Peter has often told me how much I modeled that particular verse, and the impact my behavior had upon him.

Our pastors believe him and have been encouraging forces in his life. Peter started sitting on the front row of our church (who wants to sit on the FRONT row?). When people ask Peter why he sits on the front row, he smiles and says that "it's as close as they let me get."

Sitting in church as if he is attending a fine restaurant, Peter looks at the bulletin to see what the "chef's special" is that day, and eagerly listens to our pastors share the life-changing Gospel of Jesus Christ. He good-naturedly and sincerely tells our pastors how he wants them to see first-hand the *wounded and sick restored*, and that if they are ever at a loss for sermons, to "...look down from the pulpit and see what God can do with a broken body and a sinful man."

Many of our friends have gone through messy divorces (for *far less serious reasons* than we could have!!!) yet, we're still here. The 90% divorce rate for couples living with a disability is probably much higher when you factor in moral failures; we can't say for sure because no one seems to keep or publish those numbers. It's a safe bet, however, that statistically speaking, Peter and I are in rarified air; we've been married for nearly twenty-five years. There is no explanation other than the grace of God through the redemptive work of Jesus Christ.

With remarkable visuals such as crucifixes in my hospital room to drive home the point of the cross, Peter's are no less poignant. One particular moment came unexpectedly at our church, and stands out more than others when it comes to Peter's journey.

Have you ever been in church and watched communion being served in those silver trays with the small plastic cups full of grape juice ...and wondered what would happen if one of those were dropped?

Well, guess what ...

I'm not sure how it happened, but one of the trays crashed and grape juice spilled onto the table, the floor, the *whiter than white* tablecloth, and a few startled elders and pastors ...right on the platform in front of everyone. There really wasn't any damage, since the pulpit area is all hardwood, but from the gasps that went out, it was clear the general feeling was that this was a disaster.

The elders serving the elements recovered quickly and went about their business of passing the remaining trays row by row; each elder and church member gripping the trays like wrestlers; determined not to contribute to the embarrassing scenario at the front of the church. The little cups lay scattered around, and the bright white cloth covering the table was stained deep red. I watched our pastors looking at each other, their faces displaying their questioning the protocol for such an event. Surely this had been covered in a seminary class ...somewhere?!

Evidently not.

One pastor bent down to pick up some of the scattered cups. He was the same pastor who ministered to us at our home the morning after Peter's confession. I will always remember him sitting in our den looking at Peter and stating emphatically, "Peter ...the only way through this, is you have got to die."

He then literally lay prostrate on our den carpet and prayed for our family. Peter believed him, and more importantly, believed God. Peter died that day next to our pastor lying on our floor.

Now, that same pastor was bending down to wipe up the spilled grape juice representing the saving blood of Jesus. Something happened in Peter at that point, and he left his seat, walked up the steps, and started picking up cups. Another pastor showed up with a roll of paper towels, and the three of them wiped up the juice puddle around the table and pulpit ...while hundreds of people looked on with concern. What seemed a "catastrophe" in reality served as a powerful moment for Peter as he continued wiping up the dark red liquid now trickling down the wooden stairs. One pastor earnestly whispered his thanks to Peter, but drew back with surprise at his response. With tears filling Peter's eyes, he choked out, *"He did this for me!"*

In the deafening silence, Peter's quiet sobs could be heard, and then my own joined his. Then it happened in waves, row after row of members could be heard crying. At first, the pastors thought this was a disaster; but as the beautiful white linen cloth grew increasingly red, the picture dawned upon the congregation.

No longer was Peter wiping up grape juice. In his heart, he knew this juice symbolized the blood of Christ spilled for his sinful heart. He was about to take off his suit coat to wipe up the juice, when more paper towels arrived. As the tears streamed down his face, he knew a suit coat was meaningless next to what Jesus did for him. The man who once needed every hair in place, dressed impeccably well, took more pride in his appearance than in his soul ...was now on his hands and knees in front of hundreds of people sobbing next to the very pastor who humbled himself in our den. Peter no longer cared about how he looked, his suit, or what anyone else in the church thought of him, he only focused on the reality of what Jesus did for him at the cross.

After a lifetime of looking at the menu without ordering …accepting scraps and leftovers, Peter finally understood the meal prepared just for him. What a beautiful example of the Gospel. Peter told the pastors he hoped they never washed the tablecloth; he wanted to see the stained cloth for the rest of his life as a reminder of the good news that someone else paid the debt he could never pay …that someone else said he was worth such a price.

He's an exceptional man.

Chapter 24

Some Get It, Some Don't

But pain insists upon being attended to.
God whispers to us in our pleasures,
speaks in our conscience,
but shouts in our pains: it is
His megaphone to rouse a deaf world.

—C.S. Lewis
The Problem of Pain

Pain, loss, letting go, and relational issues are universal experiences. Whether through an accident, injury, disease, advancing age, family dynamics, lost opportunities, natural disasters, political upheaval, or plain old-fashioned stupidity, life will change.

Expectations have to change, too.

If all we do is pine away for the person we once were, the job we didn't get, the spouse we never had …we can expect a lifetime of misery. Worse still, focusing on limits and losses causes the greatest loss of all. When we divert our minds into only thinking of ourselves, and what we *perceive* as losses, then we miss the opportunity for the wonderful blessings of the relationship we can have with God *right now* …even with all the unpleasant circumstances that can fill our daily lives.

During difficult moments in my life, a particular passage in the Apostle Paul's second letter to the church at Corinth continues to serve as a source of encouragement. Paul, struggling with some unnamed malady, asked God several times to remove whatever plagued him. I don't need to know what Paul struggled with; it is enough to know that he struggled. He mentioned a "thorn," and I can certainly relate to a constant stabbing pain. (I also still have a thorn-like piece of glass lodged under my chin that pokes me every now and then.) After praying for his "thorn" to be removed, here's how Paul described the response he received from Christ.

And He has said to me, "My grace is sufficient for you, for power is perfected in weakness." Most gladly, therefore, I will rather boast about my weaknesses, so that the power of Christ may dwell in me. Therefore I am well content with weaknesses, with insults, with distresses, with persecutions, with difficulties, for Christ's sake; for when I am weak, then I am strong.—2 CORINTHIANS 12:9, *NASB*

That verse hangs on my refrigerator; boasting in my weakness allows Christ's power to rest upon me. I have discovered that those who know and understand this can find peace and contentment in every season and circumstance of life. Some people get it, and some people don't.

For many years Peter has struggled with his own understanding of God and suffering. One of his more frequent arguments involved the question, "What good is it to be God, and not use divine powers to alleviate suffering?" Dealing with constant difficult realities for more than two decades continues to force our family to wrestle with Peter's and other similar issues …concerns we probably would have otherwise ignored. At age nine, struggling with deep feelings stemming from some of our family's hurts, Parker once cried out to Peter, "Why should I believe God cares about my hurts, when I see what he allows Mom to go through?"

Pastor/author Tim Keller discussed this topic in his book, *The Reason for God.*

If you have a God great and transcendent enough to be mad at because He hasn't stopped evil and suffering in the world, then you have (at the same moment) a God great and transcendent enough to have good reasons for allowing it to continue that you can't know. Indeed, you can't have it both ways.—TIMOTHY KELLER, ©2008 *THE REASON FOR GOD*

Just a few years prior to his honest and heartfelt outburst, Parker had fallen off the playground equipment at his pre-school. Peter and I took him to the pediatrician, who looked at the laceration with an experienced eye, and quickly went to work sewing Parker's chin. The local anesthetic used by the doctor helped his pain but did nothing to calm his fears; and so a terrified Parker cried and thrashed wildly; making it difficult to place the stitches. Peter put his arms around Parker and held him still while the doctor calmly ignored Parker's screams, and expertly repaired the laceration. While looking into our son's beautiful brown eyes full of fear, Peter softly repeated a simple phrase, "It's OK baby, Daddy's here. It's OK baby, Daddy's here."

"Daddy's here, Parker. Daddy's here."

Peter didn't try to explain the need for stitches, antibiotics, why a strange man with strange instruments poked at him, or any of the other things scaring or hurting Parker. He also didn't try to address the feelings flashing over Parker's face …feelings clearly screaming out Parker's heartbreak of being betrayed by those he thought loved him most. Peter just held Parker with such tenderness …and kept softly repeating to our terrified toddler,

"Daddy's here, Parker. Daddy's here."

I could almost see myself back in that critical care pod following my wreck …dealing with my own terrifying feelings of being betrayed and abandoned.

Daddy's here, Mary Grace. Daddy's here.

Only a toddler when receiving stitches, Parker expressed his feelings even more as a nine-year-old …and, sitting on the edge of his bed, he poured out his anger, hurt, and frustration of not understanding why God allowed suffering. Peter listened to our oldest son; hearing words from a nine-year-old that he himself asked …and sometimes still does.

Listening to Peter and our oldest son discussing pain and God's providence, brought to mind an ongoing conversation Peter and I maintained. Months prior to his conversation with Parker, Peter came to me with a thought he'd been tossing around in his mind. I indulge my husband in these philosophical conversations about pain and suffering from time to time, but they kind of make me tired. Hearkening back to my days in school, I *learned experientially* by involving all of my senses; talking about it frustrates me. I live it …let him ponder it!

But this conversation was different; this one really drove the point home.

"Can you recall the exact sensation of stubbing your toe?" He asked out of the blue one day.

"Not really." I replied with a great deal of puzzlement. "I don't have toes."

"That's my point," he said intensely.

"What's your point?"

"You can't remember pain!"

"Big deal …I can't forget that I'm in pain; so where's this going, because this is not exactly helping the pain I _do_ feel?"

These conversations with Peter wear me out.

"Think about it, Gracie. When you stub your toe, you react. You may yell, say 'ouch,' or other things…but whatever the reaction is, you eventually _stop_ reacting."

"Yeah, so what?"

"Well, apply that rule to other types of traumas. For example, a divorce, cancer, job loss, or even a car accident…"

Intrigued, I listened closely.

"…in each of those traumas or hurts, we react accordingly. The reactions, of course, depend upon the trauma. If the pain is so intense, like when you had your car wreck, well, then the reaction can be shock; people go into either physical or emotional shock over certain levels of trauma."

"You're losing me again, where is this going?" Peter can be so _wordy_. (God love him!)

"When we react to significant levels of trauma, particularly when it offends our sensibilities of the way life should be and what we perceive as a bad call by the universe's referee …_'God,'_ then we cry out 'foul!'"

"What?!" I asked with growing exasperation.

"We question God when things hurt us bad enough!"

Nodding with agreement, I looked at him with anticipation.

"And…"

"Since we can't remember pain ... when the pain goes away, we stop reacting; we stop questioning God."

He was really going somewhere with this, and by now, he had my full attention.

"When the surgery is successful, we get another job, a check arrives in the mail, after grass is growing over the grave, the divorce is final, or the wound heals ...as ***time travels forward***, the hurt seemingly becomes more manageable to us. We quit throwing our rage, disappointment, heartache, and/or accusations toward God, and put the 'Why, God?' questions on the shelf ...until the next trauma."

"So what you're saying is we never resolve our indignation at God ... or our feelings of mistrust towards his goodness?"

"Exactly! We don't get mad at God for a 'little bit of pain that we can handle'; but we turn on Him when the pain surpasses our 'ability' to handle it by ourselves. By hurling accusations of 'unfairness' at God, we admit what lurks in the basement of our soul ...but only for a limited period of time, and then we stuff it all back down again. If we feel those things, then every trauma will take us on the same roller coaster ride ... without dealing effectively with our distrust of God."

Listening to him, I could tell he worked at trying to wrap his arms around an even bigger truth. By this time, he was pacing back and forth with great animation as he talked.

"Here's the kicker, Gracie," he went on to say. "In the case of chronic pain, chronic trauma—if you will ...you never get to put the questions on the shelf. You must wrestle with the *'Why God?'* questions at the same intensity level they started ... until you resolve them, medicate yourself into oblivion ... or go crazy!"

Sitting down like he'd just finished a workout, he looked at me with great intensity. "Your pain, our pain, this heartache we feel, this physical pain you carry ..._never leaves_. The constant pressure continues to force the ugly mistrust and warped views I have of God all the way up to the surface ...and I must honestly deal with that mistrust."

"But isn't wanting to know 'Why' a legitimate question?"

"Yes," he replied. "Wanting to know 'why' is a legitimate question ...if we possess the capabilities to understand the answer."

> "Wanting to know 'why' is a legitimate question ...if we possess the capabilities to understand the answer."

"Gracie," he said earnestly, "Try to imagine any reason God allowed your car accident ...or my failures."

Throwing out a few possibilities, I suggested, "a powerful testimony, maybe ...or maybe so that He could use this to reach others?"

Taking a deep breath, he pointedly asked, "If that were the case ... would it make you _smack your forehead and say, 'Oh, now I get it ...I feel better now?'_"

"No," I truthfully sighed.

Not letting up, he dug deeper. "Is there any possible reason you can think of that would make you feel better about all the suffering you've endured ...including the stuff from me?"

After a long, slow breath, I answered, "No."

"Exactly," he replied with a seemingly satisfied look on his face.

He enjoys these kinds of discussions; I try to find "a happy place" while he talks.

"Gracie, our finite minds cannot grasp or feel at ease about any possible reason why a loving God allows such suffering. The 'why' question, then …is the wrong question."

"So, what's the right question?" I asked while looking at him with tears forming in my eyes …resulting from the struck nerve.

"The only possible question," he gently said, "is <u>*Who*</u>? Who is this God we serve? Who is the Lord we tithe to, pray to, and dedicate our lives to?"

Peter's journey, launched by our son's precious and heartfelt cry, clearly led him away from "resolving a question" …to embracing a relationship. Sitting on our son's bed while looking into Parker's tear-filled eyes, Peter provided …THE answer not only to Parker's question …but to the cry of so many more broken hearts. Watching from Parker's bedroom door, I witnessed a precious moment between father and son (on two levels).

"Parker, I don't know why your mother has to suffer so much. I don't know why God doesn't call a 'time-out,' and make it all go away."

Holding him tight, Peter offered his son the same hope that sustains him. "But, Parker … I do know this: God sent His Son, Jesus, who stretched out His arms for us on the cross. He gave His life willingly so that we could be saved and freed from sin …and so that this broken world could be restored. If He loves us *that much*, then I'm willing to trust Him with Mom."

Content with the answer, Parker cried in his father's arms; so did Peter.

"Daddy's here, Parker."

"Daddy's here, Peter."

Chapter 25

Not So Bruised Heel

*And I [God] will put enmity between you [the serpent]
and the woman, and between your offspring and hers;
he will crush your head, and you will strike his heel.*

—Genesis 3:15 (NIV)

There is no substitute for victory

—General Douglas MacArthur

Running into my in-laws' house during Thanksgiving one year, Parker yelled out, "Mom, come outside, we've got a snake cornered …and we thought you might want to step on him!"

Genesis 3:15 immediately flew into my head, and I excitedly jumped up and volunteered to deal with the dangerous reptile. This encounter was not my first with a deadly snake. As a young girl, I once reached to grab a poisonous water moccasin basking in the warm Florida sunshine. I already possessed a collection of frogs, lizards, and turtles in an aquarium that I kept in the trailer we lived in while Mom and Dad built the mobile home park. The snake would be a wonderful addition to my growing assortment of creepy crawling things (I could handle reptiles and frogs, but not BUGS!). Before my tiny hand touched the snake, my father seemingly instantly appeared and yanked me by the arm; pulling me out of harm's way. Rather than thanking my father, I carried a comical "grudge"; frustrated for being denied the opportunity to capture a deadly reptile.

That Thanksgiving day in South Carolina, I had my long awaited confrontation with a snake.

Stepping quickly through the crowd of cousins and in-laws, I used my heels to smash the snake's head …all while, according to Peter, having a look of profound satisfaction on my face. Although most acquainted with me clearly know I never shy away from a challenge, I don't think Peter's family expected me to take *so much* pleasure in killing this creature.

Stomp, Stomp, Stomp! It seemed exceptionally spiritual to me.

"Behold I give you the authority to trample on serpents and scorpions and over all the power of the enemy, and nothing shall by any means hurt you." —LUKE 10:19, *NKJV*

On a fall day in South Carolina, I chose to accept that verse at face value. Maybe it has something to do with me being a ninth-generation Tennessean (strange folks lived in those East Tennessee hills) but, regardless, I wanted my long-denied triumph over a snake. This particular venomous and dangerous serpent slid across the wrong driveway at the wrong time.

Chapter 25 Not So Bruised Heel

Seemingly the embodiment of all the evil and maladies endured for so long, I was determined to claim victory over this snake. Singing to myself while the writhing reptile went to its doom under my prosthetic feet, at no point did I feel any fear …or concern for my safety. Oddly while I kept crushing the copperhead, I thought the prosthetic company that made my legs should use this new activity in a marketing promotion. "We'll help you walk …and KILL SNAKES!!!"

The snake twisted and squirmed, and yet I continued to crush it under my heel. Hearing the voice of my father-in-law, I turned to look at the man who married us and helped hold us together during such painful times, his face lit up with laughter while cheering me on; "Step on him some more, Gracie, I don't think you quite got him!"

Later, I called Daddy and told him about the killing. Without any hesitation he said, "You've always had this issue with a snake!" It was almost as if he'd been expecting the call for the last thirty-five years!

Somewhat emulating Gen. 3:15, I couldn't help but notice that the artificial legs causing such difficulties, embarrassment, and pain were the very things allowing me to conquer a deadly enemy without fear. What many considered a reason to question the goodness of God, instead served as a weapon against a lifetime nemesis.

While determinedly killing a poisonous creature on a driveway in South Carolina, I received a small picture of a larger truth about the evils in this world. The devil is already defeated, and he will go on being repeatedly defeated by, from our viewpoint, the most unlikely of things: Christ's power working through our weaknesses.

Slamming into that cement abutment nearly killed me and left me permanently scarred and maimed, but Christ's power working through that evil continues to give glory to God …and defeat to a devil that would rather have me dead than praising God through weakness. When immorality slithered into our marriage, it appeared we'd be another casualty; Satan would rather us be divorced than praising God through our brokenness.

I quit focusing on the handicap and began appreciating the gift. It was a case of Christ's strength moving in on my weakness. Now I take limitations in stride, and with good cheer, these limitations that cut me down to size—abuse, accidents, opposition, bad breaks. I just let Christ take over! And so the weaker I get, the stronger I become.—2 CORINTHIANS 12:9-10, *THE MESSAGE*

While living in this broken, fallen world that the most famous serpent in history helped bring about, we will never escape heartache, pain, suffering, and even the ugliness of sin; but the story doesn't end there. God doesn't simply frantically run around trying to clean up evil and its aftermath. He is purposing His will through all of this and using it to HIS glory. Satan can do his worst, but it will never triumph over God's purposes.

Killing a poisonous reptile with my artificial feet clearly demonstrated how God uses our weaknesses, brokenness, and disabilities, to face enemies without fear; even to the point of singing praises to God while we do so. There may be things in each of our lives causing great heartache that can be used to *conquer* unfinished battles. One thing I'm learning in this walk with Christ: it's not about our strengths, but rather when we offer our weaknesses in God's service; that's where the real triumphs occur.

> One thing I'm learning in this walk with Christ: it's not about our strengths, but rather when we offer our weaknesses in God's service; that's where the real triumphs occur.

Chapter 25 Not So Bruised Heel

Each time I walk out on stage or appear on television to give God glory with my maimed and broken body, I stomp a little more on the snake. Each time Peter and I walk hand-in-hand to sit on the front row of our church, or make the decision to bow our knee to God instead of ourselves ... we crush the snake's head a bit more. Every person reading this book helps me step on the serpent with rejoicing. Without ignoring the pain, suffering, and heartache in this world, we shift our focus to HIS glory, HIS redemption, HIS Love, and HIS purpose by placing our weaknesses into GOD's hand. In doing so we live without fear, shame, and despair; confident that the victory is won.

Whatever happens, conduct yourselves in a manner worthy of the gospel of Christ. Then, whether I come and see you or only hear about you in my absence, I will know that you stand firm in one spirit, contending as one man for the faith of the gospel without being frightened in any way by those who oppose you. This is a sign to them that they will be destroyed, but that you will be saved—and that by God. For it has been granted to you on behalf of Christ not only to believe on him, but also to suffer for him.—PHILIPPIANS 1:27-29, NIV

Part IV

Enduring

...being confident of this very thing, that He who has begun a good work in you will complete it until the day of Jesus Christ;

—Philippians 1:6 (ASV)

It ain't how hard you hit;
it's about how hard you can get hit and keep moving forward.

—Sylvester Stallone, *Rocky Balboa*

Chapter 26

The Eyes Have It

And I shall push on, despite my flaws,
and present my body a living sacrifice, blemishes and all,
and believe I am acceptable to His service.

—*Where Eagles Soar*
Jamie Buckingham

Charm is deceptive, and beauty is fleeting:
but a woman who fears the Lord is to be praised.

—Proverbs 31:30 (NIV)

Although fixed for some time now, my left eye doesn't always feel normal, and I remain terribly self-conscious about it. The surgeries helped tighten the muscles around my eyes to make them relatively straight. For a while, however, weariness caused the left one to pull a little bit, and I avoided looking people straight in the eye for more than a few moments at a time.

As Peter and I continued to claim new ground, both as a couple and as individuals, we found ourselves making more and more public appearances. Performing together on stage always feels natural to us, but cameras and television interviews continue to cause me great discomfort …and I often make a fuss about where I sit in order to keep the camera from drawing attention to my eye.

In a television studio recently, I twisted and fidgeted on the couch prior to the interview in an effort to make sure the camera didn't catch my eye wandering; taxing the patience of the camera crew and floor director. After watching me repeat this nonsense for several minutes, Peter finally looked over at me and witheringly said, "Mary Grace!"

Again, the full name …what is it with people calling me by my full name when they really want my attention.

"Mary Grace," he sighed, "You have robot legs and you're wearing a skirt …I'm thinking the eyes are not what people will be staring at!"

Feeling pretty foolish, I sheepishly laughed.

Sitting in that television studio, I recalled a pivotal moment years earlier while visiting my sister's home in Florida, when I enjoyed walking around with my cosmetically covered legs; showing off shapely ankles and straight feet for the first time since my car wreck. As lovely as those legs were, I found myself sitting on the dock inwardly fuming at all the fun everyone enjoyed, while I with my pretty "cosmetically covered legs" couldn't get into the beautiful water that so clearly beckoned me.

Torn by a desire to maintain my now beautiful legs for the first time since my wreck, I also hated the idea of sitting on the sidelines …just for vanity's sake. Not content to simply take them off and then roll off the dock into the water, I wanted to feel the exhilaration of diving. After mentally wrestling with this dilemma for several minutes, I reached a conclusion and called Jim McElhiney to inquire about the legs being waterproof.

"Absolutely not!" He said without missing a beat. "As long as those legs are covered you can't get into the water; they'll blow up like balloons and will be ruined!"

Disappointed, I hung up the phone, frustrated …but not defeated. Mentally weighing the pros and cons, I considered the coverings preventing me from getting into the water that I loved so much …versus the coverings making my legs pretty and providing emotional comfort. Stewing on this for a few moments while watching my family play in the water, I made a decision; vanity had to go!

Rummaging around my sister's kitchen, I found a really good knife, and stepped outside to find a chair. If the legs would be ruined anyway, I certainly didn't want them to swell up and look like tires around my legs. I'll never forget the expression on Peter's face when he walked up from the dock to see me sitting by the pool with a knife in my hand busily, and happily, cutting the "skin" away from my legs. From his perspective, it must have been shocking. He described the scene as similar to when Arnold Schwarzenegger peeled back the skin covering of his robotic arm in his role as the Terminator.

With bits of foam and tattered skin-colored material fluttering behind me, I walked to the edge of the dock and, for the first time as a double amputee, dove into the clear water of the Florida panhandle. Soon I was tearing around on Bobby's and Andrea's Sea Doo with a sense of freedom my injuries had almost made me forget. Once again using duct tape, a miracle product if ever there was one, I secured my legs in place so we wouldn't have to use SCUBA gear to retrieve them.

I use duct tape like Nina's father used Windex in the movie *My Big Fat Greek Wedding.*

From that moment on, I decided to wear uncovered legs, permanently. I still have another pair of covered legs that I wear only when I want to take a vacation from people staring …or when my everyday legs are in the shop (one friend calls them my Sunday-go-to-meeting legs!). For years following my wreck, I dreamed of pretty legs … but now I willingly made the decision to look like a cyborg. Peter and the boys didn't seem to mind, and the comparison to "Ahhhnold's" character led to just calling them my "Terminator legs." Uncovered legs made my life easier and if they didn't bother me, I figured they shouldn't bother anybody else.

Sometimes the sight of my uncovered legs startles people, but most seem accepting of the way I look, and a few even go so far as to give me words of encouragement. But I do get a lot of stares. The way I see it, though, is that my uncovered legs serve as an "indicator" of what's going on with me as an individual. Invariably people will approach me and tell me about a family member who lost a leg, or some will go even further and tell me how brave I am to show my legs. Those "conversation starters" lead to wonderful opportunities to share my faith …as well as imparting the way God continues to sustain me through even the loss of legs. Although some individuals treat me like amputation's contagious, most are simply curious. Walking hurriedly into the grocery store wearing shorts one day, a little girl quietly followed me and stood near while I pointedly tried to look at the dairy case, hoping she'd lose interest. Finally mustering her courage, she gently reached up and tugged at my shirt and asked, "Are your legs in Heaven?"

Laughing, I looked at this precious young girl and said, "Well, yes, I suppose they are …but one day I'm going to get them back!"

Her mother appeared at that moment and seemed embarrassed, but I told her not to worry about it because "…she just gave me something wonderful to think about!"

Then Jesus called a little child to Him, set him in the midst of them, and said, "Assuredly, I say to you, unless you are converted and become as little children, you will by no means enter the kingdom of heaven. Therefore whoever humbles himself as this little child is the greatest in the kingdom of heaven.—MATTHEW 18:2-4, *NKJV*

Sitting in a television studio fussing about my eyes while wearing "Terminator legs" may seem a little odd, but my identity was not formed as an amputee …it was developed as someone with an eye problem; a defect. Entering the world with eye dysfunctions shaped my (and others') opinion of myself. The car accident came from the outside and left me scarred and disabled; the eye problem was from within and seemed to serve as a commentary on my self-worth.

That damaged sense-of-self compelled me to compensate by doing such things as having pictures taken in profile rather than facing forward. Interesting enough, I still find it much easier to walk out on stage with "robot legs" than staring into a camera. Like so many years ago while walking as a single amputee, I naturally gravitated toward compensating … by depending upon my remaining damaged leg instead of the new, unnatural feeling prosthesis. Once both legs were gone, I had no choice but to depend upon both artificial limbs … and function as a whole person rather than a "compensating" person.

> We all have some level of imperfection or defect. Those who disagree will one day change their mind when age prevails over youth.

Communication, however, occurs with the eyes more than the legs, so as I share my thoughts and heart with others, they often look at the one place that causes me the most discomfort. Admittedly, prohibiting that discomfort from detracting from my message remains challenging; I seem to instinctively want to cover the defect.

We all have some level of imperfection or defect. Those who disagree will one day change their mind when age prevails over youth. Like pain, we choose to accept certain levels of defects, but a mysterious line of demarcation exists when the defect or level of pain exceeds a perceived tolerability. At that point, and it varies from person to person, we cease enduring a defect, and instead question the goodness of God.

All of this is subjective, based upon our own sense of well-being. Often a moving target, our contentment with self can change with time and maturity. Jay Leno's protruding chin, Jimmy Durante's nose, Mel Tillis' stuttering; …defect or life-forming attribute?

It is hard to say. None of those individuals had any say-so as to those particular characteristics, and I can only imagine the teasing and challenges all of them endured. Sure a protruding chin is a far cry from a disability, but does it not have an effect on the sense of self? Some like Jay Leno turn it into an asset, but for every Jay Leno, a million others struggle to present only the perceived acceptable parts of themselves to a world they think demands perfection. In doing so, they often hide what could be an important part of their life. Sectioning off part of your life robs others of the chance to embrace you as a whole person. Constantly playing to our strengths develops what Peter calls "Popeye arms," referring to the cartoon character with the grossly exaggerated forearms, but an otherwise scrawny body; he's out of balance.

> Sectioning off part of your life robs others of the chance to embrace you as a whole person.

It doesn't mean I should go around apologizing or drawing attention to my eyes, but rather I should quit apologizing to myself about them. I'm who I am, and I can't change it (or as Popeye would say, "I yam, what I yam"). If my eye wanders while I talk to you, it's okay; it doesn't detract from me as a person ...or God's love for me. Using any perceived or classified "defect" as an indictment against God's love reflects a severe lack of understanding of God's character ...and our nature.

In God's eyes, *we're all* defective. Not simply because of eyes, chins, legs, or arms, but rather the soul itself. God sees and knows our defect, so much so that He made it possible for us to live in perfection. Christ took our massive defect upon Himself so that we don't have to be judged by an impossible standard of perfection; *He* is perfect. Putting our faith in Him, in *His perfection*, we are freed from the burden of striving for some level of "acceptable perfect."

We can just be who we are. Big chinned, crossed-eyed, stuttering sinners saved by grace ...waiting for the day when our defective bodies will be resurrected to perfection. While we wait, we can love freely from our whole heart, because we are so freely loved from His perfect heart. Singing my heart out and swinging my legs from the counter top at Carl's Café, I felt acceptance and love ...regardless of the patch over my eye. That love wasn't limited to my grandfather; that love originates from my heavenly Father ...and stays with me every day, in every situation. He knows the condition of my eyes; He made them.

As He [Jesus] passed by, He saw a man blind from birth. And His disciples asked Him, "Rabbi, who sinned, this man or his parents, that he would be born blind?"

Jesus answered, "It was neither that this man sinned, nor his parents; but it was so that the works of God might be displayed in him. —JOHN 9:1-3, *NASB*

People want an explanation of why "bad things" happen; particularly when discussing a loving God. Jesus clearly states the answer, although many people may not be comfortable with His response: "...that the works of God might be displayed in him."

Peter asked me recently if going on television is still difficult for me. Thinking for a moment, I surprised him, and myself, by replying, "I have an important message to communicate. If people are distracted by eyes, legs, or whatever other imperfections I have, then that's their problem. I can't afford to be distracted, however, from the mission I feel God has given to me; it's too important. So, if they want to stare, then they can stare. If they want to judge me by the way I look, then that's their prerogative. But, if they want to hear about the grace and power of God that is greater than eyes, legs, or anything else ...then they will see past my defects, and concentrate on Christ's power that is made perfect in our weaknesses."

Even in this broken, defective body, I am thrilled to serve God ... and don't want to miss an opportunity to do so simply because of my hang-ups or those of others. This perseverance is not a one-time decision I made while on my sister's dock in Florida; I make it every day. I don't need to look perfect; I simply point to the One who IS perfect.

Leaving Andrea's dock that day, I continued walking with uncovered legs and a growing confidence. For nearly my entire life, I had looked different. So many years ago, Granddaddy Parker communicated to me that my eye patch didn't define my worth. I think, although sad at the circumstances, he would have been proud of how I handled the way my legs look. The memories of my grandfather flooded back over me in late December 2002. Grandmother Parker lay dying at age 91. Gloomily, Peter and I loaded the boys into the car and headed south from Nashville to Fort Walton Beach in order to be with her. Already lapsed into unconsciousness at the nursing home, we kept vigil ....but leaving the room quickly saying he had an idea, Peter returned a few minutes later with an electronic keyboard he spied while entering the facility.

Setting it up in my grandmother's room, he played hymn after hymn, as Andrea and I sang softly; sitting on either side of grandmother as she slipped into eternity. I'm not certain, but I think that other than in church, it's the only time Andrea and I ever sang together ...and she has a beautiful voice. My father and his sister, Anne, joined in on "Great is Thy Faithfulness" and many other old hymns my grandmother loved. For nearly six hours, we played and sang for her. Singing with my sister for a final "goodbye" to our grandmother will always remain a precious and tender moment to me.

On January 15, 2003, I gazed at the fresh earth of my grandmother's grave nestled in the family plot in Elizabethton, Tennessee ... finally reunited with her loving husband and oldest son after decades apart. She never knew, as she lay dying with her granddaughters singing to her, Peter received a call from the inaugural committee of the newly elected Governor of Tennessee, inviting me to perform at the inauguration. Mary Emma Pouder Parker, a seventh-generation Tennessean whose family produced two Tennessee governors, would be so pleased.

More tears brimmed as my gaze shifted from the new grave ...to the weathered tombstone above bearing my grandfather's name, as well as his oldest son's ...whose precious hat I wore in the high school pageant. Although he died years before my birth, I felt strangely close to him at that moment.

Standing on artificial limbs my grandfather never had to see me need, tears continued filling my eyes while staring at his name etched in the granite; the stone keeping a silent vigil for nearly thirty years. Had he any idea the indelible mark he made on my heart? Was he aware of how God used him to help rescue a little girl struggling for acceptance ...loving and encouraging me regardless of how I looked? Did he fully realize how he helped prepare me for the brutal circumstances that would surround my life? Could he have grasped what he helped shape ...simply by loving?

The little "pirate" girl who entertained her grandfather's friends at a cheap diner was now set to sing before the present and past governors of Tennessee, the Tennessee legislature, the majority leader of the U.S. Senate and many other dignitaries attending the event, and be heard across the great state of Tennessee; the only singer performing at the inauguration …in a state full of renowned singers and recording artists; a far cry from belting out songs while sitting on the Formica countertops at Carl's Café.

Returning from my memories, I focused again on the elegant granite tombstone bearing the names of my family, and decided upon one last tribute. Holding my father's hand, while my sons and husband stood with me on a wind-swept hill in northeast Tennessee, I closed my healthy, no longer crossed eyes, and sang once more, "Heaven Came Down and Glory Filled My Soul."

Sighing, I turned to leave the graveside; prepared to step onto even larger stages. As the cold winter wind whipped my hair, I could almost smell the sea air outside the weather-beaten walls of Carl's Café. Glancing one last time at the centuries-old cemetery framed by beautiful Tennessee trees awaiting a mountain Spring, the words still echoed from a lifetime ago, *"Sing, Gracie …sing with all your heart."*

Chapter 27

We Will Stand

There is a balm in Gilead
To make the wounded whole;
There is a balm in Gilead
To heal the sin-sick soul.

—Traditional Spiritual

Following my grandmother's funeral on a Wednesday, we left the airport in East Tennessee just ahead of a snowstorm. Arriving in Nashville safely, the weather grew increasingly worse, and by Friday, Nashville experienced several inches of snow and single-digit temperatures. Loving the cold weather as I do, I had no problem with snowy days, but Governor Phil Bredesen's first inauguration was scheduled for Saturday (my birthday) …just one day away. The ceremony went on, but the parade had to be cancelled due to the snow still on the ground.

Assembled across the street from the platform, all of the platform guests met two hours before the ceremony. Karyn Frist, wife of newly elected U.S. Senate majority leader, Bill

Frist, came into the room …along with other members of the Tennessee congressional delegation. Karyn and I hit it off immediately …and I was honored a few years later when she asked me to contribute a chapter about my relationship with Daddy to her book, *Love You, Daddy Boy – Daughters Honor the Fathers they Love.*

Heading over to the platform, the staff provided everyone with blankets, and pointed out the electric foot warmers under the seats. Laughing at Peter, I rubbed my gloved hands together and wryly said, "A lot of good those things will do for me!"

Even in the nine degree cold, the inauguration went off without a hitch. My part of the inaugural ceremony was to sing a hymn, so I chose to sing "How Great Thou Art" (*a capella*, in frigid air!). I was simply introduced as "Gracie Rosenberger"; only the new and former governors, along with other guests on the platform able to see my metal shins peeking out from my hem line, recognized I was an amputee. Following my performance, I turned to embrace Governor-elect Phil Bredesen and Governor Don Sundquist. Taking the hand of Governor Sundquist, I recalled the friendship with him and his wife, Martha, and her once visiting me in the hospital during a particularly grueling stint.

Years earlier, after singing at an event at the Tennessee governor's mansion, Martha Sundquist and I quietly toured the executive residence. Both of us had endured a long day, and Martha wearily stated she wanted to "just take her shoes off and rest."

She chuckled and warmly grabbed my hand when I commented, "I know what you mean, ma'am …I just want to take off my legs and rest!"

After hugging two Tennessee governors on a bitterly cold morning in Nashville's legislative plaza, I looked down the row of dignitaries attending the gubernatorial ceremony; observing additional past governors of the volunteer state, and both of Tennessee's United States Senators. I couldn't help but reflect on the family members in my past who played such important roles in Tennessee's history; I think they would have been proud.

A few months later, while driving to speak at a church several hours from Nashville, Peter received a phone call from an aide to Senator Frist. He and then Senator Rick Santorum from Pennsylvania invited us to speak and perform at a dinner hosted by the Republican Senate Caucus for wounded soldiers at Walter Reed Army Medical Center. Accepting the invitation, we both felt the awesome responsibility of participating in such an event ...particularly as the war on terror continued providing the first steady stream of wounded military since Vietnam.

I underwent an unexpected, additional surgery prior to traveling to Washington, and for a while, it appeared uncertain if I could actually participate. Removing some pins and screws from a back surgery a few years prior, the procedure itself wasn't supposed to be particularly involved. It seems, however, that I continue to be on the far end of the curve when it comes to complications. Arriving back in my room following an hour or so in recovery, I lay quietly in bed, while Peter sat next to me reading. This was our first operation together since all the stuff came out about him, and his whole demeanor reflected this new journey.

Normally kinetic, and even borderline frantic, following surgeries with me, Peter now quietly sat beside me doing, well ...nothing. He simply stood guard and watched over me. Gazing at me after a few minutes of silence, he leapt into action when noticing the color of my face was a deep blue; I stopped breathing. As he did so many years ago during my seizure, he quickly summoned the nurses who called the code team. A "code blue" alarm blared over the hospital intercom system, and a flurry of people flew into my room to resuscitate me. Peter, who thought he knew most nurses and staff members at St. Thomas, looked on with surprise as people he'd never even laid eyes on came swooping into the room. He later commented that it seemed as if they rappelled down from the roof like "ninja-nurses."

An anesthesiologist (one Peter did not recognize) took the lead, and started to intubate me. Peter, trying to spare my vocal cords commented, "She's a singer …please use a small tube."

Not even looking up while trying to resuscitate me, the doctor never missed a beat while saying, "We know Gracie …we'll watch her cords."

Some people possess media-driven fame. At St. Thomas Hospital, mine *was medically* driven!

Once safe and breathing again, my doctor transferred me to intensive care for further monitoring. It appeared that the post-op pain medicine combined with the anesthesia medicine still in my system following the surgery; I had received too much anesthesia, causing me to go into respiratory arrest. Had Peter not been there, I would have died.

He got several *"atta-boys"* that day. One nurse who had taken care of me for years, Patrick, used to be a corpsman in the Marines, and he bragged extensively on Peter and how he kept his cool throughout the situation. It's not the only time he's saved my life …but it's probably the most dramatic.

His sense of humor still finely honed, Peter told everyone to save their adulation until they received his bill.

Other than nearly dying, everything else progressed along, but I left St. Thomas concerned about the trip to Walter Reed. Lying in bed at home, I wrestled with the trip, and felt weak and unable to participate in such an event. At that point, however, a wave of scriptures flooded through my mind recalling verse after verse of how our weakness is the opportunity for God's strength. Peter and I discussed this at length, and we both agreed that seemingly every time God provided key opportunities for us …they usually fell on the heels of an intense struggle that left both of us feeling supremely unqualified.

I suppose that's the whole point; it's His qualifications and abilities …not ours.

After resting for about three weeks, Peter and I flew to Washington for our first trip to one of the most famous hospitals in America. Walking into the historic "Red Cross Building" on post at Walter Reed, I suddenly felt as if stepping into our country's history. Beautifully paneled, the old building continues to voicelessly count the wounded warriors passing through one of our nation's most treasured military posts. Only the hardest and most callous hearts remained unaffected when visiting the campus of Walter Reed. Every building, every street, and every garden speaks the names of men and women in uniform who walked, or were carried, through the gates.

"There are so many amputees out there," was my first thought as I looked out across the audience of soldiers that night. Appreciating God's perfect plan once again, I quickly realized that the soldiers I came to visit didn't need me to be well and feeling strong; they needed to hear from someone who spent long hours in a hospital …while depending upon God for each one of those hours.

Looking at the assembled crowd, I couldn't help but be surprised at the dinner. Outback Steakhouse catered the affair, and served the meal buffet style. (If you ever have the opportunity to eat a buffet catered by Outback …I heartily recommend it!) Seated at my table, I looked around at many young men and women missing limbs, other's pushing IV poles, and still others in wheelchairs. Puzzled, I asked Peter why the army would allow a buffet for wounded soldiers, many of whom could not even walk; I have a problem with buffets myself!

As the question left my lips, I immediately learned the answer: officers, celebrities, and more importantly, the senators from the Republican Senate Caucus assembled there, all worked together to serve these young men and women.

At our table, we dined with Senator and Mrs. Chuck Grassley from Iowa and then Senator Norm Coleman from Minnesota. At my left sat a handsome man who looked familiar, but I couldn't place him. Peter stepped in and saved me from embarrassment when he introduced me to former NFL quarterback and now sports announcer, Boomer Esiason. I watched Boomer and Senator Coleman repeatedly hop up to help each new young person being wheeled into the auditorium; Boomer even offered to get *me* a plate.

Looking around the room, I recognized more and more celebrities, athletes, and political figures carrying a plate and drink to a waiting soldier. With egos checked at the door, each of these individuals displayed such humility and genuine gratitude to the young men and women bearing brutal scars from the war on terror. Watching senators serve wounded warriors stands out as one of the most meaningful memories of my life. With no media present, I'm sorry our country lacked the ability to witness such an event.

As the evening progressed, Senator Santorum presided as master of ceremonies, and he introduced speaker after speaker. Tommy Lasorda brought the house down with his humor and great stories from coaching. Even as all these speakers shared from the podium, however, I noticed the crowd continued to talk and eat, and generally remain boisterous.

At the close of the evening, Senator Santorum asked for everyone's attention and introduced us. The room grew quiet for the first time that evening, and my nerves once again felt rattled. Former Hewlett Packard CEO Carly Fiorina once stated in her book how nervous she continues to get speaking before a crowd. I sang for Carly at an event once, and Peter and I both had lunch at her table ...she hardly looked nervous. But, as much of a pro as she is, she said the butterflies still come.

At that moment, in front of a room full of powerful leaders, I felt more than butterflies. I couldn't believe they selected me to be the closer for the event, and briefly noticing the faces in this crowd, I grew even more nervous as I made my way to the stage. Leaning on Peter and taking Senator Santorum's hand, I climbed the four or five stairs leading to the platform. Even that act drew the undivided attention of the audience, particularly the wounded warriors gathered up front.

Walking on stage in a skirt, my uncovered prosthetic legs clearly visible to the assembled crowd, I couldn't help but notice how many amputees were assembled in front of me. Young men and women, not much older than Parker at the time, with scars, casts, and maimed limbs looking all too familiar, sat in wheelchairs in front of the stage; each of them staring intently at my legs, watching my every move.

Over the years, I've discovered that if Peter will open up our appearances and kind of "break the ice" it helps settle me down. I never know how to "start," and usually verbally trip and fall right out of the gate. Hearing him smoothly convey an introduction to our part in the event, I quickly whipped my head towards him when hearing his voice break. In all our years speaking and performing, I don't ever remember Peter choking up on stage, but I certainly understood why.

The sight of so many soldiers wounded in service of our country creates an almost reverent atmosphere. Until recently, these soldiers, some barely out of high school, enjoyed life at an absolute peak physical condition. Trained by the greatest military in the history of the world, words such as honor, duty, determination, stamina, and achievement served as hallmarks of their everyday lives.

Could they transition those same traits into this dreadful new set of circumstances?

The celebrities spoke from their heart, and gave encouragement to the audience; particularly Coach Lasorda. Although desiring to also offer encouragement, my role clearly involved something else: practical hope. I served as the lone speaker that night who understood the journey ahead for many of them. At the beginning of our country's war on terror, these wounded warriors were the first of their type since Vietnam …and they now saw a little of their future as I walked across the stage in state-of-the-art prosthetic limbs.

Just by watching me stride onto the platform, those who were missing limbs observed the possibilities. With each step of my prosthetic feet, I felt the eyes of extremely scared young men and women who seemed to hold their breath with every footfall. Seeing me with a husband, the women with maimed bodies causing them to feel less than beautiful realized a boyfriend waited somewhere for them. Hearing about our sons, they also realized a family still remained in their future. Lost limbs do not automatically mean lost hope.

> Lost limbs do not automatically mean lost hope.

As Peter took his place at the piano, I paused for a moment to look at the crowd. Ignoring the famous individuals gathered there, I instead turned my gaze to the anxious but eager faces clustered near the stage. Many of them struggled to understand the purpose of the wounds suffered halfway around the world. For two decades, I wrestled with purpose in injuries; knowing that if some meaning or good comes from wounds …the healing often becomes a little easier. Wounded at about the same age as these "kids," I knew the questions lurking in their hearts. Looking at me, they saw possibilities; now, I needed to help direct their eyes to *purpose*.

"Three weeks ago I had my sixty-sixth operation in twenty years. In my room after the surgery, I unexpectedly went into respiratory arrest and the code team had to be called to help me start breathing again. It was Peter who saved my life. He was sitting right beside me when I stopped breathing, and quickly got the right people to come resuscitate me. He wasn't off somewhere watching TV or working a deal on his cell phone, he was right beside me; right where God wanted him. I'm alive today because he was where he was supposed to be.

"Americans are alive today because you were where you were supposed to be. You helped keep this war away from our streets, schools, offices, and malls. You saved the lives of perfect strangers all across the country because you were where you were called to be."

The room grew even quieter. Peter observed senators locked in their own political battles in dealing with the war on terror, listening intently.

"I fell asleep at the wheel—a stupid mistake. God continues to redeem that event, but there is no honor in my injuries. My mistake cost me my legs; you offered yours. Your injuries have honor because you won them fighting for the precious God-given gift of freedom."

Signaling Peter to play the introduction, I sang his song "We Will Stand." Peter wrote this song for me as an expression of his desire to care for me. Writing these lyrics, he expressed his heart to me, and now I shared them with the precious soldiers gathered at Walter Reed Army Medical Center.

Finishing the song, I looked down at the young men and women gathered in wheelchairs as they applauded. I believe they liked the song, but their applause reached past my performance as a singer ...and validated the courage to face life with a maimed body. In me, they caught a hint of themselves a few years down the road; hope still remained for a meaningful life ...even with amputations. They clapped and cheered for every individual who refuses to be defined by wounds, disfigurement, and disability.

Afterwards we all clustered together; wounded individuals sharing a moment as members of an exclusive club. Fascinated by my state-of-the-art components, they peppered me with questions, wanted to touch the legs, and discussed so many more things involved with limb loss.

"Can we get feet like yours?"

"Do you get in the water with those?"

"Do they have a lot of cushion when you step?"

We stayed for an hour longer, until everyone had to leave. Senator Orrin Hatch of Utah and Senator Richard Shelby of Alabama tried to greet me afterwards, but couldn't reach past the soldiers. Both of them turned to Peter and smiled, graciously asking him to give me their regards.

"We're not important; she's right where she needs to be," Senator Hatch humbly told Peter.

We Will Stand

Every day I see the struggles that you face
As you fight to run a race that has no end.
In your heart I know you sail above the clouds
But the hurt just pulls you down again.

Don't let go of the hope you're holding on.
You need to see a friend will be right here all along.

I will stand with you when you cannot stand alone,
I will fight for you when all your strength is gone,
I will sing for you so all can hear your song –
Take my hand, lean on me, we will stand

In this world, filled with such uncertainty
Hearts are broken easily, and left behind
But in God's hand, we're connected by His love
And the grace that through His Son …changes lives.

Peter and Gracie Rosenberger
We Will Stand © 2001 PeterandGracie Music
Used by permission

Chapter 28

Coincidentally Designed

*For the Christian, there are, strictly speaking, no chances.
A secret Master of the Ceremonies has been at work.*

—C.S. Lewis

The Four Loves

*I have lived a long time, sir, and the longer I live
the more convincing proofs I see of this truth—
that God governs in the affairs of men.*

—Benjamin Franklin

*As Christians, we relinquish the frivolous luxury
of believing in the absurd thing called chance.*

—Peter W. Rosenberger

*I*n the mid-1990's, a young girl in Accra, Ghana,
lay in a hospital, recently hit by a car while cross-
ing the street. The doctors in Ghana removed her left

leg above the knee. Little Patience Frimpong, scared and heartbroken, now faced a life of disability in a country of few resources, and even less regard for the disabled.

Patience's mother, Comfort, dreamed of a different path for her daughter. Delivering her into this world as an un-wed mother, Comfort knew the burden fell upon her shoulders as to whether or not Patience could live a life of meaning and achievement ... instead of simply adding to the sad poverty she witnessed across her West African country.

In the early 1990's two women from Franklin, Tennessee, a small town just south of Nashville, Pam Hawkins and Debbie French formed an organization entitled Today's Choices in an effort to prevent unwanted pregnancies in young girls by equipping them to make better choices and reaching at-risk girls with the Gospel of Jesus Christ. Traveling around to local schools and churches, Pam and Debbie worked with a passion; expanding the ministry of Today's Choices.

While on a short-term mission trip to Ghana, West Africa, Debbie and her husband, Steve French, attended a local church where the pastor introduced them to Patience. Hearing the whisper of God, Debbie and Steve returned to their home near Nashville, Tennessee in the small town of Franklin, and launched an effort to bring Patience to the United States for treatment.

Spending their own money, Debbie and Steve not only purchased airfare and helped house Patience and Comfort, but arranged for a local orthopedic surgeon to treat Patience at Nashville's Baptist Hospital; practitioners at the facility also volunteered to provide physical therapy and treatment for Patience during the three months of her visit. The surgeon then referred Patience to a prosthetist just a block away from Baptist Hospital; James S. McElhiney.

Chapter 28   Coincidentally Designed

While in Nashville, Comfort accompanied Debbie and her friend, Pam Hawkins, to a local church where they made a presentation on behalf of the ministry they founded, Today's Choices. Touched by the presentation, and recognizing her own circumstances in the ministry's outreach, Comfort asked for a video of the ministry's outreach to carry with her back to Ghana. Through Patience's difficult circumstances, God wove together women from two different countries to launch an extension of Today's Choices into Ghana, West Africa.

Building a facility near the capital city of Accra, Today's Choices literally rescued young, at-risk girls and provided a safe environment for them to live ...while teaching them a trade; equipping them to be self – sufficient upon leaving the home after completing the program. Girls left the home grounded in their faith in God, able to make a living, and ready to live a life of sexual purity.

During one of her many visits to Nashville, Patience, by then a young woman, spent some time with Today's Choices board member, Edna Salyer, who spoke to Patience of another amputee woman who attended church with Edna. Excitedly telling Patience about this woman she recently met, Edna determined to arrange a meeting. Already seeing pictures of this woman on the wall at Jim McElhiney's prosthetic clinic during a follow-up visit while in Nashville, Patience enthusiastically agreed.

Shopping with Patience for clothing in Nashville, Edna excitedly shared more information about this other woman missing her limbs, and enthusiastically stated, "Patience, you and Gracie Rosenberger need to meet."

Bringing everyone together for a meal, the conversation turned to discussing the plight of amputees in developing countries. After listening for a while, Patience firmly stated, "Gracie, you need to come to Ghana and help provide artificial limbs. I will pray to God. You will come!"

Immediately after my appearance at Walter Reed Army Medical Center, Peter and I returned to Nashville for one night, and then flew to Dallas for a *Joni and Friends Family Retreat*. These camps, launched by Joni Eareckson-Tada, serve as a tremendous outreach to families with special needs members.

Knowing first-hand the stress a disability places on a family, Joni determined to do all she could to give the families a respite; if only for one week. "Short-term missionaries" raise their own support and volunteer to serve these families for a week. Whether helping feed a child with cerebral palsy, or carefully watching over children with autism, virtually every type of disability presents an opportunity for loving care from Christians desiring to share the same grace they themselves receive.

Peter and I were to lead music at a camp in Waxahachie, Texas. This small town, about an hour south of Dallas, had a new church camp/conference center nearby, and seemed perfect for the retreat. Peter and I wanted to attend in part because my grandmother Grace's sister, Lila Wilson, lived one mile from the camp.

I spent many HOT summers in the Dallas area with my grandmother at her home in Plano, Texas. Although dearly loving my grandmother, she worked ALL the time …and I always looked forward to the short trips to Waxahachie to see the rest of my mother's family; escaping the toil of working in Grandmother's garden. Aunt Lila and her husband Clarence Wilson grafted me into their family at an early age and even invited me to join their large family for their annual camping trips to Colorado. Grandmother Grace was the oldest of four girls and one brother, and Lila the youngest of the bunch; so although she's my great-aunt, she's not much older than Mom.

Chapter 28   Coincidentally Designed

Barely having time to sleep in our own bed, we left Nashville and arrived in Dallas excited to see family …and feeling a little uncertain of what a *Joni and Friends* camp would present. Right at the start, we recognized our performance style needed to adapt.

Singing and speaking at Walter Reed for the event hosted by Republican senators just seventy-two hours earlier, we had the full attention of half the United States Senate. What a difference three days can make.

In a small town in the middle of Texas, we found ourselves performing while screaming children with autism ran across the stage. As a singer, I've certainly performed at events where people kept talking, but never shrieking on stage beside me. I admit …it's somewhat unsettling. Other children who suffered from various diseases sat in wheelchairs in the audience with their spastic limbs flailing wildly, as young volunteers patiently watched over them …while weary parents took a break. All in all, I found it to be the most challenging performance event of my life; and I loved every minute of the whole experience.

John Wern, director at the time of *Joni and Friend's* international wheelchair ministry, *Wheels for the World*, came to this particular camp at the last minute to fill in for the director who had injured his shoulder two days before the camp started. Introduced to John, who can compete with Peter when it comes to a sense of humor, I felt as if I'd known him my entire life. Listening to him talk about the places he traveled with *Wheels for the World* further excited me about the vision I had upon seeing the documentary of Princess Diana helping amputees while lying in my hospital bed after relinquishing my remaining leg.

"You know, John," I gushed out while we sat around the table having lunch one day during the camp. "I have this vision for using prosthetic legs in the same manner you all use wheelchairs, and I really want to launch this in Eastern Europe. Those people you serve who don't need a wheelchair, but rather need a leg. We could help them. Then that wheelchair can be freed up to be given instead to someone who truly needs it ...and the person who receives the leg can be integrated back into the workplace, school, or whatever."

Thinking for a moment, John stated firmly, "You need to start this in Ghana."

Peter nearly choked on the bite he had just put into his mouth. "Ghana ...as in Africa?!" Laughing, he flatly told John, "I'm not taking Gracie to Africa ...**I'M** not going to Africa!"

John wasn't laughing. "If you can make this work in Ghana, you can make it work anywhere else in the world," he stated matter-of-factly. "In fact, the missionaries who help facilitate all we do in Ghana are here on furlough ...in the Dallas area."

As John kept talking, all that came to mind when I thought of Africa was heat, bugs, and more heat. Just in Waxahachie, Texas, I already felt sweat pouring over my body; how in the world would I make it in Africa?

Refusing to take "no" for an answer, John arranged for Allan and Patsy Fulton to drive down for breakfast the next morning. A little unsettled, we obediently showed up for breakfast and I shared my vision. Listening with excitement, Patsy and Allan immediately loved the idea, and went so far as to mention an amputee they recently met in Ghana.

"We've only met one amputee ...a girl named Patience, and she really wants to see something like this happen."

Incredulously, I looked at Peter and then back at Allan. "Her name wouldn't happen to be Patience Frimpong would it?"

"Well, yes it is!" He replied with a surprised look on his face. "Do you know her?"

Chapter 28 Coincidentally Designed

Out of a country of twenty million people, and many, many, amputees, the one person I *happened* to know from Ghana, who *happened* to be acquainted with a woman I *happened* to attend church with, who *happened* to be treated by my prosthetist, also knew this couple who *happened* to be on furlough, in a town where we *happened* to travel for a *Joni and Friends' Family Retreat* mainly because my dear aunt *happened* to live close by, and we were introduced by a man who normally doesn't come to these retreats, but *happened* to be filling in ...and connected us to the missionaries.

Feeling flustered, we agreed to pray about this new turn of events. John, _now_ laughing _at us_ while we tried to wrap our mind around the odds of all these things working together, assured us he'd pray about this, as well. I think it's also interesting to note that *Joni and Friends* never used that particular campsite again. The first and last time they held a retreat there was during our visit.

Leaving Waxahachie, Peter, still getting used to not working in the conventional setting he had left just months earlier ... turned to me with a resigned look on his face and said, "I suppose you think this means we're going to Ghana?"

Chapter 29

Standing with Hope

*People who regard themselves as invalids rather
than heroes will make excellent missionaries.*

—Daniel Fuller

Leaving the camp in Texas, we returned to Nashville and Peter and I continued speaking and performing. Wearing my "Terminator Legs," I walked across stages, sat on even more television sets, all while now confidently wearing my uncovered prosthetic limbs. I was invited to sing for an event with President George W. Bush, and the current senior senator from Tennessee, Lamar Alexander, also a former two-time governor, introduced me before I sang.

An avid history buff, Senator Alexander shared the story of my family's lengthy Tennessee heritage with the audience. (Peter always seems to take a twisted delight in telling people, "Don't let the fact that she's got all her teeth fool you ...she's a 'hillbilly!'") Senator Alexander also added a little known fact to the story of the Taylor boys who ran against each other for Governor (known in Tennessee as the *War of the Roses*). According to Senator Alexander, Bob and Alf's father, Nathaniel Taylor (my great, great grandfather), also ran against his sons, but he ran as a Prohibitionist. We've all heard many people complain about their family conflicts, but I would imagine dinner time at the Taylor's would trump them all.

Meeting President Bush was an amazing experience. I understand I am the first member on both sides of my family to meet a sitting U.S. President since my ancestors who served as legislators so long ago. The first thing the President noticed was my legs, and he grabbed my outstretched hand with both of his. I've met many politicians over the years, but none who seem to be as heart-driven as George W. Bush.

My performance for the President led to an invitation to open one of the evenings of the 2004 Republican National Convention in New York. Joni Tada opened the first day event with prayer, and I opened the second night with the National Anthem. Surprisingly, I learned I was the first woman with a disability to sing at a major party's convention.

Given my robotic looking limbs, it is somewhat ironic that I performed the night the real "Terminator" spoke. Governor Schwarzenegger gave the keynote address that evening, but I didn't get to meet him. They did give me his green room, the one for dignitaries, under the stage …simply to make it easier for me, since the dressing rooms for performers were further from the stage. I don't move very fast, so the RNC wasn't taking chances of missing timetables.

Grateful that "Ahhhnold" likes it cold, the thermostat in his room was set to fifty-five degrees, which suited me just fine. His room was loaded with food, and Peter helped himself. Unknown to a lot of people, we were probably the poorest people at the convention. Leaving the security of regular paychecks more than a year prior, we simply did not have a lot of money, and although the RNC put us up at the Waldorf Astoria and gave a stipend, it didn't last long in New York. Years of raising a lot of boys equipped Peter's mother on how to appropriately "stretch a meal" and she sent us to New York with a large container of homemade trail mix. Learning of this, Peter turned up his nose at it saying, "I'm not taking trail mix to New York!" After looking at some of the prices, he was the first one to dive into the enormously appreciated trail mix!

So while crowds of people began arriving at Madison Square Garden, Peter and I enjoyed a little pre-show peace and quiet in Arnold Schwarzenegger's private green room …right next to the one set up for President Bush. (We did peek into the President's room; I have to admit, it was impressive.) Peter happily grabbed sandwiches and snacks, while I felt like throwing up …again.

My robot legs attracted quite a bit of attention. I wore shorts for my rehearsal at Madison Square Garden, and it was carried live on Fox News. After my performance at the convention, Peter and I were whisked away to sit in the "President's Box" behind former President and Mrs. George H.W. Bush. Due to the position of the seats, my legs were nearly at eye level for Barbara Bush who repeatedly turned around to admire and pat the shock-absorbers and carbon-fiber material of my "shins."

A couple of years later, I sang for an event with former President George H.W. Bush, and laughingly reminded him of Barbara patting my legs. When I dove off my sister's dock, I never dreamed I'd be discussing my metal legs with world leaders …I just wanted to go swimming.

The morning after my performance, Peter and I decided to see some of Manhattan. By that time, the President had arrived and was also staying at the Waldorf Astoria, so an army of Secret Service personnel lined the walkway outside the hotel. (Peter remarked that "we're either staying in the most secure hotel in the world …or the biggest target!") Wearing shorts again, I walked past about a dozen or so agents with

Peter trailing a few steps behind me. Noticing the eyes of every Secret Service agent immediately focusing on my strange-looking legs, Peter caught them all flat-footed.

"So, you guys are checking out my wife's legs, huh?" His wide grin clearly communicated how much he enjoyed embarrassing them. Many of the agents turned beet-red, and then had to sheepishly smile themselves.

As we toured around Manhattan, we took a cab to grab a bite to eat; the driver was from Ghana. At a convenience store, the clerk's accent gave it away. Ghanaians seemed to be everywhere! Before meeting Patience, neither of us knew or had met anyone from Ghana. After our time in Texas with John Wern, I seemed to constantly encounter people from the tiny West African country.

Leaving the cab, we continued walking towards Times Square and encountered people who watched the performance the night before ... all of them were inspired by the arrangement I used. Veteran Nashville record producer, Keith Thomas, produced the track for me. I told him I needed a track for the anthem, but my version had to be different. "Keith, I sing for soldiers who had their legs blown off ...and I need to remind them of why they did it." Keith produced an unbelievable track that often chokes me up while I sing it. The directors of the convention liked it so much they played it throughout Madison Square Garden during breaks in the convention.

Preparing to leave New York, Peter received a call from the head of President Bush's advance team inviting us to stay another night and be on the platform behind the President as he accepted the nomination. Stunned, we accepted.

While waiting on the President's advance team to confirm, the RNC contact called and said he knew nothing of the arrangement, and that we should just go on to the airport and return to Nashville. Peter, mentally calculating the bill of changing flight schedules and the cost of staying a couple of extra nights at one of New York's most expensive hotels (and looking at the nearly empty container of trail mix), became quite stressed. Pacing in our lovely, but pricey room, I finally told him to sit down, read his Bible, and ask God for direction. Tensed like a stallion ready to run a race, Peter plopped in a chair, and pulled out his Bible. During this time, Peter also talked with his father who repeated the same advice I offered, and we both successfully convinced him to sit quietly in the chair. It took nearly every bit of willpower for him to be still, but he did …and I went back to sleep for a little longer.

Recalling the thought I had while watching the hurricane bearing down on the Florida panhandle years earlier, I suppose I understood Jesus falling asleep in the boat better than I once did!

An hour later, the phone rang, and the President's team assured us the details were settled …and the RNC picked up the tab. That day marked another shift in Peter's normally kinetic personality, and he adopted a new saying for moments when he's confronted with situations where he has absolutely no control: "Don't *just do* something …*stand* there!"

The next evening, while sitting on the platform looking out at the capacity crowd in Madison Square Garden, well, I have to admit …it was surreal. When the President appeared, the place went wild; the air itself seemed electrified. Trying to be comfortable, I wore sneakers and left my dress shoes downstairs. Guess who made *Time* magazine, *Newsweek*, and a host of other media in her tennis shoes? After his speech, the balloons fell, Laura Bush and the Cheneys joined the President on stage… and Peter and I were right there shaking their hands. Country star Lee Ann Womack closed the event with her hit song, "I Hope You Dance." As she sang, Peter and I, still wearing sneakers, danced on the platform.

I must say, it was an event to remember!

A month later, I traveled to Fort Campbell, Kentucky and sang the anthem again for about ten thousand troops at an event with then Secretary of Defense Donald Rumsfeld, and shortly after that returned to Walter Reed to perform for the groundbreaking ceremony of the Military Advanced Training Center. This state-of-the-art facility would provide everything needed to help soldiers with devastating wounds. Arriving in our hotel a few miles from the army hospital in Silver Spring, Maryland, Peter and I decided to walk down the street and have dinner at a *Red Lobster* restaurant. Noticing the thick accent of our waitress, Peter asked, "Where are you from?"

"I am from Ghana," she said with a smile, "But you probably have never heard of it."

Little did she know. After months of continually meeting people from Ghana, Peter threw up his hands and agreed to go to the West African country.

We officially launched the prosthetic limb outreach of *Standing With Hope* in Accra, Ghana in 2005. The dream I had while lying in a hospital bed following my second amputation took a decade to become reality. Joining us in Ghana was none other than Jim McElhiney, who serves as our senior prosthetic advisor. Working alongside one of Joni Eareckson-Tada's *Wheels for the World* teams, we put legs on amputees in one building, and across the compound, Joni's team provided wheelchairs ...just like I envisioned when talking with John Wern at the Family Retreat less than two years earlier. John also participated in the trip, along with Allan and Patsy Fulton; a long way from breakfast in Waxahachie, Texas. *Wheels for the World* provided tee-shirts for all the team members with "Wheels for the World" prominently written across the shirt, but on mine, Jim's and Peter's, I took a "Sharpie" and added *"and Limbs"* beside the logo. In my heart I knew this trip was the first step of an important journey, and although it was hand-scrawled, I felt it important that our shirts proclaim, "Wheels *and* LIMBS for the World!" I don't think Joni minded.

Taking a field trip from the clinic, Jim, Peter, and I went to meet with Patience and her mother at Comfort's home. Stepping back graciously, Peter allowed a few minutes for Patience, Jim, and me, all three of us amputees, to huddle together and experience a deep moment of poignancy while reflecting on our remarkable journey together. Through *Today's Choices* and *Standing With Hope*, this young woman, missing a leg, served as a catalyst for two ministries to launch in Ghana.

Our first patient, Jonathan Anukwa, arrived at the clinic wearing a leg, but walking horribly. Looking at the clinic director, Daniel Kodi, I felt puzzled and asked him why we were providing a limb to a man who already owned one. Taking off his artificial limb resembling a Korean War relic, we quickly learned why: Jonathan walked so poorly because the socket of the leg he wore, one he'd found somewhere, was four or five sizes too big; it engulfed his stump. To compensate, Jonathan wrapped yards of cloth around his amputated limb to wedge it into the socket. All the material stuffed into the socket made it impossible for him to bend his knee. Walking on a stiff leg, Jonathan hobbled around, but could not access the public transportation buses in order to get to work.

Calling them "Tro-Tro's," the buses in Ghana, unlike spacious vehicles in America, literally teem with people. With two different sizes, the buses built to comfortably hold eight people for the smaller, and twenty for the larger, cram so many people into every square inch of the rickety, smoke-spewing vehicles that it seems hard to breathe in them, much less comfortably stretch out a prosthetic limb. The only way for Jonathan to ride the "tro-tro" involved first removing his leg, and then hopping on to the van …where he crawled over masses of people to hopefully find a seat; all while carrying a leg that should be carrying him.

Watching Jonathan continue to unravel layer upon layer of cloth bandages and rags binding his limb, Jim turned to Peter and me and drawled, "Good Lo-word, Ah'ma change this boy's life!"

Whispering to Peter, I said, "Jim doesn't understand that HIS life is about to be changed as well."

"Change his life" perfectly describes what happened to Jonathan. He not only walked, he ran; literally "…went walking and leaping and praising God!" On a separate trip the following year, the U.S. Ambassador to Ghana visited our clinic, and Jonathan happened to drop by. Directing Jonathan to walk back and forth, Peter asked the ambassador to identify the prosthetic limb. Watching Jonathan carefully, the ambassador … guessed the wrong leg!

Jim's training model and style of fabrication continues changing hundreds of lives. The line of patients we treat contain children who lost limbs to snake bites or who were hit by cars, like Patience was so long ago, middle-aged parents suffering from diabetes …even leprosy; we've seen it all. One man's condition nearly caused me to pass out when, while showing him how to wash and care for his amputated limb, I saw maggots crawling in his stump. I once caught an interview of Franklin Graham who commented about the ministry he founded, *Samaritan's Purse,* "You can't run an organization like this from behind a desk …you have to get out there and smell it."

His comment continues to resonate with me, and referring to what the Bible calls our earthly sin nature, I call our trips, "flesh killers" because invariably we encounter events or individuals causing us to see things in ourselves that need to die …things that make us want to run back to the safety and comfort of our carefully manicured lives. Recalling my experience before my first trip to Walter Reed, I feel supremely unqualified, and am increasingly convinced of that fact every day. It's in those moments, however, when Christ's power does rest upon me; His strength is my source.

We don't simply provide a limb, but we also supply each patient with a "suspension-sleeve" and liner. I wear these items myself, and it allows the limb to stay on without belts and cumbersome attachments. The liners simply fit over the end of the limb, and the sleeve (open on both ends) rolls over the prosthesis, over the liner, and snugly on the thigh (for a below knee amputation).

The same leg and suspension sleeve system we provide to patients in Ghana costs approximately $7,000 in the United States. *Standing With Hope*'s cost is just under $700, and we're implementing steps to reduce it much further. My policy, however, is to _only_ provide a limb that I'm willing to wear myself. Representing Christ, I feel we should offer the best possible product we can. We take donated limbs, disassemble them, and recycle every available part for a patient. Although a good prosthetic foot (and knee unit for above-knee amputees) is important, our focus remains on the socket. If the socket fits poorly to the patient, then the patient won't wear the leg … even with a $15,000 foot (and some are that expensive). I've seen prosthetic limbs in the United States that I _know_ cost insurance companies tens of thousands of dollars, but, due to poor socket fit and alignment, the patient can barely walk.

Although infrequently, we continue to receive criticism about the costs of our limbs from people familiar with other organizations providing "relief-limbs." Not from another amputee or prosthetist (those who clearly understand these devices), but from well meaning individuals who simply do not understand all that is involved with artificial limbs. Peter always replies to critics, "A toilet plunger can be turned upside-down and wrapped to an amputee with duct tape …but that doesn't mean it's a good prosthetic leg!" That comment, plus the fact that I, to our knowledge, continue to be the only double-amputee woman in the world who is doing this type of work ... usually ends the criticism.

Each socket we provide, including the ones made by the technicians we train, is custom-made on site for the patient. In the case of children, as each child grows, the training we provide equips the local technicians to make adjustments to the limb, remake the socket, or often simply change the foot to reflect the growth of the patient. Recognizing the lifetime needs of amputees, our model is to partner with the host country's government to build and maintain an infrastructure able to fabricate and maintain these devices. If our team isn't there, patients can still access services from local workers trained by *Standing With Hope* prosthetists.

The long-range goal is to equip Ghana to serve as a West African hub for prosthetic development and training. Recently achieving two strategic goals within the same week, we sent our first solo team without me or Peter ...and another country (Togo) sent workers to Ghana in order to train under our program. We've also helped provide limbs to amputees in Trinidad, Nigeria, and even China.

All of this provides a unique and profound way of sharing the Gospel of Jesus Christ. Each patient not only receives a limb, but also a "Life and Limb" bag containing supplies for maintaining the prosthesis. In addition to those supplies, a laminated sheet (for durability) with instructions on one side, and the plan of salvation on the other is included. Every patient receives a Bible, and hears the message of the Gospel. Using the limb as a metaphor, we explain the cost of the leg they just received, and allow them to realize their inability to afford such a thing ...not to shame them or scare them, but to drive the point home of the value of their new limb. In the same manner, we then share the debt we owe to God's justice due to our sin ...surpasses *all of our* abilities to pay, but God in His grace and mercy, sent Jesus to pay it on our behalf.

Another patient of ours, Halima, was carried in by her son. Losing her leg to diabetes, Halima looked so thin and weak. With her son interpreting, Peter shared the Gospel to Halima; telling her about how Christ changed his life …and now he was there to offer a limb to her. Her son quickly told Peter that Halima was a Muslim, and that his mother wanted Peter to know that particularly important fact; Halima clearly communicated through her son that her devotion was to Allah.

While watching Peter, it almost seemed as if time slowed down. Without even speaking to each other, we both realized an "a-ha" experience for Peter where seemingly everything he'd ever learned or had put in him by God from day one of his life converged into one powerful moment. Recalling the first time at the student center at Belmont, I saw the Peter Rosenberger I fell in love with. The moment seemed poignant, even holy …and I knew that I was supposed to be quiet and just observe.

Up until that point, I'd never heard Peter share his faith with someone one-on-one, and it was awe-inspiring to watch how God wove everything together …and even used Peter's wonderful personality. Cocking his eyebrow, Peter gave Halima his all too familiar crooked mischievous smile and pointedly told her son, "I understand your mother is a Muslim, and I'm not here to criticize. But you need to know that this limb is from Jesus Christ …not Allah. I don't know Allah, but I do know Jesus …and He sent me here to give you this limb."

Recognizing not only Peter's sincerity, but also the fact that no Muslim missionary ever provided a limb to her, Halima gave her full attention to Peter as he continued talking while her son interpreted. Peter then asked her to remember how much God loves her …with each step she now took on her new limb. Distinguishing the God of the Bible from Allah, Peter gently broke down multiple barriers with seeming ease. Following Peter's instructions to the letter of the law, Halima walked around the clinic and stated in broken English during every step, "God loves Halima!"

A devout Muslim, Halima experienced Christianity from a new perspective. With each visit of our team to Ghana, Halima returns ...and looks fabulous. One visit she danced with Kraig Helberg, a prosthetist from Pennsylvania. Kraig is 6'7" and Halima is tiny; it was hilarious to watch them cavorting around the clinic!!

Halima proudly shared with the clinic staff that "Jesus gave her a new leg so that she could go to Mecca!" Smacking his hand against his forehead in an exaggerated sign, Peter laughed while saying, "Houston, we have a problem!" We shared the Gospel, Halima heard the Gospel. What God does with it is up to God. But if there's ever a news report of a woman with an artificial leg telling Muslims at Mecca about Jesus ... well, that's Halima.

Pulling the sheets back and looking at my own amputated limbs in that hospital room so long ago, I believed the vision God gave would come to pass. When I see the changed lives of the patients we treat, I feel such gratitude to play a part in their journey. Women, and particularly disabled women, are not valued highly in most developing countries. As I travel around the streets of Accra, and visit villages in the countryside, you should see the stares I receive. Sure my legs are "odd-looking," but that's not the only reason people stop to look. I'm not a beggar, nor do I look downcast at my condition. In fact, I boast about it in order for Christ's power to rest upon me, as the Apostle Paul stated.

Even in the United States, cultural, religious, and racial barriers are quickly broken down when people see me walking around. Once while shopping in an upscale mall near our home, a man from the top floor noticed me walking while wearing shorts ...and crisscrossing the main lobby area. Evidently inspired, he yelled out to me (in front of a lot of people!), "You go girl!" Turning red, I smiled and waved my "little girl wave" to him, just like I did as Miss Fort Walton Beach High School!

With that type of reaction in the United States, where high–tech prosthetic limbs seem pretty common, imagine the response in a developing country! As in the case with my trip to Walter Reed, it's not what I say that matters; when I walk through the door of a clinic full of amputees, I can immediately feel the eyes of everyone in the room intently watching each footstep. By simply striding into the room, I offer a glimmer of hope; not because of me personally, but rather because of what I represent: the possibilities for each and every one of them; *they too, will walk.* Women sitting forlornly in the clinic will carry their babies on two legs …or even dance with their husband. Children will run and play, without falling; no longer feeling left out of life. Fathers will return to work and provide for their families.

As I walk around the clinic greeting patients, I encourage them to touch my legs, ask questions, and stare all they wish, because, as Jim McElhiney did so long ago when I first hobbled into his clinic, I now know something each heartbroken and scared face doesn't …yet. In a matter of mere hours, these desperate lives, experiencing such difficult challenges, will find themselves, like me …Standing With Hope!

Chapter 30
Somebody Call a Priest

God uses men who are weak and feeble enough to lean on Him.

—Hudson Taylor

he most remarkable transformation of this whole venture would have to be the change in Peter. Never wanting to lead a non-profit, and certainly never wanting to take me to Africa, I find it inspiring to observe how his life has changed through this mission.

From the moment he chose to walk in God's love and grace, his life altered radically and profoundly. He loves getting on the plane and heading over to Ghana, and he e-mails or calls the technicians on SKYPE (the internet global phone network) nearly every week. Leaving his job years ago and literally stepping out in faith, Peter mentioned recently how *Standing With Hope* is the only job he's ever held that required every skill, talent, brain cell, and every other asset he possesses ...every day. Never before has he enjoyed going to work so much. At the end of the day, he knows that we made a difference; someone is walking, able to go to school, taking care of a family, and living an active life. More importantly, he knows that someone else is learning of the life-changing grace of Jesus Christ.

Working with prosthetic limbs creates many opportunities for one-on-one encounters with patients. During these encounters, we educate the patient on caring for their new limbs, share the Gospel, build friendships, and, more often than not, find ourselves witnessing poignant examples of the redemptive work of Christ in our own lives. One particular event with Peter stands out.

Examining a young man who arrived at the clinic with a seemingly well-fitted prosthesis, Peter discovered that he had not only failed to wash the liner daily per instruction, but from the smell of it, he had neglected to wash his leg in an exceptionally long time. Sitting directly over him as he pulled the liner and sleeve off his amputated limb, Peter flinched and blinked his eyes at the overpowering odor. My father's dear friend for more than fifty years, Bill Hillard (with me the night of the accident so long ago), joined our team for that trip, and out of the corner of his watering eyes, Peter spotted Bill backing up ...and Bill stood ten feet from the man.

Up until this point, Peter conversationally shared the Gospel with this young man, who happened to be Muslim. When he peeled off his liner, however, Peter could hardly speak; it reeked that badly! At first, Peter felt the stench generated from an open wound, but after checking the limb thoroughly, Peter observed no cuts or sores, and concluded the smell simply stemmed from body odor.

Recalling a *Seinfeld* episode, when someone with terrible body odor drove Jerry's car and nothing could get rid of the smell, Peter wanted to laugh at the memory of the show ...but fighting the gag reflex took all his concentration. In the TV show, Jerry Seinfeld quipped the smell was so bad, he needed "...to call a *priest*!" At that moment, Peter agreed with

Jerry's diagnosis, and, between gasps for air, hoped a priest would happen by the clinic.

Attempting to explain to this young man the importance of daily washing the limb, liner, and sleeve, Peter quickly realized he wasn't getting through. Abandoning efforts to communicate with the man, Peter, pausing for a moment, took a different approach.

Asking someone to bring him a basin of water and a clean towel ... Peter grabbed one of the bars of antibacterial soap we give each patient, and washed this man's limb himself. Late in the afternoon, with nearly all the patients gone for the day, Peter bent over this young man and gently scrubbed his amputated limb.

The setting sun streamed through the doorway of the little clinic ... almost spotlighting the event. Throughout the center, the loud noises of a prosthetic limb workshop filled the air: team members busily chiseling hardened plaster from the recently fabricated molds of other patients, and belt sanders grinding down sockets for a smooth finish. The sounds and distractions of the clinic seemed to fade away for Peter, however, as he continued bathing the stump of this young Muslim. Leaning over him, with the putrid smell of his unwashed leg filling Peter's nose, his thoughts filled with the reality of how much more foul-smelling he himself seemed to God ...before Jesus humbled Himself and washed him.

Before going to Ghana on this particular trip, Peter, knowing we treat many Muslims, studied the Muslim faith wanting to effectively share the Gospel with them. Since 9/11, Peter's struggled with Muslims, and felt conflicted about them ...a fact he freely admits. Knowing our mission, however, he determined to try and push past those feelings and somehow connect to each Muslim patient we treated.

While washing this man's leg, Peter realized he didn't have to study his faith in order to share the Gospel. In fact, it wasn't even necessary for Peter to speak. Peter knew he only needed to remember his own need for washing. All of Peter's negative thoughts toward Muslims seemed to grow fainter, as he continued performing a task he never dreamed of doing since the terrorists' attack on September 11, 2001.

The tears filling Peter's eyes no longer resulted from the foul odor of the man's limb, but rather Peter could only think of how his own sinful life brought tears to Jesus' eyes. Wryly recalling his sarcastic desire "for a priest," Peter humbly realized the presence of THE priest who intercedes for us and cleanses us. Remembering the embrace and cleansing Jesus provided to him without wearing gloves, Peter focused on his own daily need of washing.

What can wash away my sin?

Nothing but the blood of Jesus;

What can make me whole again?

Nothing but the blood of Jesus.

Oh! precious is the flow

That makes me white as snow;

No other fount I know,

Nothing but the blood of Jesus

—Robert Lowry

Does the smell of others' sin cause us to flinch, but our own does not? Looking at people through the prism of self-righteousness, do we fail to see ourselves in the light of God's holiness? On his knees ...serving someone he believed an enemy of his faith, and possibly his country,

Chapter 30 Somebody Call a Priest

Peter received a blessing we should all experience: a greater awareness of God's love and grace.

Can you love God and not love those He has asked you to love? Can He not supply you with the love you need to obey Him? God's love in you endures all things, bears all things, hopes all good things for others. His love can conquer all obstacles as it flows out from within your spirit.—FENELON, *THE SEEKING HEART*

Chapter 31

He Raised Me Up

*And I saw heaven opened, and behold a white horse; and he that sat
upon him was called Faithful and True, and in righteousness he
doth judge and make war. His eyes were as a flame of fire, and on
his head were many crowns; and he had a name written, that no
man knew, but he himself. And he was clothed with a vesture dipped
in blood: and his name is called The Word of God. And the armies
which were in heaven followed him upon white horses, clothed in
fine linen, white and clean. And out of his mouth goeth a sharp sword,
that with it he should smite the nations: and he shall rule them with a
rod of iron: and he treadeth the winepress of the fierceness and wrath
of Almighty God. And he hath on his vesture and on his thigh
a name written, KING OF KINGS, AND LORD OF LORDS.*

—Revelation 19:11-16 (KJV)

I watched a movie recently called *We Were Soldiers*. It's based on a true story that took place in
Vietnam, and I've heard Peter and others talk about
this realistic and powerful film. I had avoided watching it be-

cause tragedy and realism are not entertainment for me. If I'm going to watch something, well, I'd rather it be funny, or at least a nature film. When NBC first aired the medical drama show, *ER*, I remember friends telling me how great and lifelike the show felt …and that I should watch it. I looked at them with wide-eyed incredulity and said, "You have *got* to be kidding me …why would *I* want to watch such a show?"

But knowing Peter and I were returning to Walter Reed Army Medical Center in a matter of weeks, I recognized that when I walk into the physical therapy room full of new amputees, these young men and women need to know certain things from me. Since that first visit to Walter Reed, I journeyed back many times for various events such as prayer breakfasts, groundbreaking ceremonies, chapel, and Easter services … and each visit reminds me of the awesome responsibility and privilege of spending time with wounded warriors. I'm not a soldier; at least, not in the conventional sense, and I don't speak the same language the military uses in dealing with adversity, but I have a warrior's heart. After watching *We Were Soldiers*, I gained an understanding of the bluntness and sometime brutal language used by soldiers when facing overwhelming odds and difficulties. THAT part I understand all too well.

I was amazed at Mel Gibson's portrayal of the movie's lead character Lt. Col. Hal Moore. As shells and bullets flew around his battalion causing death and chaos, Col. Moore shouted in the face of incredibly frightened young captains and lieutenants which hill they needed to take, what creek bed they needed to secure, and what landing zone they needed to clear; simple instructions that were literally life and death tasks. There was no time to think or be anxious; just time to obey. They listened …not simply because he was a colonel, but because he spoke with authority, focus, and battle-proven experience. They also knew that he promised to not leave the field of battle until they **all** left.

Chapter 31 He Raised Me Up

The men and women I encounter at Walter Reed have arrived there from similar nightmarish situations. They have lots of doctors and nurses treating them, and celebrities coming by to cheer them up. But that's not my mission. My job (confirmed by the hospital's commanding doctor) is to point them to a new hill, a new creek bed, or a landing zone, so that these highly trained and disciplined young men and women can move forward in their lives and not be picked off by the enemy.

Taking a NEW hill can be a lengthy, bloody business. With amputees, this "hill" is a steep grade of eight to fifteen years; a long process of loss, grieving, denial, and *finally*, acceptance of the passing away of things that will never be again. Usually, this journey starts with taking a few steps at a time, and then building up to one hour, then two, and then a day… you get the picture. Depression and the desire to simply give up the hill are formidable and persistent enemies.

That's why a Col. Hal Moore is so critical; someone who continually points to the "hill" that needs to be taken. That kind of person states and re-states the mission, clearly explaining the dire risks of failing. As an amputee now for nearly twenty years, I own the process well enough to help direct newly wounded hearts and lives to the "emotional real estate" they need to conquer …in order to successfully journey down this road.

My life, accomplishments, and any impact I have on those around me is due to the Col. Hal Moore figures in my life. For many years, more than anyone else in my life, Dr. Leonard Marvin served as the key individual barking out commands in the often bloody battle that is my life. Through many skirmishes, the two of us forged a unique relationship since that morning long ago when I asked him why he didn't smile.

No commanding officer worthy of respect regards the wounds of those in his/her command lightly. Peter and I once spent time with a young soldier and his wife at Walter Reed; he'd lost both legs (one above the knee, one below) and most of his right hand. The soldier's wife mentioned that President George W. Bush visited them the week prior, and they shared that as the President left the room, he broke down and wept. The President's response touched them both deeply; that he clearly took their lifelong wounds seriously ...and personally. Not all wounds have visible scars.

Life is the ultimate battlefield where the rules of war apply in grotesque consistency. Casualties all around cause even the stoutest hearts to waiver in fatigue and despair. Desiring to mend and repair is quickly trumped by reality, but still surgeons like Leonard Marvin, MD, work valiantly to treat those they can reach. Clearly knowing the impossibility of the task, Dr. Marvin, and many like him, press on ...in devotion *to a calling* that permeates their entire being. Although never wavering from the conviction and calling, so many of these individuals, as President Bush did with that young soldier, often take the loss, devastation, and wounds ...personally. That's what separates them from mediocre leaders.

As inspiring as the "Colonels" and other leaders are, there are "sergeants" along the way who also bark out orders. After a particularly grueling surgery that required me to lie nearly flat on my back for two months, I remember freaking out at having to use the bed pan ...again. Through more than two decades, I have resisted and hated that part of my hospital experiences. Crying hysterically, I called out to Peter struggling to sleep on a cot next to me ...and begged him to help change the nurse's mind. Wearily leaving the room, he walked down the hall to appeal to the nurse on my behalf. With eyes brimming in sympathy for me, he petitioned the nurse to allow me a little more dignity ...and at least let me use the bedside commode.

Most nurses I encounter these days are younger than I, soft-spoken, and compassionate. The nurse that evening fit the profile for *Nurse*

Ratched in the movie I'm grateful to say I never watched, *One Flew Over the Cuckoo's Nest*. With a severely starched uniform, and a hat to match, she whipped around at Peter and, with a voice giving testament to years of smoking, barked, "For Heaven's sake …come with me!"

Marching into the room like a drill sergeant …and pointing a claw-like finger towards the cot, she told my husband to "Lay down right there and don't you move!" (Peter later wisecracked, "Her voice sounded so husky it could pull a dog sled!")

The starch in her uniform nearly creaking, she turned to me and said in no uncertain terms what would happen next …and that I didn't get a vote! Both of us hastily responded with a "Yes Ma'am!" After doing what needed to be done, she straightened the room, fluffed my pillow, and pulled the covers over me. Lying as still as possible to avoid the nurse's wrath, what Peter witnessed next genuinely touched his heart. Not wanting to budge an inch, he peered out of the corner of his eyes and witnessed this crusty and "tough as nails" nurse leaning over me. With her thin, bony fingers tenderly holding my hand, we listened to her humbly beseech God to provide comfort, rest, and calmness to her charge. Patting me on the hand and throwing a glance over at Peter, who quickly shut his eyes and pretended to be asleep, she then soundlessly left the room. For the most part, that event ended my decades' long struggle with bedpans. Still trying to avoid them whenever possible, I don't get upset about it as in the early days …mostly. Recalling all the older patients I first encountered while in the hospital, I couldn't help but laugh and admit that maybe getting older ***does*** help you stop caring about such things …particularly when a nurse with a countenance more intimidating than Clint Eastwood is involved.

Following my first amputation, Dr. Marvin gave his report to Peter in that long hallway at St. Thomas Hospital, but had a distant look in his eyes. Later, I learned why. Because I lived and accomplished so many things …he considered me as one of his greatest successes. When my legs were amputated, he considered those surgeries as failures. One day, in a rare moment of candid conversation, he mentioned that to me. Grabbing him by the shoulders, I looked at him in the eyes and convinced him otherwise.

Several years ago, St. Thomas Hospital recognized my surgeon's long standing achievements and inducted him into the Seton Society; Saint Thomas Health Services' honorary hall of fame for individuals who have dedicated themselves to Saint Thomas Hospital and to the community, and have carried on the tradition of service begun by Saint Elizabeth Ann.

Sister Mary Kay Tyrell, then vice-president of St. Thomas, asked me to surprise my surgeon at the event with a performance specifically for him. Although quickly agreeing, things grew a little dicey when my internist admitted me to St. Thomas that week with a pulmonary embolism in each lung. Certain medicines, along with a lengthy stay earlier that year where I lay flat on my back for a while (and endured the hated bedpan moments), worked to make favorable conditions for blood clots, and sure enough …I experienced two pulmonary emboli.

Other than being on Coumadin for the rest of my life and having blood work at a lab on a regular basis, everything gratefully turned out alright *(those clots can kill you!!)*, and St. Thomas safely discharged me the day before the event. Although given permission to perform the next evening, my internist insisted I leave after the performance.

Walking to the microphone, I spoke for a few moments, but no words could effectively describe the unusual relationship forged between a patient and an orthopedic surgeon for more than a quarter century. Pausing for a second or two, I started the song I chose for the evening *a capella,* and then Peter, at the keyboard behind me, joined in on the chorus. Pouring my heart into every note, I performed "You Raised Me Up."

Chapter 31

At the end of the song, the black-tie audience gave a standing ovation, many of them crying. Normally quite reserved, my surgeon left his seat, walked in front of the audience full of his peers, and held me. In front of a thousand people, he not only hugged me, but ...*he smiled.* Knowing the difficult week I had, he then looked over at Peter and said with his "Col. Hal Moore" voice, "Take her home." Peter nearly saluted.

Our ultimate Col. Hal Moore is Christ. In our darkest, most frightening moments, His voice is clear and full of authority; never at a loss for what needs to be done ...even if it's something like dealing with bedpans. The steps we take are often terrifying, but He constantly reminds us of His presence. As we daily "take hills" in our lives, it is Christ's voice directing, challenging, encouraging us ...and He also prays for us right in the middle of our anguish and humiliation.

Therefore He is able also to save to the uttermost (completely, perfectly, finally, and for all time and eternity) those who come to God through Him, since He is always living to make petition to God and intercede with Him and intervene for them. —HEBREWS 7:25, *THE AMPLIFIED BIBLE*

He not only sees our trials and injuries, but He takes each wound we receive personally; so much so that He even went so far as to take those wounds upon His own body.

But he was wounded for our transgressions, he was bruised for our iniquities: the chastisement of our peace was upon him; and with his stripes we are healed.—ISAIAH 53:5, *KJV*

He's with us until we *__all__* leave the field of battle, and at the end of the day, we *__will all__* sing to Him, "You Raised Us Up."

Then, He'll hold us tight ...and smile—for all eternity.

Chapter 32

Bubble Wrap...
Who da Thunk?

*It had long since come to my attention that people of
accomplishment rarely sat back and let things happen to them.
They went out and happened to things.*

—Leonardo da Vinci

"om, can I use one of your old legs in the closet
for a science project?"

Probably not a question heard in most houses,
but certainly not an odd request in our home. Around the dinner table one night, Grayson mentioned a science teacher at
school discussing a national contest for middle school students
to create a new use for Bubble Wrap®. Sealed Air Corporation, along with the National Museum of Education, sponsored
this nationwide challenge in 2006. The National Museum of
Education worked with several large organizations for similar

contests across the country, but this was Sealed Air's first time, and they featured their best known product, Bubble Wrap®.

For some time, Grayson, then 14, listened to us discuss a particular dilemma involving the patients we treated; they wanted cosmetic coverings for the artificial limbs we provided. Although I don't often wear them, I still own a pair of covered legs, and each covering costs nearly $1,100; hardly a figure we could afford for the patients we treat in Africa. The cheapest cosmetic foam covering available costs about $200, and again, it meant that someone getting a cosmetic covering would prohibit someone else from actually getting a leg.

The subject advanced to the top of the list of important tasks when the clinic director in Ghana sent an e-mail to Peter and mentioned a teenager named Daniel who desperately wanted a covering for the leg we provided to him earlier that year. While playing soccer, Daniel broke his leg, but instead of repairing the leg, the doctors in his town simply amputated it below the knee. The harsh reality is that qualified orthopedic surgeons are not readily available in developing countries, so "Civil War" type medicine often serves as the norm. Amputation serves as a quick and less expensive solution to things such as infected insect bites, snake bites, trauma, and disease. For the patients we see, trauma remains the number one cause for children missing limbs.

Jim McElhiney put a limb on Daniel, and the fifteen-year-old boy walked, ran, and could even play soccer when we left. But his "robot-looking" leg made him an easy target for teasing from other children; he felt dreadfully self-conscious about how different he looked. Mr. Kodi, the clinic director asked if we could provide some type of covering for Daniel's limb. E-mailing him back, Peter assured him we would try, but inwardly he felt doubtful about a solution.

When Grayson mentioned the contest, everything seemed to click. What started as a contest for a new use for Bubble Wrap® became a mission to solve a real-life problem. Huddling around one of my old legs, Peter and Grayson wrapped some scraps of the packing material around the leg. You could see the wheels turning in Grayson's eyes, and he felt like he had something.

For nearly all his young life, Grayson, an avid Lego collector, tinkered around with all sorts of things. Taking scrap pieces of wood, he made wild inventions and hilarious toys. Once he built a brake system for a skateboard using bricks strung along on a chain. Sitting on the skateboard, he mounted the bricks behind him and headed downhill on the road in front of his grandparents' home. Picking up speed, he waited until just the right moment, and then …hurled the bricks behind him. Clattering on the chain holding them together, the bricks served as drag to help slow him down. Peter nicknamed it the "Death mobile."

Grayson had previously, but unsuccessfully, entered other contests for companies like Lego, but the Sealed Air Competition went far beyond simply building a cool toy. Part of the contest required the student to have a mentor, so Peter took Grayson down to Jim McElhiney's office, and left the two of them together. Working with Jim, Grayson used a heat gun and packing tape to form the shell of a leg around an endo-skeletal below-knee limb. Jim placed a limb he recently covered on the table in front of Grayson to serve as a model, and Grayson worked on the shape for about an hour. Carefully sculpting the outline of a calf, and shin, Grayson periodically popped a bubble or two to adjust the shape to meet his approval. Once he felt the form resembled Jim's expensive "skin" covering the leg perched on the work table, he pulled a flesh-colored stocking over the limb, and then re-evaluated his work.

With the hose on the limb, he noticed a few bumps, and so taking a needle, he simply popped the bubbles creating arcs in the shape of the limb. Finally finishing his prototype, he stepped back to admire his work, and realized he had created something special. Holding the leg Jim made against the one he just made, he realized that, from a short distance away, the difference seemed negligible. Jim's cost a lot of money. Grayson's used recycled Bubble Wrap®, packing tape, and $15 flesh-colored hose.

Putting together the packet to submit the entry, Grayson and Peter mailed it off to the National Museum of Education, and life returned to normal. Truthfully, we all forgot about the contest. We knew Grayson innovatively discovered a way to provide a low-cost covering for Daniel (and others), so our focus turned to the real-life application of this invention. Looking over the contest rules and guidelines, it appeared Sealed Air Corporation looked for marketable ideas of things that could be sold. Grayson's project met an important need, but didn't seem to fit into the contest parameters, so we all felt Sealed Air would like the idea, but not go anywhere with the "Bubble Wrap® Covering for Endo-Skeletal, Below-the Knee Prosthetic Limbs."

Months later, a woman called, and introduced herself as the executive director of the National Museum of Education. Loving Grayson's project, she notified him of his selection to the semi-finals. Grayson now needed to submit a working prototype of the limb. Using the same leg, Grayson made a new version of the prosthetic limb covering and mailed it to the museum's headquarters in Akron, Ohio. A local paper found out about his status as a semi-finalist, and interviewed Grayson. Although frequently on camera with things that Peter and I do, this was Grayson's first solo interview.

A month later, another call came, and this time, Grayson made the finals. As one of three finalists, he would travel to New York, tour the Sealed Air plant where they make Bubble Wrap®, and attend an awards dinner at the Rainbow Room on top of Rockefeller Center. Word got out about the finalists, and requests for interviews arrived daily; at one point, three local network television affiliates filmed Grayson at Jim's office demonstrating how to create these coverings.

Jim made my right leg and treated me while I was pregnant with Grayson. I find it extremely meaningful to see the friendship between my youngest son and my prosthetist.

Arriving in New York, Sealed Air put us up at the Marriott at *Times Square,* and we enjoyed a wonderful time as a family. On the second evening of the trip, a light snow fell, and so Parker took his younger brother out to enjoy the snowfall in *Times Square* ...making a wonderful memory for our two sons. The snow seemed to hush the frenzy normally so descriptive of *Times Square* and Manhattan.

At the awards dinner, we prepared Grayson for an "honorable mention"; his idea being a good one, but not a "money-maker." The other two finalists entered marketable submissions that could easily fit into a kit and be put on a shelf, whereas Grayson's, although meeting a need, didn't seem to quite meet what the judges at Sealed Air wanted.

The judges disagreed with us; Grayson's submission was exactly what they wanted and represented the company's commitment to innovative solutions for real problems. Winning the grand prize, Grayson accepted a $10,000 savings bond, a wonderful trophy, and launched a continuing journey of public speaking, service, and leadership. In his acceptance speech, he mentioned the young boy, Daniel, and his desire to help him fit in with his friends. Grayson went on to thank me for being the inspiration for the whole thing, and brought tears to the eyes of scientists and top-level executives from Sealed Air Corporation.

Following the awards banquet, we returned to our hotel room and called family and friends to celebrate Grayson's award and accomplishment. The next day (Sunday), we enjoyed sightseeing in Manhattan and had a wonderful time ...but had no idea how Grayson's and our family's life would change in a matter of hours. The following morning, his fifteenth birthday, the media blitz started when the awards were publically announced, and Grayson started off with a mention in *USA Today*. Within hours, our phone was ringing off the hook. Grayson spent his birthday conducting interview after interview …including a reporter from the *Associated Press* who called us while in transit to finish taping a segment for the *Today Show* (they filmed our whole family for the feature …and even taped me ice-skating, with Peter's and Parker's help at Rockefeller Center!). Just before blowing out the candles on his birthday cake in our hotel room, Grayson finished up the day doing a radio interview with the BBC from London. Over the next few weeks and months, he found himself in *People Magazine*, in virtually every prosthetic limb trade organization's magazine, countless blogs and online magazines, textbooks, and conducted dozens of local, national, and international radio interviews.

Later that year, Grayson traveled to Ghana with Peter and a *Standing with Hope* team for a real life implementation of his now award-winning invention. Sealed Air Corporation sent over rolls and rolls of Bubble Wrap® for Grayson to use, and, eagerly getting off the plane in Accra, Grayson knew the name of his first patient: Daniel. Arriving at the clinic, he excitedly asked the clinic director, Mr. Kodi, about meeting Daniel. With a sad look in his eye, Mr. Kodi pointed to a prosthetic leg leaning against a shelf in the lab. "Grayson, I am so sorry to say that Daniel died last month as a result of Malaria."

Crestfallen, Grayson turned away with hot tears in his eyes. This young boy, about Grayson's own age, had a new leg and could walk … only to be struck down by a disease all too common in West Africa. All the media, fame, and excitement seemed to fade away from Grayson as he stood in a dusty clinic in Ghana, facing the brutality of life in a shocking way. A disease virtually unknown to him, certainly something never dealt with in his nice, clean school ... killed a boy his own age who just wanted to play soccer with his friends and not be teased for the way he looked; a harsh reality for our fifteen-year-old.

Setting his jaw, he looked at his father and Mr. Kodi, and stated that he would like to be the one to disassemble Daniel's leg in order to re-use the parts for someone else. Nodding with great pride and love for our son, Peter agreed and handed Grayson the limb. Retreating to a work table in the corner of the lab, Grayson carefully dismantled the leg that his mentor, and my prosthetist, made for Daniel a year earlier. Once finished, he put the pieces in the inventory room, and, with a heavy sigh, turned his attention to the other patients filling the clinic.

After a successful trip to Ghana, a sober and focused Grayson returned to the United States. Speaking at a national prosthetic convention in Las Vegas, he interacted with prosthetists and suppliers from around the country; all of whom knew Grayson's story. A week later, we flew to Detroit where he received a *da Vinci Award* presented by the Michigan chapter of the *Multiple Sclerosis Society*. Presented to individuals and organizations for inventive solutions to help people with disabilities, Grayson won for the brand new student category: *da Vinci Apprentice* (in reference to Leonardo da Vinci's apprentice). Receiving his award from Mr. Chet Huber, Jr., the head of General Motor's ONSTAR program, Grayson addressed the audience of nearly fifteen hundred people with a message of service ...and innovation with purpose.

From earlier mission trips to Haiti as a child with Peter's parents, to Ghana, to even working with us at a Joni and Friends retreat with disabled children, we've tried to expose him to needy people as much as possible, in order to foster a desire to serve, lead, and use his life and skills to touch others.

On his second trip to Ghana, Grayson felt more confident about his Bubble Wrap® application, and quickly went to work covering the limbs we made. On this trip, Parker also joined us, and we had a wonderful time with the whole family. My father also traveled with us, and he and my nephew, Drew, led the construction efforts of building shelves, chairs, and benches for the waiting room. With the loud noises of saws, hammers, and other tools filling the clinic, Grayson quietly approached Peter with an unusual dilemma; the man next in line to receive a covered limb was a bi-lateral (both legs) amputee …like me. Our prosthetic team made both legs for the man, but Grayson had only made coverings for single amputees …using the patient's remaining leg as the model so that both limbs matched.

"Dad, this man doesn't have a leg for me to measure." He told Peter. "How am I going to know what shape to mold the covers?"

Looking at him while working on another limb himself, Peter replied, "You're just going to have to figure something out."

Hours later, Peter asked Grayson about the man's legs. "Well, I looked at this man, and he seemed to be about the same size as me, so I used my own legs as measurements," Grayson replied. Filled again with pride and affection for our youngest son, Peter hugged him and complimented him on his ingenuity and compassion.

In 2008, the National Museum of Education honored Grayson with an induction into the Young Inventors Hall of Fame, and he also currently serves on their student board of directors. He continues to speak and conduct interviews, and plans to return to Africa for additional trips. A friend once asked Peter how we keep Grayson from letting the fame and attention go to his head. Thinking for a minute, Peter replied, "We've introduced him to the President of the United States, and we've introduced him to a person in Africa with leprosy …who has toes, fingers, and even limbs rotting off. That's a pretty good balance."

Chapter 32 Bubble Wrap... Who'da Thunk?

Something as simple as packing material and a science contest charted an amazing course for our son. His story inspired a lot of people, and he even kept a blog while in Africa for the widely read student magazine, the *Weekly Reader*. Grayson's own words better reflect the impact on his life of seeing a need ...and meeting that need with the simple materials in his possession:

"...I felt pretty nervous about the whole thing. Besides that, the only 'blueprint' for making these Bubble Wrap coverings was in my head, and now I had to teach it to adults, which also felt a little strange. I told my Dad how I felt. He smiled and said I'd be fine, and would really like the staff.

I worked with a man named Welbeck, who was about sixty years old, and a longtime employee of the clinic. We started on a Monday, and by our last day he was able to make a covering better than some of mine. It didn't hurt my pride any, because that was my goal; teaching them, not showing off.

When I first came up with this, it seemed like a really good idea, but I have to admit, I wondered if the people would want a Bubble Wrap covering. It seemed a long way from the prosthetic lab where I first made this, and I was scared that people wouldn't like them.

But I didn't need to be afraid. Everyone wanted a covering. They loved it! Not just our new patients, but some of the first patients Dad and Mom treated came in just to get a covering.

I observed the slums in the capital city of Accra, while I was in Ghana. People were roaming the streets half-clothed, with flies all over them. I wondered what would happen to them. Would they die in some nameless alley, from disease most Americans have never even heard of? Do they know the Lord? It opened my eyes to a world that's hard to imagine and harder to describe. Seeing such poverty and horrible living conditions helped me realize that I need to be more grateful for the many things I take for granted here in the United States.

In Africa, I realized I'm in a big story, in a much larger world. Winning the Bubble Wrap contest gave me a platform to speak not only to America, but also the world.

I want my message to be, 'Anyone can make a difference, even a woman who's missing both legs ...or a teenager with Bubble Wrap.'"

—GRAYSON ROSENBERGER, *9TH GRADE, AUGUST 2007, NASHVILLE, TN*

Chapter 33

In Pain You Shall Bring Forth Children

To the woman He [God] said, "I will greatly multiply your pain in childbirth; in pain you shall bring forth children."

—Genesis 3:16 (NASB)

Hey Mom, put your leg on ...you've got to come see this!

—Parker Rosenberger, age seven

During one particular visit at Walter Reed Army Medical Center, I met a young, single mother who just lost her leg. The downcast look on her face broke my heart, and we sat and talked for a while.

"I feel so guilty for what I'm putting my kids through," she said while tearing up.

Asking her about the last time she saw her children, she flatly told me she didn't want them coming to the hospital and "seeing her like this." By keeping her children away from observing their mom struggling, she felt as if she offered them some level of protection. Peter stepped in at that moment and pointedly asked her to tell him about her children. Learning about her oldest, a thirteen-year-old boy, Peter emphatically shared with her his thoughts on the subject.

"Let me tell you what allowing your son into this part of your life can do for him," he said forcefully. "You're giving that boy the opportunity to love the most important woman in his life …without demanding something back. He's learning to give, without expectations; to be more self-reliant and independent, while at the same time more sensitive to the needs of someone who is hurting. This son of yours will KNOW how to love a wife one day. He will KNOW how to love someone who cannot always respond in kind. He will KNOW how to respectfully treat someone with a disability. THAT's what you can do for your son by involving him in your recovery and challenges!"

Looking at Peter with amazement, the young mother took a deep breath, straightened her shoulders, and smiled for the first time.

"I guess I never looked at it that way." Her sheepish grin brightened the whole room.

Holding her hand, I looked at her in the eyes and said with confidence, "You're going to be just fine! Don't try and parent as if you're not disabled; engage them in, through, and with your disability. The point is not to be the perfect mom …it's just to be MOM!"

Raising children through the challenges we've faced as a family continues to be a difficult journey. When I look at our sons, I see outstanding men of God who have purpose, focus, and a desire to reach others who are hurting. They could have so easily chosen to rebel against the pain so keenly felt in our home. Parker and Grayson opted for a different life; they chose to face the pain in their lives …instead of medicating.

Since carrying Parker and Grayson, I've daily prayed for them. We've made many, many, mistakes along the way, but God has graciously covered our sons in raincoats and galoshes to keep stuff off them. I encourage mothers to pray daily for their children (born and unborn). Scripture is full of accounts of God's tender responses to praying moms. If they come home with tattoos and nose rings …pray. If you find your time with your son limited to visiting hours at a prison …pray. If your daughter is drinking, pray. If the doctor tells you that your child has cancer, PRAY. If your doctor tells you to take a test in order to make the "proper choice…." PRAY.

One morning we talked with a waitress at Waffle House who had spent the night before at the county jail bailing out her daughter. That afternoon, a friend of ours who served in Congress had to bail his child out of jail after he was arrested for driving while intoxicated. Children have a way of leveling the playing field of life …providing all of us ample opportunity to hit our knees.

We've had a great deal of help from many individuals. Family, teachers, friends, and a wonderful set of godparents …none other than one of my oldest friends who met me while I lay unconscious at St. Thomas Hospital so many years ago: Sam Clarke and his wife, Marianne. Sam, who serves on our board of directors, and Marianne, along with both sets of grandparents, pray daily for our family …and we are truly grateful.

I learned to be a mother from a hospital bed, and I also learned legs aren't required to be a mom; a perfect body is not necessary to love *and be loved by* your children. I've

…a perfect body is not necessary to love and be loved by your children.

been to football games and baseball games in wheelchairs, on crutches, with legs, without legs, wearing casts ...you name it, I've rolled out as best I could. I've packed lunches from my wheelchair, and, while in so much pain that I couldn't see straight, I still helped with homework. Every chance they get, my sons tell me how proud they are of me ...and are never ashamed of how I look, or what I can or cannot do. In fact the only thing that ever embarrasses them about me has nothing to do with my disability. Parker will affirm that my excessively loud cheering at his baseball games caused him to pull his hat way down over his eyes ...far more than my being in a wheelchair, having robot legs, or anything else.

It's hard to hide, however, when you're the pitcher ...so, sorry Parker! After throwing fabulous *strikes* that were called *balls* by an evidently blind umpire, Parker was mortified to hear his mother's loud voice scream out, "C'mon Ump, that was a strike...you're breaking my heart!"

To fathers, I share something that Peter started doing years ago. During the first few painful months of Peter's new walk, he heard a sermon from well-known minister, T.D. Jakes. In his message, Bishop Jakes recalled his own father's death. Only sixteen at the time, he shared how he stood at his father's grave and "...nearly lost my mind!" In his heart he screamed to his daddy's grave, "You can't leave! You haven't told me what you think of me!" Sobbing, Bishop Jakes cried out his despair over never knowing what his father thought of him.

"Did I measure up? Were you proud of me?" These and other questions troubled this famous minister for many years.

That message affected Peter profoundly, and he determined *that day* to ensure our sons never lived another moment without knowing how their father felt about them. "Whatever battles they fight in life, they will never have to look over their shoulder and wonder if their father loved them, accepted them, or was proud of them," he often tells me ...and them.

Chapter 33 In Pain You Shall Bring Forth Children

I can't count the number of times I've heard him bless our sons, affirm them, and assure them of his love for them. He hugs them, kisses them, prays with them, and is involved in every part of their lives. In addition to lively conversations about world events and politics (Grayson's and Peter's favorite subject), they have frank discussions about sin, repentance, sex, godliness, and character.

So, to every father …let your children know how you feel about them. Tell your daughter she's beautiful. If she's a few pounds overweight or even wearing a patch over her eye, *convey to her heart* how precious and pretty she is to you. Let her *feel your* acceptance. Don't ever qualify it by saying, "I love you, even though you're …" That destroys a girl, and you condemn her to drinking from the sewer instead of the clean water that she cries for. She craves affirmation, and if she doesn't receive it from you, *who will it* come from …and what will she do to obtain it?

I don't know many men who dream for their daughter to grow up and pose for a centerfold, yet it happens. Where are those fathers? How does a precious little six-year-old girl who wants to wear a pretty dress and be considered beautiful …evolve into living a life full of immorality?

Affirm your son's masculinity. If he can't throw a ball or do something as well as you do, find something he does do …and spend time with him doing it together. Let him see you pray. Fathers, let your sons watch you humble yourself before your Savior. Let them know how much you need a Savior. How will they know if you don't tell them?

When our sons learned about their father's mistakes, we wept together as a family, but I did not dishonor Peter in front of them. I admit, I have had my bad moments…but I apologized afterwards. Peter comically (and ruefully) comments, "You ain't never been kicked …until a woman with metal legs gives you the boot!" I think Parker and Grayson handled it well enough to the point that they enthusiastically agreed to the story being told in this book. Peter still works against his natural inclination of compensating for his past; he wants to play to his strengths and look "large and in charge" with them. But when he makes himself transparent and vulnerable to our sons, that's when their hearts connect with him on a level that is powerful and real.

Peter struggled for years with how our sons would react when they finally learned about his failures. My sons are sad about my legs and injuries, but they respond to me based upon how I handle those things. They do the same with Peter ...*and with me*, regarding our failures. Peter clearly shows our sons the path to the cross; he also communicates how great his own need is for a Savior. By doing so, they are provided with a model.

> The years have taught us that by heaping acceptance and love on our children, while not ignoring shortcomings or faults, we equip them with strength and confidence ...which in turn enables them to carry hope and leadership to a harsh world desperately needing both.

When mistakes are made, we are candid with our sons, and invite them to join us at the foot of the cross ...daily. I don't know any perfect parents. But I do know that engaging children, with or without limbs, with or without a *spotless life*, helps detangle the knots that form in their young hearts; knots that can quickly twist and snarl into a huge mess.

We don't make our sons long for our approval and expressions of love, but instead pour it on them lavishly. Our Heavenly Father does that for us. He extravagantly cascades His love and blessings on us. The years have taught us that by heaping acceptance and love on our children, while not ignoring shortcomings or faults, we equip them with strength and confidence ...which in turn enables them to carry hope and leadership to a harsh world desperately needing both.

To the best of our abilities, we've guided our sons to reach out to those who are hurting ...with the same hope that continues to sustain our family. Several years ago, Parker traveled to Tunisia, North Africa to spend time with my brother-in-law, Tom Rosenberger, and his family. Tom works as a diplomat for the United States Department of State, and is one of the top Arabic speakers in our country's government. While enjoying a tour of Tunisia, even riding camels in the Sahara desert, Parker also had a mission to explore the amputee community for *Standing with Hope*. Tom arranged a meeting between Parker and a local man, Mr. Tebib, whose wife lost both of her legs when a truck crashed into their home. Sitting at Tom's house in Tunis, Parker, nineteen at the time, found himself sharing an unusual bond with a middle-aged, Muslim man from North Africa.

As Tom worked to interpret for the two, he suddenly realized that even the language barrier disappeared as these two men shared a powerful moment reflecting on the most important woman in their lives ... each of whom lost both legs. Later, Tom told Peter that until that point, he'd never witnessed diplomacy of the level Parker and Mr. Tebib shared. Surpassing religion, marital status, nationality, and age, these two men transcended diplomacy and formed a friendship rarely seen in today's international relations environment.

Parker left Tunisia a changed young man; so much so that he chose to major in international relations ...and hopes to lead teams for us. Borrowing from his trips to West Africa with *Standing with Hope*, and his brief internship with Senator Bill Frist (where he learned of the senator's passion for global health initiatives), Parker wrote a stellar paper during his freshman year in college about the merits of medical diplomacy. In his paper, Parker wrote:

Medical diplomacy and assistance succeeds where other types of diplomacy are jeopardized due to economic, religious, and cultural differences. Healthy individuals help make healthy productive communities, which in turn lead to prosperous countries. By uniting different cultures into a common goal of caring for the sick and wounded, medical diplomacy and assistance helps build strong partnerships, which can expand to additional diplomatic opportunities such as labor, trade, and environmental concerns. In light of the distrust and intra-cultural hatred, so prevalent in today's world, diplomacy is infinitely better than military actions, and medical diplomacy has a proven history of succeeding even when traditional diplomacy fails. To paraphrase an axiom used by medical practitioners, "it is difficult to hate the one who is saving the life of your child or loved one."

Our sons watched us walk, often crawl, to the foot of the cross; and have witnessed God's provision of grace in our family's life. As they step into whatever paths God has for them, they do so from a foundation of faith built on trusting God through heartache, loss, and pain. In doing so ...they can offer others what they themselves daily depend upon.

Blessed be the God and Father of our Lord Jesus Christ, the Father of mercies and God of all comfort, who comforts us in all our affliction, so that we may be able to comfort those who are in any affliction, with the comfort with which we ourselves are comforted by God.—2 CORINTHIANS 1:3-4, *ESV*

Chapter 34

Left Behind

God doth not need either man's work or his own gifts.
Who best bear his mild yoke, they serve him best.
His state is kingly: thousands at his bidding speed,
and post o'er land and ocean without rest;
They also serve who only stand and wait.

—John Milton

Something clicked while listening to our pastor's sermon on disappointment, just days before a return trip to Africa. His message described the Apostle Paul's personal battle with infirmity, and Paul's undisclosed "thorn in the flesh." Paul really struggled with his infirmity prohibiting him from participating in specific mission trips. It hit hard when our pastor said that Paul's condition in today's terms would be like him [Paul] showing up to preach in a hospital gown with one hand holding the flaps together in the back. (I have some experience in this area.) We all look at Paul as a hero of the faith, and rightly so, but history seemed to paint Paul as rather physically pitiful in appearance.

Leaving church, an unsettled feeling in the pit of my stomach prepared me for my own "thorny" struggle.

After being prepped by a powerful sermon on Sunday, Monday brought devastating news. Less than three days before our team was to leave for Africa, Dr. Marvin firmly told me I should not go on the trip. Since 1983, he had never prohibited activities; he usually wanted me to try anything I felt up to doing (within reason).

A pain medication snafu sent me into intensive care for two nights, and that, combined with regulating the blood thinner I'm taking because of pulmonary emboli, forced the situation to an unpleasant decision. Learning of my daily painful challenges prompts many people to question why I even try to go to Africa, or anywhere for that matter. But it's going to Ghana, to Walter Reed, and other places that help me see purpose in some of the more difficult things in my life. The thought of getting left behind breaks my heart.

I begged my doctor for 24 more hours to make the decision with some new blood work, and he agreed. "Four o'clock tomorrow afternoon in my office. We'll make the decision."

I prayed all night and into the day that my blood work would come back with good news, and that he would, with certain stipulations, allow me to go. The next day at his office we discovered my lab results were worse than the day before. Unfortunately, that wasn't all. Not only could I not go, but now I had to be on 24-hour watch …and I couldn't even leave Nashville to go to my parents' home in Florida for at least a change of scenery. To top it off, someone had to drive for me and check me while I slept to make sure I was breathing …or I'd have to be admitted.

Peter and Grayson and the team were leaving in less than thirty-six hours, Peter's parents weren't available, and my parents were in Montana. It came down to Parker, who was working for my brother-in-law in

Florida. He dropped everything and drove up to Nashville to be with me. Hauling me back and forth to the hospital every two days, AND sleeping on the couch in our bedroom in order to check my breathing, was not his idea of a fun way to spend any part of his summer, but he did it …and he did it with love and concern for me. He showed a true servant's heart.

Four days later, Dad showed up from Montana to relieve Parker. He brought a new baby monitor and an old cowbell from Montana. He even demonstrated (often) how to use the cowbell properly if I needed him for anything. After a couple of practice sessions, it sounded like a herd of cattle in our house …and I halfway looked around to see if a stampede would appear through our den! He told me later that he didn't trust the cowbell or the monitor …so he checked on me every hour anyway.

Early Friday morning, I received a call and the ID showed Peter's cell number. The whole team and all the workers from the clinic clustered around Peter, who put the call on speakerphone (our cell bill was a bit high that month). While crowding around the phone, the Ghanaian prosthetic technicians all wore the new lab coats we provided them (my former college roommate, Nancy, embroidered each technician's name onto the jacket). Peter and I felt the technicians trained by *Standing with Hope* deserved to be donned with the coats in order to show the proper respect to their work …and the accomplishments they achieved in developing their skills. Peter had a prayer service with them before patients were seen, and he asked me to sing over the speakerphone. For just a few moments, I was able to participate as part of the team …from my bedroom in Nashville.

A few days later I got another call from Peter. They discovered the prosthetic arm parts they took were the wrong size. The tiny parts needed to be expressed over, in order to make the arms we promised for our patients. One patient in particular, Lateef, came on a bus from Lagos, Nigeria. For nearly a year, Lateef's father, Emmanuel, e-mailed Peter from an internet café in Lagos begging for arms for his son Lateef. An electrical accident at age eighteen burned both of Lateef's hands, and he lost them below the elbow. For the last three years, Lateef could only eat like a dog, lapping up his food from a bowl squeezed precariously between his scarred stumps.

The arms promised to Lateef now seemed unattainable due to a simple mix up in components. Hanging up from my conversation with Peter, I called our friend, Fran Jenkins, at Fillauer Corporation in Chattanooga. Fran and I worked quickly, and she helped me compile all the necessary parts, and make DHL's afternoon shipment. The shipping company maintains an office in Accra, and Peter let them know to look for the package carrying the tiny parts.

On the last day of clinic, a DHL driver arrived on a motorcycle, with the vital box of arm parts securely strapped to the back of his bike. Already ten o'clock in the morning, Peter and the team worked quickly to beat the mandatory electricity curfew for later that afternoon. Our team leader that trip, Randy Roberson, threw himself into assembling the prosthetic arms while the rest of the group wrapped up the work from the busy clinic.

Working against the clock, Randy never missed a step while his hands rapidly assembled tiny pieces that helped move the cables to control the "hands." As the sun slowly lowered into the west, the other prosthetist from that particular trip, Halima's giant dancing partner, Kraig Helberg, joined Randy. With Kraig now working on the left arm, Randy focused on the right. Lateef and Emmanuel patiently and gratefully looked on as these men furiously assembled devices normally built over a couple of days in the United States.

Towards the end of the process, the power went off. Finished with all the electrically powered equipment needed to fabricate the arms, the problem became "light." As the sun sank behind the trees and buildings to the west, the light failed and the clinic soon grew dark. Transferring the process outside, Randy and Kraig placed Lateef in a chair in front of the team's van, and with the headlights directly on their patient, they continued their work. Holding Peter's video camera above Lateef so that the bright camera light could serve as a spotlight on the tiny pieces, my nephew, Drew, carefully followed Randy's and Kraig's hands with the shining beam to help them see their work.

Finally, putting down hammers, pliers, and other tools, Randy and Kraig helped Lateef don his new prosthetic limbs. Pushing what remained of his arms through the harness, Lateef shrugged his shoulders to help shift the devices until he had a comfortable fit. Holding out his credit-card-shaped hotel key, Peter motioned for Lateef to take it from his hands. As Lateef extended his right arm, the tension on the cables running through the harness across his back pulled on the shiny hook at the end of the molded "fore-arm."

With everyone holding their breath, Lateef gingerly centered the now split hook over the card in Peter's hand. Relaxing his arm and shoulder muscle, the hook closed tightly and Lateef pulled the card from Peter's hand. Cheering wildly, the whole team broke into applause as Lateef's smile nearly outshone the van's headlights illuminating the exuberant crowd.

As they closed that trip's clinic in prayer, Lateef's father paused for a moment to address Peter. "Sir, you gave me your word that you would help my son." Peter, looking down at the ground as tears filled his eyes, heard this precious, humble man go on to say, "Jesus said that if you do this to the least of these you do it unto me. Sir, you have helped the least of these, and I am grateful."

Now everyone felt tears rolling down their cheeks. Grabbing Lateef's new hand, Peter gathered the group around them to sing the same hymn I offered to God the day I became a double-amputee, and the same hymn Peter sang on a freight elevator as he walked away from a job that represented his efforts and not God's:

"Praise God from Whom All Blessings Flow!"

Our patient, Lateef, has two new arms and can feed himself because I was left behind. Others are walking and lifting new hands to praise God, and I participated in all of that ...even from Nashville. It's painful for me, and my family, to accept some of the realities of my life, and I don't always know why God allows certain things. I'm learning, however, that I don't have to go and look for purpose and meaning in my difficulties. The things I deal with don't even have to make sense to me. They make sense to God, and I trust Him. Periodically, He permits me to see things along the way that show meaning and purpose. Those moments are encouraging ...but they're only glimpses. The rest of the time, I'm stepping out on faith.

Chapter 35

Friendly Fire

The broken soldier, kindly bade to stay;
Sat by his fire, and talked the night away,
Wept o'er his wounds, or tales of sorrow done,
Shoulder'd his crutch, and show'd how fields were won.

—Oliver Goldsmith, *The Deserted Village*

*I*n the physical therapy room at Walter Reed, Peter and I met a young corporal who not only had lost a leg, but also had freckled bits of shrapnel still peppering the shin area of her remaining leg. The tiny fragments work themselves out over time, but can look awfully disconcerting. Peter, harkening back to our first meeting as students on the campus of Belmont University, didn't skirt the issue but directly asked about her injuries. Noticing the tiny pieces of metal just below the skin of her leg, he asked her with complete deadpan, "You haven't been hunting with vice-president Cheney, have you?"

The face of the young corporal lit up with laughter, and she quickly looked around the room …almost as if making sure it was permissible to laugh at the reference to the former vice-president's famous hunting mishap. Breaking the tension of her pain and despondency, she opened up and, after talking for a few moments, her voice lowered as she quietly asked, "Will I ever get a boyfriend?"

Thumbing towards Peter, I quickly let her know, "Hey, I found this guy!"

Interrupting me, Peter (with a feigned look of worry) admonished, "Gracie, we're trying to cheer the girl up ...hasn't she suffered enough?"

At that point, we all started laughing. But, through the laughter, we still addressed the heart issues: *What will happen to me? Will I be loved? Will I be accepted?*

On our next visit to Walter Reed, we connected up with the young soldier, and she not only was walking superbly, but looked like a different person. Her confidence, smile, and general overall sense of "I'm going to get through this" seemed to flow out of her ...and after lots of hugs, we all knew the road ahead, although full of challenges, was bright and exciting.

But that's not always the story for wounded warriors.

So many truths are hammered home during my visits to Walter Reed. In many respects, Peter and I regard the army hospital as one giant metaphor for the church. Highly skilled warriors struggling with devastating wounds are found not only on *Ward 57* at Walter Reed, but in church pews and pastors' offices across the country. Some marriage issues can feel like amputations; *I believe I am uniquely qualified to make that statement.* Relationship discord can

> Some marriage issues can feel like amputations; I believe I am uniquely qualified to make that statement.

result in lifetime heartaches and produce many casualties. Observing wounded soldiers often provides a picture of what confronts many of today's pastors.

One such encounter stood out during our most recent visit to Walter Reed. While visiting freshly wounded soldiers performing physical therapy in the Military Advanced Training Center (MATC) on campus at Walter Reed (I sang for the groundbreaking of that facility), we met a bitter young man whose wounds resulted from *friendly fire*. Although an accident, he was struck down by his own team.

In his mind, as he looks down at his amputated leg, he doesn't even get the bragging rights to say he lost it ***for*** his country …rather, he thinks he lost it ***because*** of his country. Of course that's not true …and he's a hero for even enlisting, but those are hard feelings to fight.

Walking over to greet him, he rudely snapped at me. Lying on his back while working out on a physical therapy table, he could only see me from the waist up. The physical therapist working with him looked embarrassed, and quickly tried to cover for me by telling the young man I was welcome there ... and had a lot of practical advice worth hearing.

Disbelieving the therapist, he snarled back with a hateful comment. Momentarily stunned, I regained my composure, and, while holding on to a railing, propped my prosthetic leg near where his head rested on the low workout table.

He not only noticed my artificial foot beside him *(encased in a beautiful shoe, I might add),* but his eyes turned to watch me balancing on my other artificial leg, as well.

"You're not the only amputee in here, big guy." I said, while looking him squarely in the eye.

The *soldier in him* quietly nodded at me, and he grew silent.

Ten feet away, Peter listened to a man who, although he had lost both legs, cracked jokes with a contagious sense of humor. Cutting up with him (as Peter often does), the soldier's face quickly clouded over, however, when Peter pointedly asked him how things were back home.

Looking down at his new prosthetic legs, he whispered out, "My marriage is on the rocks ...and it doesn't look good."

The loss of his legs didn't keep him from joking, but the wounds of his heart silenced the laughter.

Friendly fire.

Peter asked a mother if her son's father had been up to the hospital. Looking over at her son's newly amputated left leg, as well as the halo device holding the pins piercing his right leg ...her jaw tightened as she flatly said, "He left years ago, and good riddance."

Friendly fire.

How many of us deal with deep wounds caused by those closest to us? How many of us have caused damage to the ones we love and swore to protect? Sometimes "friendly fire" wounds are compounded with the shame of the wound itself ...we feel like our wounds come with dishonor, and our fists clench with a rage that wants to choke the one(s) who hurt us. Other times, we realize with horror how poorly we treated those counting on us, and the guilt and shame fill us with despair.

> Christ is *the* wounded warrior who presents His own wounds, not only to communicate perspective, but also to demonstrate His love for each of us.

We can all recall those things that cause tears to pour from our eyes ... the things driving us to lash out at the ones who hit us with "friendly fire." In our pain, we might even strike at people who are simply trying to encourage us.

I propped an artificial limb on a physical therapy table to help a hurting young man gain perspective and, *hopefully*, see he can move past the horrific injury that altered his life. Christ is *the* wounded warrior who presents His own wounds, not only to communicate perspective, but also to demonstrate His love for each of us. He didn't just prop a metal leg on the table; He laid down His life and was Himself wounded …for our sins. His wounds made it possible for ours to be healed. He never clenched His fists, but rather stretched out his hands and received the nails.

Knowing ***that*** has given me the courage to face my own "friendly fire" events, including the self-inflicted one so many years ago; even today, looking at my wounds is still difficult …after all these years.

But when I look at HIS wounds, I am strengthened to know that HE redeemed my soul …and is redeeming my wounds. He even uses my broken body and wounded heart to play a small part in the redemption of others' hurts; maybe even yours.

For a lifetime, I've trusted God with my trauma and disability. Beyond my wildest dreams, He's reached into what most thought was a senseless tragedy ...and used it to comfort wounded warriors, broken hearts, and many others struggling with "friendly fire."

But it was our sins that did that to Him, that ripped and tore and crushed Him—our sins! He took the punishment, and that made us whole. Through His bruises we get healed.—ISAIAH 53:5, *THE MESSAGE*

Chapter 36

Kwame's Dilemma

Then Peter said, "Look at us!" So the man gave them his attention,
expecting to get something from them. Then Peter said, "Silver or gold
I do not have, but what I have I give you. In the name of Jesus Christ
of Nazareth, walk." Taking him by the right hand, he helped him up,
and instantly the man's feet and ankles became strong. He jumped to
his feet and began to walk. Then he went with them into the
temple courts, walking and jumping, and praising God.

—Acts 3:2-8 (NIV)

Hear Him, ye deaf; His praise, ye dumb, your loosened tongues employ;
Ye blind, behold your Savior come, and leap, ye lame, for joy.

—O' For A Thousand Tongues to Sing
Charles Wesley

While patients wait for the new limb *Standing with Hope* provides at the clinic in Ghana, Peter often joins them in the waiting area to hear individual stories and discover more about the people we treat. In a room full of amputees, the discussion invariably turns to God and why He allows suffering and loss. During one trip, Kwame, a farmer who lost his leg to diabetes, expressed particularly strong views proclaiming his disappointment with God for allowing such widespread misery. Peter theologically sparred with him for a while, using everything he'd learned through his own journey of questioning God; but Kwame didn't budge. Propping his amputated limb on his crutch, Kwame continued to list his indictments against God for allowing this mess of a world we inhabit. Several of the team, including me, grew frustrated with Kwame's loud accusations about God's goodness and justice, or in his opinion, the lack thereof.

Interestingly enough, Kwame's comments sounded uncannily similar to ones I've heard expressed by friends, family … and me since donning an eye-patch for the first time or strapping on prosthetic limbs.

While Kwame shared his disappointment with God, the team continued working on limbs and treating patients. Muslim, Christian, Buddhist—we treat patients from every faith, or even no faith at all. Our job is to provide the best artificial limbs possible, and be faithful to share why we do this work; results are God's department. Peter often states, "We're in sales, not management."

After properly fitting the prosthesis, we sit down individually with each patient, provide them with a *"Life and Limb"* bag, and share the message of the Gospel. As each patient is unique, so is this one-on-one time we have when distributing Life and Limb bags. Sitting down with Kwame, Peter's work was cut out for him. Kwame, an older, smaller man, continues to remain active and is in great shape, so the prosthetists put a high performance foot on his new, custom fit limb. We are able to use high-end recycled prosthetic feet from patients in the U.S., who discard them for a variety of reasons *(i.e., death, upgraded, or no longer needed devices, etc.)*

Noticing something particularly familiar about the prosthetic foot Kwame now wore, Peter looked closely and discovered a foot that once belonged to me. Looking at the man now wearing my foot, Peter smiled and said, "Kwame, I know you have a lot of hard feelings toward God. But every time you find yourself blaming God for this world's misery, I want you to look down at that foot. Rather than blame God, remember that Gracie trusted Him with her loss and pain, and chose to offer God her life; broken body and all."

Gone were all the objections and accusations, Peter had Kwame's full attention.

"Because Gracie chooses to trust God, you are now able to walk without crutches *on her foot*; Kwame. You are literally standing because of her faith!"

Kwame smiled. Where theological arguments failed, a foot prevailed.

Later, as Kwame prepared to leave, one of the team's prosthetists walked by him, carrying a limb for another patient. Kwame grabbed her hand, and asked her to pray for him. While she prayed, Kwame stood straight and proud ...*with no crutches!* The foot Kwame is wearing once helped me stand next to the President of the United States. Now, it's helping carry Kwame to a higher office.

I heard about His healing, of His cleansing power revealing,

How He made the lame to walk again and caused the blind to see;

And then I cried, "Dear Jesus, come and heal my broken spirit,"

And somehow Jesus came and brought to me the victory.

—**Victory in Jesus**, Eugene M. Bartlett

I once heard a great statement: *"Jesus was a carpenter, and he doesn't even waste the sawdust."* God is using a foot once gathering dust in the back of my closet, to point a man to Christ. Our Lord transforms broken bodies, used limbs, sinful lives, Bubble Wrap, and even two fish and five loaves into beacons of His redemption.

What an amazing paradox: painful things, things representing embarrassment or shame, sources of discouragement, and even things meant for evil become blessings to others and reflect glory to God when offered to Christ. Nothing I can say will answer Kwame's, yours, or even my questions about the misery in this world. Instead, like I did for Kwame, I offer *what I have* to equip you to continue standing with hope.

Epilogue

"Pain relief" is not a worthy life goal.

—Gracie Rosenberger

By enduring constant pain and loss for nearly thirty years, I believe my story can effectively address the heartache and disappointments in yours. My tale goes beyond a car accident, marriage issues, amputation, or even severe, chronic pain …instead this story chronicles a broken woman learning to daily trust God with the setbacks and harsh realities of life. As in the case when I propped my foot beside the soldier lying on a workout table at Walter Reed, I've shown you my injuries, mistakes, betrayals, and even successes …in order to point you to the ONE who redeems it all.

In September 2009, I underwent my seventy-third operation since the car accident. Three of the pastors on staff at our church visited me at the hospital prior to surgery. Peter brought them into the holding area where two anesthesiologists had unsuccessfully attempted (three times) a sciatic block for my left leg before taking me into the operating room. The stabbing pain caused by their efforts nearly sent me into the stratosphere, and I sobbed and groaned in agony.

For the first time, my pastors witnessed the most common part of my life …but one most do not see. Clearly affected by my suffering, I heard the somberness in the voice of one of them as he cried out to God on my behalf; struggling on how to even pray for me. Understanding my circumstances lay beyond their ability to change …they also each recognized, much like Peter did when he held Parker as the doctor stitched the laceration in our son's chin, the futility of attempting to even ask the "why God" question while watching me weeping in the tiny, curtained-off area. Understanding *why* something is happening, even *if* we could comprehend it, does little to ease pain. The ministry of my pastors that day rose higher than the desire to fix or answer any of the questions always lurking near tragic circumstances; their mission was to be *with* me.

The United States military launched a chaplains' initiative years ago entitled a "ministry of presence." Peter's father, who served as a U.S. Navy chaplain for more than thirty years, played a part of the initial campaign of chaplains working to more directly connect to the troops in the trenches, at sea, or wherever needed. Although U.S. military chaplains have served alongside troops since the Revolutionary War, this initiative worked to officially define the pastoral ministry for men and women in uniform.

Peter and I know many chaplains standing with deployed and wounded warriors alike in their various struggles. From the physical therapy room to the guard towers in Afghanistan, the mission of these chaplains soars higher than providing answers or change to the often horrific circumstances they experience in ministering to military personnel. Like our pastors who visited me in the holding area before surgery, their _ministry of presence_ reflects the same assuring love that whispered to my heart, "Daddy's here, Mary Grace."

Epilogue

That ministry of presence serves as a continual thread through my own journey of heartbreak, loss, suffering, and other intensely painful struggles. Not over by a long shot, and barring a miraculous intervention from Christ (which I still pray for), I will wake up tomorrow in more pain than most people can imagine, strain to roll over and transfer to my wheelchair, put my legs on, join hands with my husband ...and face another day. Motivational phrases and catchy theological "bumper-stickers" can't sustain the level of challenges I struggle with; it takes more. That "more" is the ministry of _God's_ presence; He never abandons us through the long and often terrifying _valley of the shadow of death._

Yea, though I walk through the valley of the shadow of death, I will fear no evil: for Thou art with me.—PSALM 23:4, *KJV*

In allowing you to see some of my hurts and fears, as well as things I've learned along the way, my prayer is that this story serves as a beacon ...pointing you more clearly to Jesus, who remains with me; leading, strengthening, and often carrying me through paths infinitely more frightening than the treacherous "black-diamond" ski slope I once tried at the top of Big Sky ski resort in Montana. Like my foot that Kwame now wears, I offer this book to help equip **_you_** to stand and walk with confidence; strengthening you with the same strength that I daily, *often hourly*, receive.

All praise to the God and Father of our Master, Jesus the Messiah! Father of all mercy! God of all healing counsel! He comes alongside us when we go through hard times, and before you know it, he brings us alongside someone else who is going through hard times so that we can be there for that person just as God was there for us. We have plenty of hard times that come from following the Messiah, but no more so than the good times of his healing comfort—we get a full measure of that, too. —2 CORINTHIANS 1:3-5, *THE MESSAGE*

In a moment of compassion, Peter held my hand one morning as I groaned to meet another day. "It's okay, Baby," he said tenderly. "It won't always hurt. One day, you won't have to be in pain anymore."

Snapping my head around to him, I surprised him with a forceful reply. "Don't tell me that! I know that one day I'll be in Heaven and live eternally in a pain-free body!" I said while clenching my teeth against the searing sensations coursing through my back and into what remains of my legs.

"Don't tell me that!" I gasped again while straining to sit up. "Rather, remind me of the work I still need to do here…even in this broken body."

Patrolling the camp watching for enemies, an army sergeant doesn't need to hear about going home …he needs the chaplain, the brother, the father, the friend who is ministering to him in those lonely and scary hours to remind him of the mission, and the importance of the task at hand.

One day <u>*I will stand*</u> before my Savior in perfection; completely and eternally pain-free. The next time I feel the ground under my restored feet, it will be in the presence of Jesus. I will dance and laugh and sing His praises with all the countless others who wait to mount up with wings like eagles, and run and not grow weary.

But they that wait upon the LORD shall renew their strength; they shall mount up with wings as eagles; they shall run, and not be weary; and they shall walk, and not faint.—ISAIAH 40:31, *KJV*

One day …*I will fly!!* While I'm waiting, however, there's work to be done. I choose to continue *standing with hope*; waiting on what <u>**I know will come**</u> to pass. I refuse to sit in the stands, or check-out because my challenges are too hard. I want to live—even injured and hurting; because I know that in God's hand, my broken body is now being used to reach others who hurt.

Epilogue

As I struggle with the difficulties of each day, constant reminders help direct my eyes to Christ. When Parker introduced me to his girlfriend, Viveka Kellgren (now his wife), she presented me with a gift to mark the occasion; a crucifix from her and her mother, purchased on a recent trip to Israel. Viveka and her mother had no idea of the significance of the gift, and I treasure the little crucifix that permanently knitted our hearts together. Holding the gift from my future daughter-in-law, I thought of Sister Euphemia …and how she helped set my broken feet, and eventually my artificial feet, on the path of trusting Christ exclusively.

To the best of my ability I've borne witness to what I've seen, touched, and experienced while journeying on this road. Although many other painful days may come my way, I've made my decision, and like Halima did that day in a dusty clinic in Ghana as she walked on her new leg, I continue to trust God with each step of my artificial feet; *"God Loves Gracie!"* My hope, sin, pain, dreams, loss, and desperate need of a savior are all placed upon the One wounded for me; on Christ and Christ alone.

Not a single moment of my suffering escapes the attention or providence of my Savior. His *ministry of presence* is actively involved in reminding me of the mission …while weaving redemption through every broken bone, every laceration, every screaming nerve, every conflict, and every sin. In this book, I've related only a portion of what I've witnessed and lived through, but all my experiences come together to form one strong conviction: **The glory Christ will receive from the redemption of my suffering will be greater than if these things had never even occurred.**

Our Scrapbook

With Daddy
(Jim Parker) and
wearing my first
eye-patch

Singing (with my
eyes closed)
while sitting on
Daddy's lap

Last picture taken of me (with undamaged legs) before the wreck. Photo by Bill Hillard

Side view of what was left of my car.

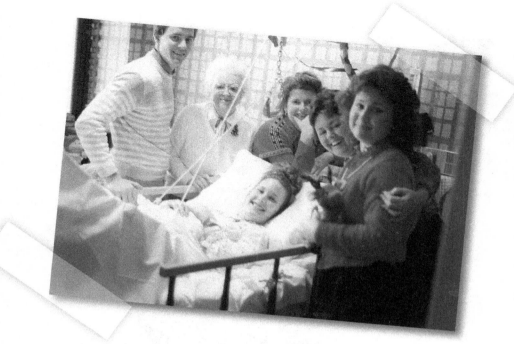

Celebrating Christmas a month after my wreck. Left to right: Bobby Killingsworth, Grandmother Parker, Aunt Anne Parker, Carol Parker, Andrea Parker Killingsworth

Peter and I on our honeymoon. We were just children!

Peter and I performing at an Easter Sunrise Service at Walter Reed Army Medical Center. Photo courtesy of Billy Graham Evangelistic Association

A light moment with Jeff Foxworthy following our performances at a charity event.

With my family
(photo courtesy of Michael Gomez)

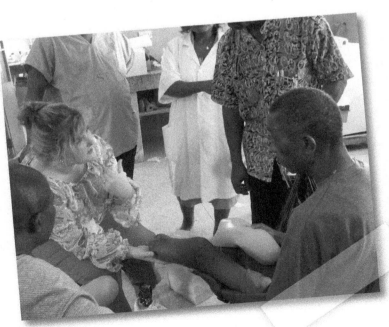

With one of *Standing with Hope's* patients in Ghana

My precious
sons, Parker
and Grayson

Peter took me
skiing for my
birthday!